"When Amanda Gorman delivered her spoken word at the 2021 inauguration of President Joe Biden, she took her listeners to a place beyond mere prose. As music and poetry can often do, her hearers and viewers were transported, and in measure transformed, because what she gave us sang. All the way to our deepest places of pain and longing, her beautiful, melodic honesty drew us toward hope that lies beyond the prosaic. This miraculous singing is what preaching can manifest. What this very fine book by Noel Snyder underscores is not that music matters per se, but that the spiritual formation of the preacher is what creates the breath from which the singing of the sermon can also rise in the lungs and lives of others. It's not the vocal cords alone but the *ruakh* offered up from the preacher's soul. May this profound work make more sermons rise and sing better because of it!"

Mark Labberton, president of Fuller Theological Seminary

"*Sermons That Sing* is essential reading for anyone exploring homiletics as it relates to theology and the arts. Noel Snyder masterfully provides a map to orient us into an expansive conversation where musicality and preaching converge for a melodious dialogue and the power and possibilities of Christian proclamation within the arts are given their due with honor."

Trygve Johnson, dean of the chapel at Hope College

"In *Sermons That Sing*, Noel Snyder avoids mere academic abstraction in favor of substance that generates formative praxis and constructive theology. From Barth to Begbie, from the contours and cadences of tonal harmony to the modal interchange of modern jazz theory, Snyder articulates a musical homiletic in which the relationship between preaching and music is more than merely metaphorical. Through substantive engagement of music theory, musicology, and homiletic theory, Snyder demonstrates how the structures and characteristics of music (such as synchrony, tonality, repetition, and teleology) fulfill a similar function in sermons. By moving beyond music as an illustration for predetermined homiletic techniques, Snyder invites the reader into a new creative and reflective space where the study of harmony fuses with schema of Scripture and the patterns of homiletical communicative action. As a musician and songwriter who is also a preacher and theologian, I found this book to be both intellectually and spiritually satisfying, drawing the reader's curiosity and imagination into the interplay between music and homiletics. Snyder excels by pointing out analogies between music and preaching, and then pointing beyond those surface level similarities toward the more significant deep structures present within both disciplines. These structures function as instruments in the economy of salvation, facilitating the work of the Spirit in the people of God in ways that are deeply creaturely and yet all caught up in the beauty and holiness of God's redemptive, sanctifying, and sonic work. This book is a must-read for those interested in relinquishing neither the role of art and beauty nor the constructive task and praxis of Christian theology, but who long to see their interplay proceed to deeper, more substantive, and spiritually formative integration."

John Frederick, lecturer in New Testament at Trinity College in Queensland, Australia, and author of *Worship in the Way of the Cross*

DYNAMICS OF CHRISTIAN WORSHIP

SERMONS THAT SING

MUSIC AND THE PRACTICE OF PREACHING

NOEL A. SNYDER

Foreword by JEREMY BEGBIE

Academic

An imprint of InterVarsity Press
Downers Grove, Illinois

InterVarsity Press
P.O. Box 1400, Downers Grove, IL 60515-1426
ivpress.com
email@ivpress.com

InterVarsity Press® is the book-publishing division of InterVarsity Christian Fellowship/USA®, a movement of students and faculty active on campus at hundreds of universities, colleges, and schools of nursing in the United States of America, and a member movement of the International Fellowship of Evangelical Students. For information about local and regional activities, visit intervarsity.org.

Scripture quotations, unless otherwise noted, are from the New Revised Standard Version Bible, copyright © 1989 National Council of the Churches of Christ in the United States of America. Used by permission. All rights reserved worldwide.

While any stories in this book are true, some names and identifying information may have been changed to protect the privacy of individuals.

The publisher cannot verify the accuracy or functionality of website URLs used in this book beyond the date of publication.

Cover design and image composite: David Fassett
Interior design: Jeanna Wiggins
Images: vector musical background: © Katerina_Androinchik / iStock / Getty Images
       white wall background: © Nadine Westveer / EyeEm / Getty Images

ISBN 978-0-8308-4933-8 (print)
ISBN 978-0-8308-4934-5 (digital)

Printed in the United States of America ∞

InterVarsity Press is committed to ecological stewardship and to the conservation of natural resources in all our operations. This book was printed using sustainably sourced paper.

Library of Congress Cataloging-in-Publication Data
A catalog record for this book is available from the Library of Congress.

P	24	23	22	21	20	19	18	17	16	15	14	13	12	11	10	9	8	7	6	5	4	3	2	1
Y	41	40	39	38	37	36	35	34	33	32	31	30	29	28	27	26	25	24	23	22	21			

TO CLAY SCHMIT

who taught me how to listen for the music of the gospel—

and more importantly, how to make it sing

CONTENTS

FIGURES

FOREWORD

JEREMY BEGBIE

PREACHERS AND MUSICIANS have not always been the best of friends. The one is adept with words but easily threatened by the near-magical powers of that slightly awkward and touchy music director. The other is adept at calling forth the deepest things of the human heart yet is often frustrated at how hard it is to talk about music with the pastor.

Noel Snyder knows the problem well. But even more, he is aware that the supposed divide between pulpit and keyboard, sermon and sound is anything but neat and clear-cut. *Preaching has its own musicality*—it is, after all words sounded out, a kind of speech that often veers toward song. A large swathe of scholarship on the origins of music and language suggests they have a common root—in a primordial, bodily embedded, emotive "musilanguage" that predates both music as we know it and the kind of referential language we use every day. And the main purpose of this musilanguage, it seems, was to ensure social cohesion, to bring and keep people together. Music and language, it seems, were never meant to be set against each other.

Snyder is an experienced musician and active preacher, adept at living comfortably in both worlds. For Snyder, music offers not only a multifaceted metaphor for numerous dimensions of preaching; it is also a conduit of the Holy Spirit's work *in* preaching. With this in mind, and in writing that is theologically astute and refreshingly practical, he offers us a rich and absorbing exploration of the interplay between musicology and homiletics, to a degree no one has attempted before. As a practicing musician-preacher myself, I can vouch for the fact that you will never see these activities in the same way again. More importantly, you will never *hear* them in the same way, and for that you will be profoundly grateful.

ACKNOWLEDGMENTS

I AM GRATEFUL TO MANY friends, family members, colleagues, and conversation partners who have helped to make this book a reality.

John Witvliet's chance comment over lunch ten years ago set the trajectory for this project at its inception. Mark Labberton's and Clay Schmit's careful reading and encouragement brought shape and depth to this project throughout its development.

My "preaching and the arts" colleagues at Fuller Theological Seminary, especially Eric Mathis, Joseph Novak, Ahmi Lee, Jeff Frymire, and Vadim Dementyev, provided much-needed clarity, perspective, and good humor as I was first developing these ideas. My colleagues at the Calvin Institute of Christian Worship, especially Satrina Reid, Joanna Wigboldy, Maria Cornou, Becky Snippe, Kristen Verhulst, and Kathy Smith, provided feedback, encouragement, and support as the project neared completion.

The thoughtful engagement of the many Calvin Theological Seminary students who interacted with a written draft, especially Ryan Shelton and Chan Jang, was a great help in sharpening these ideas. The masterful editorial eye of Karen DeVries strengthened the first draft immensely.

David McNutt's energy, warmth, and insight proved invaluable in improving my writing and preparing this book for publication. I am grateful to the whole team at IVP.

And finally, without the support and sacrifice of my wife, Heidi, and my children, Jude, Hazel, and Nona, this book would have remained nothing but a nice idea. I love you and am grateful for you.

INTRODUCTION

I WAS ONE YEAR INTO my first pastoral call, and there was a minor controversy developing among the church's leadership regarding our approach to worship music. Planning worship and providing musical leadership were among my primary responsibilities as associate pastor. Yet I was working within a format that had been developed decades earlier at this church, long before I had assumed this role. Like many churches in the midst of the "worship wars" of the 1980s and 1990s, this congregation had resolved the conflict between "contemporary" and "traditional" worship music by offering separate services featuring each of these styles. Every Sunday morning, there was a first service that was "traditional," and a second service that was "contemporary."

When I was beginning my time as worship pastor, many of the staff, elders, and musicians in the church had told me that the distinction between these two services was by no means absolute, since we would regularly sing a contemporary praise song or two in the traditional service and a traditional hymn or two in the contemporary service. Yet the general stylistic distinction between these two services remained, and the senior pastor and I did our best to honor the approach to worship that the church leadership had settled on years before.

Then the senior pastor took a call at another church, and in the absence of our much-beloved leader various conflicts began to emerge. One of these conflicts (predictably) had to do with the music. There were some among the church elders and influencers who thought that we should sharpen our approach to contemporary worship by refraining from singing any traditional hymns in the second service. In the opinion of this group, our second service had become too dreary; only newer, more upbeat music should be included going forward. This seemed too simplistic to me, and I thought moreover that we should wait to develop a more comprehensive approach with our next senior pastor. I remember having a meeting with some of our elders about this issue, at which one of the elders mused aloud about the familiarity of this conflict. "Why is it," he said, "that churches always seem to fight about the music?"

To me, the cause of the conflict was relatively straightforward. Our senior pastor had left a month or two earlier, and we were all experiencing varying levels of grief from his departure. For some, that grief was finding expression in the various controversies that were arising around the church about different issues, including the issue of worship music. In my opinion, it was a pretty simple case of scapegoating: grief working itself out as irritation at various short-comings that were perceived among the remaining pastors, staff, and programs.

There was one detail about this particular conflict, however, that puzzled me. In the perception of the group complaining about the worship music, there had been a distinct shift toward a more traditional style of music in the second service following the senior pastor's departure. But to the best of my knowledge, I had not changed anything in my approach to selecting and leading worship music. How was it, then, that some had perceived a shift where others, including myself, had perceived none? I certainly was not conscious of making any changes in my approach to the music, since I thought it was vital to maintain as much stability as possible in the interim term between senior pastors.

That's when another hypothesis began to emerge. Might it be, I wondered, that there had in fact been a major change to our worship music after all, except that it was not the music of our congregational song that had changed? Might it be that the music that had changed was the music of the former pas-tor's homiletical voice and liturgical presence, which was now replaced by the very different music of our interim pastor's preaching and presence? Might it be that this was the musical change these individuals were sensing, without identifying it as such?

Whatever the answer might have been in that particular instance, I am convinced that, in the practice of preaching more generally, musicality is indeed a powerful yet underappreciated aspect of the overall aesthetic, rhe-torical, and theological import of sermons. Moreover, as a musician myself, I have long been cognizant of the specifically *musical* instincts that I bring to the craft of preaching, without being able to account for how exactly these instincts might take shape. This book is one attempt to provide such an account. More specifically, what is undertaken here is a sustained analysis of *the musicality of preaching* by bringing the art of music into deep theoretical and practical conversation with the art of preaching.

The overall goal of this study is thus similar to the goal of James K. A. Smith's *Imagining the Kingdom: How Worship Works*, in which the field of liturgical studies is brought into conversation with the field of philosophical anthropology in order to gain a more thorough understanding of the specific means by which worship practices might serve as "conduits of the Spirit's transformative power," practices by which "the Spirit marshals our embodiment in order to rehabituate us to the kingdom of God."[1] In a similar way, this book brings the fields of musicology and homiletics into conversation, and, through a thorough examination of three shared characteristics between music and preaching (synchrony, repetition, and teleology), identifies deep theoretical and practical resonances, with the metaphor of music ultimately emerging as a powerful means by which to better understand the theological and formative potential of the practice of preaching.

Or, to give another example, in *Glimpses of the New Creation: Worship and the Formative Power of the Arts,* W. David O. Taylor examines the formative potential of the arts in worship through the idea of the "singular powers" of each art form. How, Taylor asks, "might the 'logic' of visual art, in contrast to, say, the 'logic' of music, open up an opportunity to form a people at worship?"[2] He elaborates:

> A painting, for instance, does not unfold over time like a song does. A linen banner does not expire in the way that a musical note does. A cast-iron sculpture does not bend to the subjectivity of a particular audience as in the case of an anthem, which is sung one way by a professional choir and in a rather different manner by untrained folk.[3]

These differences, among many others, are what Taylor means in referring to an art's "singular powers," and his book examines a full range of art forms

---

[1] James K. A. Smith, *Imagining the Kingdom: How Worship Works* (Grand Rapids, MI: Baker Academic, 2013), 15.
[2] W. David O. Taylor, *Glimpses of the New Creation: Worship and the Formative Power of the Arts* (Grand Rapids, MI: Eerdmans, 2020), 3.
[3] Taylor, *Glimpses of the New Creation*, 3.

through this lens. The ultimate goal is to gain a better understanding of how "our community's practices of art in worship [might] form us in the triune life."[4]

These concepts of *singular powers, formative potential, conduits of the Spirit's transformative power,* and *rehabituation to the kingdom of God* will be helpful to keep in mind throughout the present study of music and preaching, which seeks to illumine a subset of this broader line of inquiry. The core question of this book is, What are some of the key characteristics (or singular powers) of music that might inform and overlap with the practice of preaching, and how might preachers who draw on these musical instincts contribute in specific ways to the formation of worshipers? Or, to use more technical language, What might a homiletical theory that draws on musicology look like? This book is one attempt at developing such a musical homiletic.

The overall shape of this project is relatively straightforward. In the first chapter, the current state of the conversation between music and preaching is assessed through a survey and analysis of eight major contributors. Following that, a methodological exemplar and a theological guide for the remainder of the project will be identified and briefly discussed. In the second through fourth chapters, one shared characteristic between music and preaching will be analyzed per chapter, followed by discussion of some of the literal and metaphorical resonances that are found, as well as the resultant implications of those resonances for the theory and practice of preaching. Finally, the theological significance and formative potential of each shared characteristic will be assessed through the identification of a particular virtue that may be associated with each individual characteristic. In the fifth chapter, the musical homiletic that has been developed in the first four chapters will be summarized and assessed, and then demonstrated in practice through an analysis of an original sermon. In this way, I hope by the end of this project to convincingly demonstrate the potential of a musical homiletic to provide a better understanding of some of the ways in which "the Spirit marshals our embodiment in order to rehabituate us to the kingdom of God" in the practice of preaching.

Even so, there may be some who are not convinced of the ability of the musical metaphor to bring valuable insight to homiletical theory. To some

---

[4]Taylor, *Glimpses of the New Creation,* 3.

people, this project may appear to be little more than a novelty. Even those who might be open, in theory, to interdisciplinary explorations of this sort—comparing preaching and theater, for instance—may believe that the arts of preaching and music are too disparate to be capable of true and deep theoretical exchange. Beyond urging these skeptics to reserve judgment until they have considered this project in its entirety, my simple response to the question of the musical metaphor's value is to point to the priority of sound in the Christian faith. If "faith comes from what is heard" (Rom 10:17) and if "we walk by faith, not by sight" (2 Cor 5:7), then it is appropriate for preachers and homileticians to pay close attention to the only art form that relies entirely on sound and hearing.

Although it is possible for this point to be taken too far,[5] there is a connection in Scripture between *hearing* and *faith*, whereas there is also a connection between *sight* and *certainty* (or, at least, the idolatrous desire for certainty).[6] This is not to minimize the irreducibly *embodied* and *contextual* nature of preaching or to dismiss the important distinction between speech and music. It is simply to suggest that there are important insights to be gained from an examination of sound—and more specifically, musical sounds—if for no other reason than that preaching and music occupy such a prominent place in the worship life of Christian churches throughout history and around the globe. There is much to learn about the created world, the nature of listening and hearing, and the call to sound forth the gospel through a conversation between the art of music and the art of preaching. All who have ears to hear, let them listen.

---

[5]See, for instance, Stephen Webb's helpful caution against *ableism* (the stigmatization of those with disabilities)—or more specifically, *audism* (the stigmatization of those with hearing difficulties)—in his examination of preaching and the theology of sound. Stephen Webb, *The Divine Voice: Christian Proclamation and the Theology of Sound* (Grand Rapids, MI: Brazos Press, 2004), 51-55.
[6]Michael Horton, *The Christian Faith: A Systematic Theology for Pilgrims on the Way* (Grand Rapids, MI: Zondervan, 2011), 85-94.

1

THE CONVERSATION BETWEEN MUSIC AND PREACHING

FOUR MODELS

RECENTLY ON SOCIAL MEDIA, a friend of mine admitted his initial insecurity as a younger preacher in a predominantly African American church because he did not practice the traditional Black church preaching techniques of "whooping" or "tuning up." He said that he eventually came to accept that preaching with authenticity and clarity would serve him better than trying to mimic those traditional homiletical norms, which he did not feel he could embody authentically. Of course, since musicality is perhaps the most distinctive quality of the techniques my friend referenced, his preaching may seem less "musical" without them. Yet I wonder if there may still be a healthy measure of musicality in my friend's preaching despite his eschewal of some of the more overtly musical phenomena that characterize the predominant homiletical style of his ecclesial tradition. Perhaps my friend has more musical instincts than he knows, if only he were given more tools to identify them.

This chapter will explore a variety of musical-homiletical methods, situating the phenomenon of "whooping" among a much wider range of options for integrating musicality into preaching. Preachers should find inspiration in knowing that there is more than one model for integrating musical instincts into the practice of preaching.

PREACHING AND THE ARTS

The practice of Christian preaching has a long history of dialoguing with other artistic disciplines. The most popular and longstanding conversation partner is most certainly the art of rhetoric, chiefly as developed in the ancient Greco-Roman oratorical tradition.[1] Ever since Augustine rigorously defended the use of rhetoric in his classic homiletics textbook, *On Christian Doctrine*, preachers have been urged to carefully consider not only what to say but also how to say it. This necessarily involves artistic considerations and aesthetic judgments.[2] If one is to admit the necessity of "arming oneself," as Augustine so vividly pictures it, to defend truth against falsehood through aesthetic training,[3] then a flourishing of dialogue between homiletics and other artistic disciplines seems almost inevitable.

However, as Lucy Lind Hogan notes, the practice of preaching has not always had an easy relationship with art and aesthetics, for at least three reasons. The first reason, according to Hogan, is the enduring opinion that the truth of the gospel should be so compelling in and of itself that it should not need artful presentation. Secondly, there is often a distrust of imagination and creativity, which are seen as dangerous tools in the hands of a fallen humanity. The third reason, Hogan writes, is the fear of paying too much attention to the desires of the listener, which could lead to an erosion of respect for God's revelation.[4] Influential voices of modern times have voiced similar concerns about artistic considerations factoring too prominently in the

---

[1]See O. C. Edwards Jr., *A History of Preaching* (Nashville: Abingdon Press, 2004), 11-14. Lucy Lind Hogan notes a division of the discipline of rhetoric from that of poetics in the classical world, with rhetoric traditionally referring to "the rational, intellectual, and logical dimensions of speech and language," while poetics traditionally "dealt with poetry, drama, and literature; with the aesthetic and emotive or affective dimensions of language and form." Over the centuries, however, the two have become one: "While rhetoric was originally conceived as the preparation of persuasive arguments, it eventually came to be equated with a more poetic disposition. . . . Oratory was no longer viewed as political persuasion; rather it was seen as a fine art, as poetics." Hogan, "Poetics and the Context of Preaching," in *The New Interpreter's Handbook of Preaching*, ed. Paul Scott Wilson (Nashville: Abingdon Press, 2008), 173-74.

[2]Hogan subsumes artistic considerations under the general oratorical category of *poetics*. See Hogan, "Poetics," 174-75. It is important to note, however, that the separation of form and content—the *what* and the *how* of preaching—is ultimately artificial and unsustainable. As G. Lee Ramsey writes, "Influenced by recent language studies, it is almost a homiletical truism that form and content are inseparable." G. Lee Ramsey, *Care-full Preaching: From Sermon to Caring Community* (Eugene, OR: Wipf and Stock, 2012), 69.

[3]Augustine, *On Christian Doctrine*, 4.2. The translation of the Latin title, *De doctrina christiana*, as *On Christian Doctrine*, is somewhat misleading, and may perhaps more accurately be translated, *Teaching Christianity*. See Edwards, *History of Preaching*, 106.

[4]Hogan, "Poetics," 174. For a thoughtful response to the fear that aesthetic considerations will lead to idolatry, see Thomas H. Troeger, *Wonder Reborn: Creating Sermons on Hymns, Music, and Poetry* (Oxford: Oxford University Press, 2010), 14-18.

practice of preaching. For instance, in an 1866 lecture on what it takes to be a great preacher, the theologian Horace Bushnell stated, "In preaching... the artistic air kills everything."[5] A more contemporary homiletician, David Buttrick, is similarly reticent to label preaching an art, preferring the term "craft" instead.[6]

Despite these lingering concerns, however, many North American preachers and homileticians have warmed considerably in recent years with respect to homiletical appropriations of the arts. Some credit for this greater openness is likely due to H. Grady Davis's influential preaching manual, *Design for Preaching*, which compares novice preachers to novices of any other art form and counsels them to cultivate "all the sense and skill [they] can" in developing into skillful practitioners of the art of preaching.[7] The sermon itself, Davis argued, should be regarded as a "living organism" that springs naturally from the material at hand, "showing nothing but its own unfolding parts."[8] Championing this "organic" understanding of sermon form, Davis freely compared preaching to other arts, especially those arts that unfold as a movement in time: music, drama, and storytelling.[9]

Inspired by such comparisons, and with a renewed commitment to an artistic understanding of preaching, an interdisciplinary conversation has emerged among homileticians who are eager to apply the study of other arts to homiletical theory.[10] For instance, in *Performing the Word: Preaching as Theatre*, Jana Childers draws on dramatic theory and selected dramatic performance practices in order to develop a more "lively" homiletic.[11] Alyce

---

[5]Horace Bushnell, "Pulpit Talent," in *The Company of Preachers: Wisdom on Preaching from Augustine to the Present*, ed. Richard Lisher (Grand Rapids, MI: Eerdmans, 2002), 88.

[6]"Preaching is always more craft than art." David Buttrick, *Homiletic: Moves and Structures* (Philadelphia: Fortress, 1987), 193. This statement seems to assume that "art" is ultimately self-referential, created "for its own sake," whereas "craft" is necessarily directed toward some end outside of itself. For a more positive view of the purpose of art, especially in relation to worship and preaching, see Clayton J. Schmit, *Too Deep for Words: A Theology of Liturgical Expression* (Louisville, KY: Westminster John Knox, 2002), 23-25. For a rebuttal of Buttrick and a defense of beauty and aesthetics in preaching, see also Troeger, *Wonder Reborn*, 11-14.

[7]H. Grady Davis, *Design for Preaching* (Philadelphia: Fortress, 1958), 12-13.

[8]Davis, *Design for Preaching*, 15.

[9]Davis, *Design for Preaching*, 163-64.

[10]For a contemporary defense of understanding preaching as an art, see Schmit, *Too Deep for Words*, 84-86. See also Charles L. Rice, *The Embodied Word: Preaching as Art and Liturgy* (Minneapolis: Fortress, 1991).

[11]Jana Childers, *Performing the Word: Preaching as Theatre* (Nashville: Abingdon Press, 1998).

McKenzie and Sondra Willobe have similarly ventured into the world of creative writing in search of insights that can help nurture the artful use of language in preaching.[12] Charles Bartow and Clayton Schmit have explored the power of poetic devices for deepening the artistic potential of homiletics,[13] and Thomas Long and Mike Graves have proposed homiletical strategies drawn from the study of the literary and generic forms of the Bible.[14] These many conversations between homiletics and other artistic disciplines have borne much homiletical fruit in recent decades.[15]

PREACHING AND MUSIC

If, as this book argues, musicality is a powerful yet underappreciated aspect of the overall aesthetic, rhetorical, and theological import of sermons, one might also expect to find a burgeoning dialogue between music and preaching, which is indeed the case.[16] Several studies comparing music and preaching have emerged in recent years, and each represents a unique methodological approach to this interdisciplinary conversation. While each methodology has certain advantages, there are also unique challenges and drawbacks to be noted. The remainder of this chapter will assess the current state of the conversation by examining eight major contributions to the musical-homiletical conversation, grouping them into four major methodologies—or four models. This will provide a starting point for the musical homiletic developed in subsequent chapters of this book. An examination of existing studies will help to identify some of the most prominent themes and insights that emerge when comparing the art of music to the art of preaching.

---

[12]Alyce M. McKenzie, *Novel Preaching: Tips from Top Writers on Crafting Creative Sermons* (Louisville, KY: Westminster John Knox, 2010), and Sondra B. Willobe, *The Write Stuff: Crafting Sermons that Capture and Convince* (Louisville, KY: Westminster John Knox, 2009).

[13]Charles L. Bartow, *God's Human Speech: A Practical Theology of Proclamation* (Grand Rapids, MI: Eerdmans, 1997), and Schmit, *Too Deep for Words*, chap. 5. See also Walter Brueggemann, *Finally Comes the Poet: Daring Speech for Proclamation* (Philadelphia: Fortress, 1989), 1-11.

[14]Thomas G. Long, *Preaching and the Literary Forms of the Bible* (Philadelphia: Fortress, 1989), and Mike Graves, *The Sermon as Symphony: Preaching the Literary Forms of the New Testament* (Valley Forge, PA: Judson Press, 1997).

[15]For a recent treatment of preaching in relation to the visual arts, see also Daniel Louw, "Preaching as Art (Imaging the Unseen) and Art as Homiletics (Verbalizing the Unseen): Towards the Aesthetics of Iconic Thinking and Poetic Communication in Homiletics," HTS 72.2 (December 2016): 125-33.

[16]The attraction of these two disciplines is not difficult to understand, given the prominence of both music and preaching in ecclesial life, and especially the centrality of each in Protestant worship. Moreover, since music is a performing art, possibilities abound for its relation to performance in preaching.

The musical homiletic advanced in this book will draw on many of the themes and insights of these extant works, but will ultimately pursue a unique course.

Music in preaching: Thomas Troeger and Luke Powery. Methodologically speaking, perhaps the most straightforward method for framing the conversation between music and preaching is that of Thomas Troeger, developed most fully in *Wonder Reborn: Creating Sermons on Hymns, Music, and Poetry.*[17] This method involves the inclusion of performed music—with or without texts—in the sermon itself, and therefore might be referred to as the *music in preaching* method.[18] The driving issue behind Troeger's method is the "spiritual barrenness of a church that is without art," having needlessly repudiated the spiritual and religious roots of beauty.[19] Therefore, Troeger proposes a method by which preachers can reawaken wonder in the lives of their congregants, helping people to "intuit and experience anew the divine realities to which the Bible gives witness" through the inclusion of hymns and music in the actual preaching event.[20]

The *music in preaching* method advocated by Troeger goes beyond the oft-used homiletical technique of quoting hymns or other musical works for the purpose of illustration. Rather, Troeger presents "a particular way of using these arts as a resource for the very substance of what a preacher says."[21] Hymns and musical compositions can thus "serve as the 'text' for a sermon in the same way that preachers regularly use a passage or theme from the Bible."[22] Not only might this method serve as a vital means of reawakening wonder in a spiritually starved church; it might also help the Western church to become reacquainted with "its own treasure house of great artworks that are inspired by the gospel and alive with the Spirit."[23] These works are too often ignored, Troeger believes, although they represent a vital source of

---

[17]Thomas Troeger, *Wonder Reborn: Creating Sermons on Hymns, Music, and Poetry* (Oxford: Oxford University Press, 2010).

[18]For a summary of this general method, see also Thomas Troeger, "Arts," in *The New Interpreter's Handbook of Preaching*, ed. Paul Scott Wilson (Nashville: Abingdon Press, 2008), 177-79.

[19]Troeger, *Wonder Reborn*, 18.

[20]Troeger, *Wonder Reborn*, 24.

[21]Troeger, *Wonder Reborn*, 23.

[22]Troeger, *Wonder Reborn*, 23.

[23]Troeger, *Wonder Reborn*, 26. Recent empirical research shows the apparent benefits of such an approach, correlating the resilience of faith communities in the United States, in part, with the value they place on the arts. See Robert Wuthnow, *All in Sync: How Music and Art Are Revitalizing American Religion* (Berkeley: University of California Press, 2003).

spiritual insight. Incorporation of hymns and musical compositions into preaching can help reacquaint the church with its own spiritual resources, and more importantly, can ultimately teach both the preacher and the congregation how to be more attuned to the movement of the Spirit in the soundscape of their lives.[24]

One of the many examples Troeger provides of this approach is an original sermon based on two "texts," a biblical text (Jer 8:22-9:1) and an African American spiritual ("There Is a Balm in Gilead"). The sermon begins by lamenting the contemporary state of our world, with its religious violence and spiritual hunger. From there, Troeger examines features of the text from Jeremiah, with its haunting question, "Is there no balm in Gilead?" Troeger then uses the spiritual "There Is a Balm in Gilead" itself as a sort of musical midrash, an interpretive key for answering the question raised by the Jeremiah text.[25] Noting the oppressive conditions in which the spiritual arose, Troeger presents this as an example of "the ability of enslaved Africans to transform sorrow into joy."[26] This then leads into a concluding section in which a single voice or instrument begins to sound the melody of "There Is a Balm in Gilead," while Troeger speaks over the music, demonstrating the possibility of moving from the question ("Is there a balm in Gilead?") to the affirmation ("There is a balm in Gilead.") in our contemporary context. At the conclusion of the sermon, the whole congregation joins together in singing the spiritual.[27] Music and preaching are thus paired in the most concrete possible way, with the inclusion of performed music in the sermon itself. Troeger's text includes many other examples of this *music in preaching* method, with the musical selections deriving mostly from the corpus of Western classical, "sacred" music.[28]

A similar method to Troeger's is found in Luke Powery's *Dem Dry Bones: Preaching, Death, and Hope*.[29] However, whereas Troeger incorporates a

---

[24]Troeger, *Wonder Reborn*, 85.

[25]On the similarities of Christian hymns and the postbiblical rabbinic tradition of midrash, see Troeger, *Wonder Reborn*, 30-34. Troeger presents a cogent argument for understanding hymns as midrashim.

[26]Troeger, *Wonder Reborn*, 46, quoting Arthur C. Jones.

[27]Troeger, *Wonder Reborn*, 42-48.

[28]In chapter 3, Troeger demonstrates the possibility of preaching on certain features of music itself, noting, for example, the musical idioms through which J. S. Bach conveys certain theological themes by interweaving the performance of several Bach pieces with Scripture and sermon. An excerpt from this sermon will be included at the end of this chapter.

[29]Luke A. Powery, *Dem Dry Bones: Preaching, Death, and Hope* (Minneapolis: Fortress, 2012).

moderate range of musical genres, from J. S. Bach to African American spirituals, Powery focuses exclusively on the spirituals as a resource for homiletics. Powery's primary thesis is that the African American spirituals, understood as "musical sermons," can provide an antidote to the "candy theology" of so much contemporary preaching in which the reality of death is either ignored or denied.[30] The incorporation of the spirituals into one's preaching life, Powery maintains, is one way to keep preachers grounded and instruct them on the spiritual dynamics of hope. Not surprisingly—and therefore true to the name *spiritual*—Powery's homiletical method incorporates much pneumatology, paying special attention to the resurrection imagery found in Ezekiel 37, in which the Spirit breathes new life into the dry bones of exiled Israel.[31]

Our daily existence, Powery writes, is full of "little deaths," which preachers deny at their own peril.[32] As a model for telling the "gospel truth" in such a spiritual climate, Powery undertakes a textual analysis of the spirituals, while also remaining "sensitive to their musical soundscape."[33] Like Troeger, Powery sees great potential for "enhancing the theory and practice of preaching" by integrating the music of the spirituals into preaching, even viewing them as "musical sermons" in their own right and thus valuing them as "a significant theological and cultural resource for contemporary preaching."[34]

Though Powery focuses mainly on the texts of the spirituals, rather than their musical qualities, and analyzes them primarily in order to demonstrate strategies for engendering hope in the midst of intense suffering and death, he also notes a fascinating connection between the spirituals themselves and the Black preaching tradition. Indeed, as Powery explains, it is highly probable that many of the spirituals arose in the context of the intoned slave sermon.[35] He writes,

> The creation of the spirituals through the extemporaneous musical sermonic delivery of preachers in conjunction with the congregational responses was apparently a common feature. Through the call and response of preacher and

---

[30]Powery, *Dem Dry Bones*, 2-6.
[31]For a more comprehensive pneumatology for preaching, see also Luke A. Powery, *Spirit Speech: Lament and Celebration in Preaching* (Nashville: Abingdon Press, 2009).
[32]Powery, *Dem Dry Bones*, 3. Powery borrows this phrase from Gordon Lathrop.
[33]Powery, *Dem Dry Bones*, 13.
[34]Powery, *Dem Dry Bones*, 13.
[35]Powery, *Dem Dry Bones*, 22.

congregation, a song arose that I would argue is itself sermonic; musicologist
Eileen Southern names this class of spirituals "the homiletical spirituals." Other
accounts suggest that the spiritual originated when a song leader was so moved
by a preacher's sermon that he or she interrupted the sermon by answering him
with a song. Nonetheless, the spiritual was rooted in the preaching moment.[36]

Powery notes strong scholarly suspicions that the slave preachers themselves
were the main creators of the spirituals. With such a significant degree of
overlap, Powery argues, the spirituals can be a powerful homiletical resource
for deepening the gospel-shaped spirituality of preacher and listeners alike.

The musicality of preaching: William Turner and Martha Simmons.
Though Powery's main engagement with spirituals is through their texts, his
research on the connection of spirituals to the Black preaching tradition, along
with his counsel regarding the use of spirituals in developing a truly *spiritual*
homiletic, takes him a step beyond Troeger's *music in preaching* method to a
closely related method in the music and preaching conversation, the *musicality of preaching* method. In this method, preaching itself is seen as music—or
at least, as having musical qualities—and is analyzed as such. Indeed, Powery
straddles this line himself, not only in his own analysis, but also in his own
homiletical practice, in which he has been known to break into song at various points, interweaving music and the spoken word throughout his sermons.
Powery's own homiletical theory, however, remains more focused on spirituals as a musical resource to be used in preaching than it does on the musicality of preaching itself.

Another homiletician, William C. Turner, has developed the other emphasis, focusing more on the musical qualities of sermons themselves. In a chapter titled "The Musicality of Black Preaching,"[37] Turner notes the historical
biases that have prevented researchers from understanding the performative
aspects of Black preaching. Quite unfairly, Turner writes, Black preachers
have often been viewed as being devoid of intellect and training.[38] However,
drawing on Evans Crawford's concept of "biformation" (i.e., formation on

---

[36]Powery, *Dem Dry Bones*, 22.
[37]William C. Turner, "The Musicality of Black Preaching: Performing the Word," in *Performance in Preaching: Bringing the Sermon to Life*, ed. Jana Childers and Clayton J. Schmit (Grand Rapids, MI: Baker Academic, 2008), 191-209.
[38]Turner, "Musicality," 193-95.

two levels simultaneously), Turner demonstrates the manner in which the rhythm and intonation of Black preaching can work in conjunction with the intellectual content of the sermon, rather than against it, in order to feed both the mind and the spirit of the congregation.[39] Using a whole repertoire of musical-homiletical tools, Black preachers communicate with sonic authority and seek to achieve spiritual unity among the congregation. Crawford calls this phenomenon "the hum": when the people and the preacher resonate together in the Spirit, and "the ether" pulsates with "mystic harmonies."[40]

Noting Henry Mitchell's strong resistance to the "toning down" of Black preachers through seminary education shaped by Enlightenment values, Turner seeks to reinforce the value of musicality in Black preaching, inasmuch as "the musicality of the African American sermon expresses what is beyond the literal word. It takes rational content and fires the imagination and stirs the heart."[41] To strip the sermon of this musical quality would be to restrict its spiritual power and lessen its meaning, for "communication occurs not only through the meaning denoted by the words, but in the surplus that seeps up and through the spaces between the words."[42] The musical signals delivered by the preacher "are below the threshold of formal syntax and grammar. Yet they are clear as crystal within the cultural matrix in which preaching is a musical moment."[43]

While Turner's chapter indeed describes several features of typical Black preaching that are best understood "musically," nonetheless it serves perhaps more broadly as a defense of musicality in the production of meaning in Black preaching. With this as the central focus, less attention is given to analysis of the musical mechanisms themselves that might be operative in Black preaching or the ways in which those mechanisms might relate to the spoken word.[44] Yet with the emphasis placed on musicality as a significant element in preaching, Turner's work might still be seen as complementary to that of Powery, as well as to the earlier work of Henry Mitchell and Evans Crawford.

---

[39]Turner, "Musicality," 196.

[40]Turner, "Musicality," 196.

[41]Turner, "Musicality," 199.

[42]Turner, "Musicality," 207.

[43]Turner, "Musicality," 208.

[44]Turner's chapter does list many musical features used in Black preaching, such as expression, meter, cadence, rhythm, and musical style. However, it seems that the aim is not to catalog or analyze these musical sounds in themselves, but rather to reflect more broadly on the contextual meaning of these musical features. See Turner, "Musicality," 197.

It is noteworthy, however, that despite the high degree of overlap between music and preaching observed by Powery and Turner, the work of these two homileticians subsequently focuses less on specific properties that are unique to musical sounds themselves, and more on the contextual, spiritual, and theological implications of musicality in preaching. In contrast to this emphasis, the work of Martha Simmons—another practitioner of the *musicality of preaching* method—places much greater emphasis on musical sounds themselves. In a chapter titled, "Whooping: The Musicality of African American Preaching Past and Present,"[45] Simmons examines the quality of *tonality* that has historically given African American preaching such a distinctive sound. More commonly known as "whooping," this tonal quality of much African American preaching has other names as well, including "squalling, pulling it, intoning, humming, and zooming."[46] Whatever term is used, this tonal/musical quality in preaching "remains dearly loved and sought after in a large proportion of African American churches."[47]

Acknowledging the notorious difficulty of defining the phenomenon of whooping, Simmons nonetheless argues that it should be understood primarily as *melody*—pitches that are "logically connected and have prescribed, punctuated rhythms that require certain modulations of the voice, and [are] often delineated by quasi-metrical phrasings."[48] Moreover, as Simmons explains, whooping should be distinguished from two other common phenomena in African American ecclesial settings, the practice of tuning (which is often used by laity during well-known, commonly used prayers) and the use of cadence (sometimes accompanied by rhyme).[49] Simmons offers a helpful perspective on the ongoing use of musicality in African American preaching by tracing the deep historical roots of the practice of whooping up to its present-day manifestations, from the tonally rich speech of West African slaves to the various uses of rhythmic tonality among contemporary African American preachers.

---

[45]Martha Simmons, "Whooping: The Musicality of African American Preaching Past and Present," in *Preaching with Sacred Fire: An Anthology of African American Sermons, 1750 to the Present*, ed. Martha Simmons and Frank A. Thomas (New York: W. W. Norton, 2010).

[46]Simmons, "Whooping," 864. Cf. Turner, "The Musicality of Black Preaching," 197-98.

[47]Simmons, "Whooping," 864.

[48]Simmons, "Whooping," 865.

[49]Simmons, "Whooping," 865-67.

Simmons's analysis is notable for its more intentional use of musical terms to name various sonic qualities of African American preaching past and present. Drawing on Jon Michael Spencer's analysis of the connection between African folk song and Black preaching, she even identifies the tones used in whooping as aligning with the pentatonic scale.[50] Simmons furthermore delineates the many varieties of whooping, from those with a "smooth" style to those whose whoop sounds more like a growl, a hack, or a guttural gasp. The categories of tempo, volume, cadence, and call-and-response all receive attention in her analysis of various periods and exemplars of whooping.

Like Turner, Simmons defends the musicality of African American preaching against the charge of theological shallowness or unsophistication, although she does acknowledge some of the more common criticisms of whooping.[51] In the end, Simmons insists, the musicality of African American preaching is a powerful homiletical art form that deserves respect: "Famous whoopers . . . should be saluted and studied for their theological depth, homiletical imagination, mastery of metaphors, and ability to make the Word come alive."[52]

The *musicality of preaching* method employed by Turner and Simmons uses musical terms to describe distinctive qualities of human speech—especially, in this case, as these musical qualities occur in Black preaching traditions.[53] The result of this approach is that the art of music *as music* does not receive significant attention, with the focus remaining primarily on the musicality of speech patterns. Thus far in this survey, then, Troeger is the only homiletician who has called attention to sonic qualities specific to the art of music itself.[54]

---

[50]Simmons, "Whooping," 871-72.

[51]Among the criticisms she notes are the possibility of using whooping to cover a sermon's weaknesses, the possibility of disingenuous showmanship, the possible credence whooping might give to negative cultural stereotypes of African Americans, and the possibility of using whooping to overshadow a preacher's moral failure. See Simmons, "Whooping," 881-82.

[52]Simmons, "Whooping," 883.

[53]See also Teresa L. Fry Brown's discussion of musicality in sermon delivery in *Delivering the Sermon: Voice, Body, and Animation in Proclamation* (Minneapolis: Fortress, 2008), 36-38.

[54]For instance, Troeger introduces the final movement of Fauré's Requiem, with which he interweaves the spoken words of a sermon, with these words:

The Requiem starts with a strange-sounding sustained note. Even if we are not musically trained, its peculiar sound makes us wonder where it will lead. Will it blossom into a minor or major key? Will our prayers for the dead make us only sadder, or will our hearts brighten with confidence that the departed have been welcomed into God's eternal care? By the conclusion of the piece we have our answer. The Requiem ends in D major. It ends with the same kind of steady confidence that characterizes the apostle Paul's affirmation that

Yet because Troeger's primary aim is to utilize music *in* preaching as a means of evoking wonder among one's hearers, the actual conversational exchange between the two fields, music and preaching, remains limited. Music is used primarily in an illustrative way in Troeger's work, and thus is not allowed to generate a more significant theoretical engagement with the art of preaching.

Preaching as music: Kirk Byron Jones, Eugene Lowry, and Mike Graves. In order to engender a more substantive interaction, therefore, a more robust method is needed—one that enables attention to the unique properties of music itself, as well as to the theological trajectory of contemporary homiletical theory. Such a method will likely need to involve deeper, more sustained, modes of interaction, such as metaphor. Several contemporary homileticians have pursued this line of inquiry, developing a sustained metaphorical relationship between music and preaching. Among these homileticians are Kirk Byron Jones, Eugene Lowry, and Mike Graves. This might be called the *preaching as music* method.

Jones develops the *preaching as music* method in his book, *The Jazz of Preaching*.[55] Like Troeger, Jones affords significant attention to the art of music itself—specifically jazz. Going beyond the literal inclusion of music in sermons, however, Jones develops a broad metaphorical relationship between jazz and preaching. He begins with an examination of the nature of sound and the sound of jazz. "Jazz is sound-making on purpose," Jones writes. "Its reason for being is to make, celebrate, and discover new sounds."[56] In the same way that jazz musicians play notes, Jones maintains, preachers play words: "Good preachers play words well. They know that how a word sounds is as important as what it means, that the sounding of words can work wonders with their meaning."[57] Preaching and jazz have much in common, according to Jones, including the value of communal storytelling, the evasion of easy definition,[58] and the primacy of listening over playing/speaking.[59]

---

nothing in all of creation "will be able to separate us from the love of God in Christ Jesus our Lord." (Troeger, *Wonder Reborn*, 107)

[55] Kirk Byron Jones, *The Jazz of Preaching: How to Preach with Great Freedom and Joy* (Nashville: Abingdon Press, 2004).

[56] Jones, *Jazz of Preaching*, 30.

[57] Jones, *Jazz of Preaching*, 31.

[58] There is a "beyond-ness" to both crafts. Jones, *Jazz of Preaching*, 39.

[59] Jones, *Jazz of Preaching*, 27-41, 47-59.

These metaphorical resonances are only the beginning, however, as Jones develops the metaphor of *preaching as jazz* further by exploring creativity and improvisation among jazz artists and preachers. Creativity, writes Jones, involves *curiosity, openness, risks,* and *grace*.[60] Improvisation involves *play, variety, daring,* and *mastery*.[61] In the concluding chapters, Jones examines the features of dialogue, pain, and joy in both jazz and preaching. Overall, *The Jazz of Preaching* serves as an admonishment for preachers to tap into the deep well of energy, creativity, and emotion that is found in the art of jazz. Such an effort, Jones believes, will be richly rewarding to those who pursue it.[62]

While *The Jazz of Preaching* indeed develops the conversation between music and preaching in a deeper, more sustained manner than other authors do, relating the two metaphorically while also affording due attention to jazz music itself (and perhaps even more attention to jazz musicians themselves), the book nonetheless stops short of demonstrating or analyzing any specific musical techniques or practices that constitute the art of jazz. Jones may have succeeded in persuading preachers to explore the sounds and practices of jazz music in greater depth, and perhaps even to adopt an understanding of themselves borrowed from the world of jazz, but he has not done so through an exploration of jazz music as musical sound. Rather, Jones relies mostly on the testimony and reflections of jazz musicians and critics in order to develop a metaphorical relationship between preaching and jazz that is based more on extramusical phenomena associated with music-making in a jazz idiom.

The *preaching as jazz* metaphor receives a much fuller treatment, however, in the work of another homiletician, Eugene L. Lowry. In *The Homiletical Beat: Why All Sermons are Narrative*, Lowry gathers several musical metaphors to illustrate and support his narrative homiletic.[63] Of course, Lowry's main concern throughout the initial chapters of the text is not necessarily the

---

[60]Jones, *Jazz of Preaching*, 70-75.

[61]Jones, *Jazz of Preaching*, 86-95. For a comprehensive reflection on improvisation with reference not only to specific practices such as preaching, worship, and biblical interpretation, but indeed in relation to all of life, see Bruce Ellis Benson, *Liturgy as a Way of Life: Embodying the Arts in Christian Worship* (Grand Rapids, MI: Baker Academic, 2013). See especially chapter 3 on jazz improvisation.

[62]Indeed, Jones has doubtless seen the benefits of this method firsthand, as this text has grown out of a seminary class he has taught on preaching and jazz. See *Jazz of Preaching*, 15.

[63]Eugene L. Lowry, *The Homiletical Beat: Why All Sermons Are Narrative* (Nashville: Abingdon Press, 2012).

development of the *preaching as music* metaphor per se, but rather the advancement of a *temporal* understanding of preaching, over against a *spatial* understanding.[64] As Lowry argues, the meaning of the word *narrative*, when applied to preaching, is encapsulated in H. Grady Davis's memorable line, "The proper design of a sermon is a movement in time."[65] Thus Lowry's major concern is advancing a homiletical method that is more about *temporal plot* than *spatial construction*.[66] In defense of his broader claim that all sermons are narrative, and as an example of the development of tension and resolution in temporal sequence, Lowry uses several examples drawn from melodic and harmonic sequence in jazz music.[67]

One such example occurs in a section detailing the "episodal" sermon form of David Buttrick and Thomas Troeger. Lowry refers to episodal preaching as *vertically plotted mobility*, which he contrasts with his own, *horizontally plotted*, narrative form.[68] Drawing an analogy from jazz music, Lowry details the difference between two types of improvisation. In traditional jazz improvisation, the musician "focus[es] on the tune's melody line throughout the performance, that is, work[s] more traditionally, more horizontally." However, "other, more progressive style musicians improvise with a greater focus on the harmonic structure."[69] He likens the traditional improvisational style to his own horizontally plotted mobility, while Buttrick's episodal preaching he compares to vertically plotted mobility: "His narrativity moves forward by means of episodal (or vertical) blocks. Buttrick and I may come out quite similarly by the time the sermon is concluded. Yet our routes are somewhat differently shaped."[70]

---

[64]This indeed is a recurring theme throughout Lowry's work. See especially *Doing Time in the Pulpit: The Relationship between Narrative and Preaching* (Nashville: Abingdon Press, 1985) and *The Sermon: Dancing on the Edge of Mystery* (Nashville: Abingdon Press, 1997).

[65]Davis, *Design for Preaching*, 163. See Lowry, *Homiletical Beat*, 6.

[66]"When I use the term narrative sermon or narrative preaching normatively, I refer to the arrangement of ideas that takes the form of a homiletical plot. . . . I am talking about the arrangement of ideas that happens by means of the human voice, moment-by-moment-by-moment." Lowry, *Homiletical Beat*, 17.

[67]Accompanying the book is an audio recording of at least one of the lectures on which the book is based, which enables a far greater understanding of the musical metaphors Lowry utilizes. Lowry, *Homiletical Beat*, 49.

[68]Lowry, *Homiletical Beat*, 35-46.

[69]Lowry, *Homiletical Beat*, 37.

[70]Lowry, *Homiletical Beat*, 38.

This is the first of many such examples through which Lowry explores a metaphorical relationship between music and preaching, detailing various options for conceiving homiletical strategies in musical terms. Other examples include a symphonic strategy for transitioning between homiletical "movements"[71] and a large-scale analogy linking Aristotle's *Poetics* to the blues.[72] In the latter example, Lowry interweaves various jazz selections, both sacred and secular, throughout his presentation of Aristotle's four plot stages, noting various similarities between musical and homiletical strategies along the way. This chapter in *The Homiletical Beat*, titled "Encountering the Aristotle Blues," is actually the print transcript of a live "jazz lecture" in which Lowry intersperses the spoken word with the live performance of jazz music.

Lowry's "jazz lecture" is particularly notable in that it is perhaps the most ambitious attempt of any contemporary homiletician to metaphorically link music theory with homiletical theory. Moreover, there is surely more meaning in the live performance than can be expressed on the written page. In this regard, then, Lowry's *Homiletical Beat* furthers the musical-homiletical conversation in important ways, affording nonspecialists the opportunity to learn from musical insights, and connecting musical sounds directly to homiletical strategies. Lowry's *preaching as music* method pays due attention to both the art of preaching and the art of music in themselves. It remains somewhat unclear, however, what Lowry's main counsel is for preachers who would like to integrate musical insights into their homiletical theory, apart from learning to listen more closely in music for moves they can make in preaching.[73]

A third homiletician who has pursued the musical-homiletical conversation through the *preaching as music* method is Mike Graves. In *The Sermon as Symphony: Preaching the Literary Forms of the New Testament*, Graves undertakes a similarly large-scale musical metaphor for preaching, albeit with considerably less precision than Lowry.[74] Seeking to build on Thomas Long's

---

[71]Lowry, *Homiletical Beat*, 39-40. The strategy is that of a thin narrative line that can provide continuity in a sermonic transition, much the way a thin instrumental line can provide continuity in a transition between two symphonic movements.

[72]Lowry, *Homiletical Beat*, 49-73.

[73]Lowry, *Homiletical Beat*, 73. See also Lowry, *Homiletical Beat*, 50, on how Lowry learned to preach the same way he plays jazz piano.

[74]Mike Graves, *The Sermon as Symphony: Preaching the Literary Forms of the New Testament* (Valley Forge, PA: Judson Press, 1997).

book, *Preaching and the Literary Forms of the Bible*, Graves urges preachers to consider *form-sensitive preaching*—preaching which is "sensitive not only to the literary form but also to the genre and devices of a given text."[75] Although Graves does not attempt to sustain the musical metaphor throughout, nonetheless he opens the book with several meditations on music and preaching, counseling preachers to prepare form-sensitive sermons in a manner "akin to composing music."[76]

Graves claims no special musical knowledge or training, and he uses the musical metaphor quite loosely (and abundantly) in the opening chapters.[77] Although the book is ultimately less about music than about literary form, his use of the musical metaphor nonetheless points in several potentially fruitful directions. For instance, Graves explores the oral/aural nature of form-sensitive sermons by appealing to the relationship between musical scores and performed music.[78] Similarly, Graves's identification of *mood* and *movement* as the two primary components of form-sensitive preaching is aided by the musical metaphor, with preachers being urged to listen to the "music" of the biblical text (i.e., the mood and the movement) and to train their ears to hear more skillfully.[79] Finally, Graves also reflects on the pressing need to teach congregations how to listen to the music of the biblical texts, and perhaps the music of our own preaching as well, rather than simply relying on the performance of the material itself to convey its full meaning.[80]

As noted above, however, Graves's work is ultimately more about literary form than it is about music, and thus the *preaching as music* method remains underdeveloped here. Although pointing in several potentially fruitful

---

[75]Graves, *Sermon as Symphony*, 6. Graves notes that whereas Long's text "considered mostly the larger genres of both the Old and New Testaments (for example, psalms, proverbs, epistles) and only one of the smaller forms (parables)," he focuses "exclusively on several New Testament forms, looking at ten distinct forms as found in the New Testament." Graves, *Sermon as Symphony*, 5-6.

[76]Graves, *Sermon as Symphony*, 24.

[77]Music terminology is scattered liberally throughout the opening chapters. For instance, the opening chapters themselves are subtitled "movements" and a section on debates about sermon structure is titled "The Battle of the Bands." Graves, *Sermon as Symphony*, 3, 15, 26, 30.

[78]Graves, *Sermon as Symphony*, 11-12, 15-16.

[79]Graves, *Sermon as Symphony*, 12-14, 18-20.

[80]Graves, *Sermon as Symphony*, 27-30. Here the full implications of the musical metaphor are somewhat unclear. Is music a metaphor for the biblical text, for form-sensitive preaching, or both? Are preachers supposed to be teaching their congregations how to hear the biblical text, their preaching, or both?

directions, the conversation between music and preaching undertaken by Graves does not afford the art of music significant analytical attention, nor does it attempt to, since the musical metaphor is used rather loosely in the advancement of Graves's form-sensitive homiletical approach.

What musicians know: Clayton Schmit. One final method for comparing music and preaching is probably best categorized as a subset of the *preaching as music* method, yet is significant enough to warrant a separate treatment. This more narrowly defined method for metaphorically relating preaching to music, which might be termed *what musicians know*, is employed by Clayton Schmit in his chapter, "What Comes Next? Performing Music and Proclaiming the Word."[81] In this method, musical techniques and skills are metaphorically related to aspects of homiletical theory and performance. As Schmit argues, there is a wealth of skill and insight that musicians have acquired that might be useful to preachers: "I believe that there is something to be learned [by preachers] . . . through a close look at the nature of music and the habits of musical performance," writes Schmit.[82] In this particular chapter, the musical knowledge that Schmit believes will be of use to preachers is the skill of knowing *what comes next.*[83]

Schmit describes the art of preaching as being centrally and primarily the performance of the Word—an external activity—surrounded by two internal sets of activities: preparation and archiving.[84] When compared to the art of music—another externalized activity—it becomes even more apparent that preaching, like music, comes fully into being only when it is performed for, and heard by, others.[85] Schmit continues the musical metaphor by analyzing the performance habits "that release music's qualities of inevitability and anticipation."[86] "All music," writes Schmit, "is built on

---

[81]Clayton J. Schmit, "What Comes Next? Performing and Proclaiming the Word," in *Performance in Preaching*, ed. Jana Childers and Clayton J. Schmit (Grand Rapids, MI: Baker Academic, 2008), 169-90.

[82]Schmit, "What Comes Next?," 169.

[83]Schmit, "What Comes Next?," 170.

[84]Schmit, "What Comes Next?," 173-75.

[85]Schmit, "What Comes Next?," 174-77. Schmit draws out three further lessons from reflection on the practice of musical performance: first, that preaching requires adequate preparation; second, that preaching requires reception by listeners; and third, that each sermon is a spontaneous event that changes with each performance, even if the sermon is being reused. Schmit, "What Comes Next?" 179-80.

[86]Schmit, "What Comes Next?," 181.

conventions that create a sense of inevitability which in turn advances a sense of anticipation in the performance."[87] Skillful composers and performers become adept at creating and maintaining this sense of inevitability and anticipation among their listeners.

Schmit elaborates even further on the conditions necessary for creating musical performance habits, as well as on the specific habits themselves, leading ultimately into a reflection on the theological implications of the musical-homiletical metaphor: "The task of the practicing preacher is to exercise regularly the habits of announcing inevitable grace."[88] This, Schmit maintains, is the larger theological significance of developing a sense of inevitability and anticipation in preaching. In conclusion, Schmit notes several further musical performance practices that he believes preachers might find helpful in their own homiletical practice, among which are habits of relaxed awareness and memory in the moment of delivery.[89]

Schmit's *what musicians know* method[90] is surely the most noteworthy and successful of any of the musical-homiletical efforts surveyed here, for at least two reasons. First, Schmit is the only homiletician to draw extensively on the work of musicologists and philosophers of music in his analysis, thus affording the art of music its own distinctive voice in the conversation. It stands to reason, after all, that a fruitful conversation between music and preaching would require a serious engagement with both musicology and homiletical theory, and indeed Schmit accomplishes this. Second, Schmit's thorough integration of theological and practical insights ensures that his project does not result in a reductionist, "helpful hints" approach to *what musicians know*. Schmit is obviously interested in more than sharing musicians' performance tips with preachers. Through an analysis of musicians' habits and the means of forming those habits, alongside an exploration of the dynamics that create inevitability and anticipation in music, Schmit envisions a comprehensive revitalization of both the preacher's own theological vision and the necessary theological habits that nascent preachers are advised to

---

[87]Schmit, "What Comes Next?," 182.
[88]Schmit, "What Comes Next?," 187. This assertion will be more fully explored below, in chap. 4.
[89]Schmit, "What Comes Next?," 187-88.
[90]It is perhaps more accurate to say that Schmit makes use of both the larger (preaching as music) and the smaller (what musicians know) metaphorical methods, though his main emphasis remains with the smaller.

acquire.[91] This will be an important point to remember as the theological vision of Jeremy Begbie is examined for its potential fruitfulness in the musical-homiletical conversation.

THE STATE OF THE CONVERSATION

Having surveyed eight major contributions to the preaching and music conversation, with four distinct methodological models among them, some evaluative comments are now in order. It seems that there are two crucial points of divergence in determining an appropriate methodology for creating a dialogue between music and preaching. The first crucial methodological decision is the degree to which the comparison of music and preaching will be literal or metaphorical. Of the authors surveyed above, Troeger, Powery, Turner, and Simmons opt for a more literal rendering of the interaction between the two arts, whereas Jones, Lowry, Graves, and Schmit prefer a more metaphorical comparison.

The second major methodological decision is the degree to which the art of music *as music* will have a distinctive voice in the analysis, or whether it will be appealed to mainly on extramusical terms, for its incidental or emergent qualities. Of the contributors surveyed above, Troeger, Lowry, Schmit, and Simmons are the most thorough in their use of music theory and terminology, noting various operative mechanisms within musical sounds themselves, whereas Powery, Turner, Jones, and Graves are much less attentive to the analysis of music itself, keeping theology, sociology, homiletical theory, or even the texts to which works of music are set as their primary points of reference.[92] These two methodological points of divergence can be visually represented as two intersecting axes, allowing the methodological positions of each contributor to be plotted on a graph, as shown in figure 1.1.[93]

---

[91]See especially Schmit, "What Comes Next?," 185-87. Additionally, Schmit examines the anticipatory practices of listeners.

[92]These categorizations are deliberately broad, and it is acknowledged that there is a high degree of variance among the authors and even within each author's work. Some aspects of each author's approach may in fact fall on the other side of each of these methodological fault lines. In broad terms, however, these points of divergence are quite evident among the contributors and do indeed serve as distinguishing methodological factors in the musical-homiletical conversation.

[93]It should be noted that the four methodological quadrants that are created by these two methodological axes do not map neatly onto the four methodological models presented above. For instance, William Turner and Martha Simmons, while both representing the "musicality of preaching"

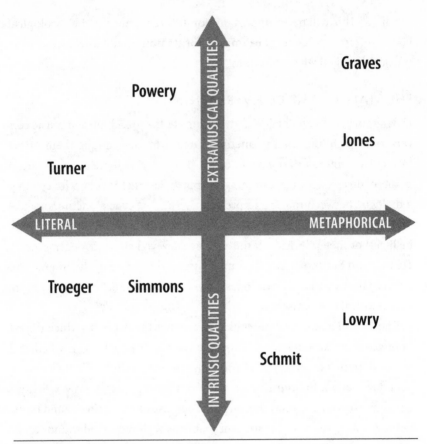

Figure 1.1. Methodological decisions

Of course, there are benefits and drawbacks in each of these methodo-logical decisions. One of the greatest benefits of developing a more literal comparison between music and preaching is that the resultant conversation is more likely to remain rooted in the actual listening life of preachers and congregations. For instance, Troeger's music in preaching method is of direct practical import, and his pastoral aims are clear: to address the spiritual bar-renness of a modern ecclesial context devoid of art, helping to renew a sense of wonder in the listening habits of preachers and congregations through the creative inclusion of music in sermons. Moreover, given the historical con-nection of African American spirituals and the Black preaching tradition,

model, fall on opposite sides of the "extramusical qualities-intrinsic qualities" axis, placing them into different quadrants in figure 1.1.

along with the undeniable musicality of Black preaching, it seems natural that Powery, Turner, and Simmons would focus their analysis more on the literal interplay between the two arts in practice.[94] A more literal comparison between music and preaching helps to ensure the practical import of the study.

The drawback of this methodological decision, however, is that it limits the potential resonances that might be discovered through a more sustained theoretical and metaphorical interaction between the two arts. In addition, engaging music and preaching on a more literal level may tend toward an unhelpful instrumental reason, in which music is seen primarily as a helpful tool for generating interest *for interest's sake* in preaching. To be sure, Troeger, Powery, Turner, and Simmons all take pains to avoid this tendency. Powery's strong pneumatological focus, in particular, seems to distance his work significantly from various types of instrumental reason that might hinder the fruitfulness of such a project.[95] Nonetheless, in the popular reception of such a methodology, the tendency toward instrumental reason is often difficult to avoid, and the reductionism that coincides with such a reception can have detrimental effects.

The great benefit, then, of maintaining a metaphorical interaction between music and preaching is that this method preserves a much greater theoretical space in which the resonances between the two arts might be more fully explored and the knowledge and understanding of each practice

---

[94]This brings to the fore the important insight that vocal music and speech exist not as entirely separate entities, but rather as two ends of a spectrum. This connection, as Powery, Turner, Simmons, and many others have shown, is preserved much more strongly in the African American preaching tradition than it is in Euro-American preaching. One thinks also of ancient music, which no doubt sounded much different than what we hear as music today. Although nearly impossible to recreate with absolute confidence, ancient chant is thought to have been much farther along the spectrum toward speech than is modern vocal music. See, for instance, Jeremy Begbie, *Resounding Truth: Christian Wisdom in the World of Music* (Grand Rapids, MI: Baker Academic, 2007), 73-74, 85. For a recent scientific analysis of the overlap between music and language, see Aniruddh D. Patel, *Music, Language, and the Brain* (New York: Oxford University Press, 2008).

[95]A recent analysis by Stephen Guthrie of the pneumatological implications of the New Testament command to sing "psalms, hymns, and spiritual songs" (Eph 5:19; Col 3:16) may provide further theological support to Powery's work connecting the "musical sermons" of the spirituals with the practice of "spiritual" preaching. See Steven R. Guthrie, "The Wisdom of Song," in *Resonant Witness: Conversations between Music and Theology*, ed. Jeremy S. Begbie and Steven R. Guthrie (Grand Rapids, MI: Eerdmans, 2011), 382-407. The theological connection Guthrie identifies here will be more fully explored in the following chapter.

deepened.[96] The danger, of course, is of stretching the metaphor too far, resulting in incoherence. Music and preaching both make use of the same materials—sound and time—but they use irreducibly different mechanisms in the creation of their respective arts. A metaphorical method thus requires far greater precision, or else it risks complete failure. The other concern of the metaphorical methodology is that it risks practical irrelevance. Certain resonances between music and preaching that might initially seem to generate groundbreaking insight for homiletical theory over time might prove to be of questionable practical import in the training and regular ministry life of preachers.[97] It would be far better in that case to remain grounded in a methodology that allows music and preaching to interact more in practice, rather than solely in theory.

The other crucial methodological decision is whether music will mostly be analyzed as music through engagement with musicology or music theory, or if it will instead be engaged primarily in extramusical terms, noting its incidental or emergent qualities. The benefits of engaging music in its own artistic integrity are similar to the benefits of the metaphorical approach: the potential for a richer theoretical yield and the avoidance of reductionism. A further benefit is the balance of the two disciplines; after all, a true conversation needs equal interaction between the two parties. The risks are also similar: precisely because music retains its own artistic integrity in its means of shaping sound, some musicological concepts may not be easily relatable or translatable to preaching, the latter art obviously nonexistent without the use of language. In some cases, there may be more traction to be gained through reflection not on music theory itself, but rather on some of the emotions and experiences that are generated through the art of music, as Powery, Jones, and Graves all note.

---

[96] A similar impulse lies behind Mark Porter's use of the term *resonance* to explore "the multidirectional and multidimensional complexes of relationships that surround Christian musicking." It is precisely because the concept of resonance is based in the materiality of musical sound while also spilling over "into other realms of experience, perception, meaning, and significance" that the term acquires its analytical power. Mark Porter, *Ecologies of Resonance in Christian Musicking* (New York: Oxford University Press, 2020), 7-8. See chapter 1 for a fuller exploration of the interaction between the literal and the metaphorical (or perhaps the physical and the metaphysical) dimensions of musical resonance.

[97] This is an enduring concern in Jeremy Begbie's *theology through the arts* project. For a discussion of this critique and a defense of the practical/performative import of his work, see Begbie, *Music, Modernity, and God: Essays in Listening* (New York: Oxford University Press, 2014), 214-16.

A METHODOLOGICAL EXEMPLAR: JANA CHILDERS

What is needed, therefore—and what this project attempts to sustain—is a kind of methodological middle ground, an approach to the musical-homiletical conversation that remains as close as possible to the center of both axes on the methodological plane (or, perhaps more accurately, a methodology that moves freely among—and draws equally from—all four quadrants). What is needed, in other words, is an approach that captures insights for preachers drawn from both a literal and a metaphorical interaction with music, while also giving the art of music *as music* a significant voice in the conversation, paying careful attention to the intrinsic qualities of musical sounds while also considering the incidental or emergent properties generated by performing and listening to music.

This is indeed the methodological approach found in another *preaching and the arts* project, Jana Childers's book *Performing the Word: Preaching as Theatre*.[98] Unlike many of the extant musical-homiletical projects, Childers's treatment of the relationship between theater and preaching is full-length. Moreover, it is devoted solely to drawing homiletical insights from the world of theater. The great value of Childers's method is found especially in the middle path she creates between the literal and the metaphorical, a crucial methodological point of departure in the musical-homiletical conversations explored in this chapter. Although clearly preferring the metaphorical, Childers approaches the relationship between the two arts through their commonalities, or shared characteristics, which goes beyond emotional (or other extrinsic) effects. Childers clearly identifies common dimensions in what each art creates within its own artistic integrity, noting both intrinsic elements of "how theater works" and emergent properties of "what theater does" contextually.

The three shared characteristics Childers identifies between the art of theater and the art of preaching are the role of action, the role of distance, and the role of performance.[99] An analysis of each of these commonalities enables her to find "overlapping terrain" that is neither wholly metaphorical nor wholly literal. The latter chapters of the book make use of the more specific methodology of

---

[98]Jana Childers, *Performing the Word: Preaching as Theatre* (Nashville: Abingdon Press, 2008).
[99]Childers, *Performing the Word*, 39-52.

what actors know, highlighting performance basics,[100] methods for the performance and interpretation of written texts,[101] and habits and skills of actors that
are relevant to preaching.[102] The final chapter broadens the theatrical metaphor,
comparing the art of theater to the worship service as a whole.[103]

Childers's methodological focus and consistency make her a worthy exemplar in the musical-homiletical conversation, in that she finds a balanced
position on the metaphorical/literal spectrum and she also allows the art of
theater to retain its own proper artistic integrity, attending to both its intrinsic and emergent qualities. However, one way that Childers seems to unnec-
essarily limit herself in this project is her seeming reticence to draw out the
broader theological implications of this interdisciplinary study. If Childers
aims to provide, as she writes, "a model of preaching that is by nature a creative
event and whose purpose is to open us to God's movement," might she not
want to propose anything further about what specific Christian virtues or
dispositions might be cultivated if theater is to serve as a generative model
for helping preachers work "not only with words on a page but with performed
words"?[104] Might there not be further implications that could be explored
regarding our understanding of the movement of God, the life of the church,
and the nature of pastoral ministry, if preachers are to follow Childers's guidance toward a more lively homiletic based on a theatrical metaphor? Or, to
borrow David Taylor's language, might there not be a more robust account
to be given of the formative potential of *preaching as theater*, in conversation
with a theological analysis of the "singular powers" of theater within God's
creative and redemptive purposes?[105]

A MUSICAL-THEOLOGICAL GUIDE: JEREMY BEGBIE

For this reason, then, it is necessary to involve a more robust theological guide
as well in this musical-homiletical conversation, in order that the temptation

---

[100]Childers, *Performing the Word*, 57-77.
[101]Childers, *Performing the Word*, 78-98.
[102]Childers, *Performing the Word*, 99-120.
[103]Childers, *Performing the Word*, 121-145.
[104]Childers, *Performing the Word*, 35.
[105]See Taylor, *Glimpses of the New Creation*, chapter 8, for an analysis of the formative powers of the
theater arts in worship. See also Todd E. Johnson and Dale Savidge, *Performing the Sacred: Theology and Theater in Dialogue* (Grand Rapids, MI: Baker Academic, 2009).

toward instrumental reason might be rigorously avoided. Jeremy Begbie is well suited to serve as such a guide. As Schmit notes in his own study, Begbie is undoubtedly the foremost theologian in the interdisciplinary conversation between music and theology.[106] Moreover, Begbie's methodological clarity and consistency deserve careful attention. Throughout his work, Begbie evinces a disciplined and sustained intention to discover new areas in which the church's theological understanding might be renewed through the medium of music.

Music, in Begbie's work, is an avenue through which not just practical insights but *new theological vistas* can be discovered. As he states in the introduction to one of his major works,

> The reader is invited to engage with music in such a way that central doctrinal loci are explored, interpreted, reconceived and articulated. It will be found that unfamiliar themes are opened up, familiar topics exposed and negotiated in fresh and telling ways, obscure matters—resistant to some modes of understanding—are clarified, and distortions of theological truth avoided and even corrected.[107]

Schmit's own commitment to "seeing music not merely as an analog for preaching," but further, "to inquire about music's essential qualities and discern from them theological principles that can inform the theology and task of preaching" is no doubt a result of his choice to follow Begbie's method.[108] Reductive instrumental reasoning, though a lurking danger in much musical-theological discussion, is nowhere to be found in Begbie's writing.[109] This theological clarity is what makes Begbie an indispensable

---

[106]Schmit, "What Comes Next?," 170. For a thorough, more general overview of the more general field of *theological aesthetics*, or *theology and the arts*, see Richard Viladesau, *Theological Aesthetics: God in Imagination, Beauty, and Art* (1999; repr., Oxford: Oxford University Press, 2012). See also Daniel J. Treier, Mark Husbands, and Roger Lundin, eds., *The Beauty of God: Theology and the Arts* (Downers Grove, IL: InterVarsity Press, 2007).

[107]Jeremy S. Begbie, *Theology, Music and Time* (Cambridge: Cambridge University Press, 2000), 5. As Begbie states elsewhere, "To 'get inside' a fresh language means that I will discern more, understand more. . . . Something similar happens when we 'get inside' the arts and explore the Christian gospel from the 'inside.' Our discernment and understanding are enriched. We discover more." Jeremy Begbie, introduction to *Beholding the Glory: Incarnation through the Arts* (Grand Rapids, MI: Baker Academic, 2001), xi.

[108]Schmit, "What Comes Next?," 171.

[109]See, for instance, Begbie's critique of immanentist, unitarian accounts of transcendence in the arts in Jeremy Begbie, *Redeeming Transcendence in the Arts: Bearing Witness to the Triune God* (Grand Rapids, MI: Eerdmans, 2018). As Begbie insists, the idea of transcendence must not be reduced to generalized accounts of God's presence and relationship to the world, based solely on

guide in this project, as without his insight some of the most pressing theological issues in this interdisciplinary terrain might be left unacknowledged or unexplored.

A brief examination of Begbie's approach to theology and the arts—or, more specifically, his approach to *theology through music*—will help to demonstrate the importance of his voice for the musical-homiletical conversation. Methodologically, Begbie's *theology through music* project might best be understood as a theology of the created world, or more specifically, a theological analysis of some of the aspects of the created world that are illumined and even transformed through musical processes.[110] The care and transformation of creation is thus a prominent feature of Begbie's musical theology. The name of one of his early works, *Voicing Creation's Praise*, demonstrates this emphasis.[111]

Eschewing the nature/culture dichotomy, Begbie posits a "theological imaginary" through which creation and culture can be understood, not as opposed to or distinct from one another, but rather together. This "imaginary" includes distinct visions of both artists and the created world:

> The artist, as physical and embodied, [is] set in the midst of a God-given world vibrant with a dynamic order of its own, not simply "there" to be left wholly as it is, or escaped, or violently abused but there as a gift from a God of uncontainable generosity, a gift for us to interact with vigorously, form, and (in the face of distortion) transform, and in this way fashion something that, in at least some manner, can be heard as anticipating by the Spirit the shalom previewed and promised in Jesus Christ.[112]

---

the supposed ability of humanity to apprehend these things, but rather must be rooted in the specific scriptural revelation of God's trinitarian transcendence, radiating outward to the world God creates. See especially pp. 122-26.

[110]See the discussion on "natural theology" and the "theology of nature" in Alastair Borthwick, Trevor Hart, and Anthony Monti, "Musical Time and Eschatology," in *Resonant Witness: Conversations between Music and Theology*, ed. Jeremy S. Begbie and Steven R. Guthrie (Grand Rapids, MI: Eerdmans, 2011), 271-72. See also Begbie's examination of this issue in *Theology, Music and Time*, 274-75, and *A Peculiar Orthodoxy: Reflections on Theology and the Arts* (Grand Rapids, MI: Baker Academic, 2018), 139-40. Given his strong emphasis on the self-revelation of the triune God, Begbie quite obviously falls on the side of a "theology of nature" rather than "natural theology."

[111]Jeremy S. Begbie, *Voicing Creation's Praise: Towards a Theology of the Arts* (New York: T&T Clark, 1991). For a comprehensive treatment of these themes, see especially part 3.

[112]Begbie, *Music, Modernity, and God*, 104. See also *A Peculiar Orthodoxy*, 142.

Begbie's theological analyses of the music of J. S. Bach are but one instance of such a theological vision in action.[113] The potential resonances that might be found by extending this understanding of the artist's vocation into a more comprehensive vocational vision of *the preacher as artist* are immense.[114]

Indeed, Begbie's careful and unique approach to theology and the arts is on full display in his many scholarly publications. To give another example, in his groundbreaking book *Theology, Music and Time*, Begbie pursues a thorough inquiry into some of the dynamics of created temporality—and our relationship with it—that are illumined by the practices of making and hearing music. For the purposes of this musical-homiletical conversation, it is important to note that such "illumination" or "rearticulation" of certain doctrinal loci is distinguished from mere "illustration" of such topics.[115] Rather, through the creative enactment of temporal processes, practical and theoretical knowledge itself is deepened and expanded. Begbie is especially keen throughout his writing to distinguish himself from instrumental reason, which is ultimately what "illustration" amounts to.[116]

Begbie's overarching hope for his theological project, he writes, is not only that specific doctrines would be revitalized, but even that the very way theology is done would be refreshed. "One of the most obvious challenges music will present is to ask theology if it is prepared to integrate a 'performative' mode into its work."[117] Similarly, the musical homiletic developed in this book seeks to integrate both a performative and a systematic-theological mode into homiletical theory, as these two modes are kept apart far too often in the homiletical literature and in the training and development of preachers. Just as preaching itself should never be reduced to merely the practical

---

[113]See "Created Beauty: The Witness of J. S. Bach," in Begbie and Guthrie, *Resonant Witness*, 83-108; and "Disquieting Conversations: Bach, Modernity, and God," in *Music, Modernity, and God*, 41-72.

[114]This is very much in line with the theological vision developed by Trygve David Johnson in *The Preacher as Liturgical Artist: Metaphor, Identity, and the Vicarious Humanity of Christ* (Eugene, OR: Cascade, 2014). As Johnson argues, the theological "imaginary" that shapes preachers' understanding of their homiletical identity is of crucial importance in the practice of preaching.

[115]This was a major critique of Begbie's work in Adrienne Dengerink Chaplin, "The Theological Potential of Music: An Evaluation of Jeremy Begbie's *Theology, Music and Time*—A Review Essay," *Christian Scholar's Review* 33, no. 1 (Fall 2003): 125-33.

[116]See especially Begbie's response to Chaplin in Jeremy Begbie, "The Theological Potential of Music: A Response to Adrienne Dengerink Chaplin," *Christian Scholar's Review* 33, no. 1 (Fall 2003): 135-41.

[117]Begbie, *Theology, Music and Time*, 280.

"application" of truths that have been previously established by systematic theology or biblical studies, so also should the performative mode of preaching not be reduced to the mere "delivery" of a message that has previously been established by written words on a page.

Begbie's scholarship consistently aims to demonstrate "what can be done when we are prepared to 'listen' in a concentrated way" to the insights that emerge when the art of music—or even the performative mode more generally—is allowed a significant voice in theology.[118] Despite the undeniable benefits of incorporating this performative mode into theological discourse, however, a persistent concern remains with regard to the relationship between linguistic and non-linguistic arts, which has immediate implications for the methodology of the musical-homiletical conversation. A common objection raised by Begbie's critics is that his approach to theology and the arts results in music serving as little more than a convenient conceptual illustration of a preestablished, linguistically formulated doctrine. Indeed, Begbie himself admits that theology "is inescapably committed to a certain form of primacy with regard to language, not through its own choosing but by virtue of the nature of God's own self-presentation."[119] Nonetheless, Begbie remains firmly convinced that music can play a role in the formation—not merely the illustration—of doctrine.[120]

The criticism is not easily dismissed, though, that Begbie's manner of conducting the musical-theological conversation amounts to nothing more than "the bringing together of two types of verbal language—musical [i.e., language about music] and theological—along with their associated thought patterns; not two different media."[121] Indeed, William Dyrness charges that in Begbie's *Theology, Music and Time*, despite the conceptual benefits it affords, "music is still only a metaphor; it is a giver of insight."[122] Begbie responds to Dyrness's charge by recalling that at the fundamental level music is a practice —or rather a twin set of practices, music-making and music-hearing—and it

---

[118]Begbie, *Music, Modernity, and God*, 9.
[119]Begbie, *Music, Modernity, and God*, 202.
[120]Begbie, *Music, Modernity, and God*, 203-7.
[121]Begbie, *Music, Modernity, and God*, 215.
[122]William A. Dyrness, *Poetic Theology: God and the Poetics of Everyday Life* (Grand Rapids, MI: Eerdmans, 2011), 151, quoted in Begbie, *Music, Modernity, and God*, 215.

is to these practices that musicological analysis attends.[123] Of course, Begbie allows, music can "reveal the grace of the Creator directly" and function iconically "without directly associated texts."[124] However, in order to make such claims "with any integrity" there needs to be some recourse to normative language and conceptuality. Otherwise, any claim to direct musical mediation of the divine "is vulnerable to being dismissed as vacuous."[125]

Yet despite this deft rejoinder, there is something ultimately unsatisfying about characterizing Begbie's project as "theology through music," as most of his work still consists of *writing about music,* not *making music.* Perhaps a more accurate description of his project would be "theology through musicology."[126] Begbie has indeed participated in scores of musical performances that might be classified as "theology through music." No doubt the meaning of the music in these performances has been enhanced by the use of some accompanying language. However, when the musician then steps back and reflects verbally on theological insights generated through music, he is no longer doing "theology through music," but rather "theology through musicology." This is not to devalue Begbie's work in any way, but rather to seek the most accurate description of Begbie's immeasurable contribution to contemporary theology.[127]

The difficulty involved in characterizing Begbie's theological method, along with Begbie's own attempts to answer his critics and defend his approach to theology and the arts, provides a helpful parallel through which to reflect on

---

[123]Begbie, *Music, Modernity, and God,* 216.

[124]Begbie, *Music, Modernity, and God,* 216.

[125]Begbie, *Music, Modernity, and God,* 216. Note the similarity to the criticisms of "whooping" that Simmons catalogs in her chapter on the musicality of African American preaching. Perhaps the most persistent concern, she notes, is that the musical-homiletical practice of whooping could too easily substitute for sound theological teaching. See Simmons, "Whooping," 881-82. See also Cleophus J. LaRue, *Rethinking Celebration: From Rhetoric to Praise in African American Preaching* (Louisville, KY: Westminster John Knox, 2016).

[126]Begbie's observation that, at the core, his writing attends to musical *practices,* not to any reified object called "music," should not significantly affect the accuracy of this designation; musical practices and performances are precisely the subject matter of musicology as well.

[127]One exception to this general evaluation of Begbie's methodology is Jeremy Begbie, ed., *Sounding the Depths: Theology through the Arts* (London: SCM Press, 2002). This text stems directly from an arts festival that occurred in Cambridge in September 2000 and comprises introductions to, and excerpts of, the artworks themselves, followed by theological reflections on the works and performances. In that sense, this particular compilation remains much closer to the methodological ideal of "theology through music," rather than "theology through musicology."

the methodological decisions involved in the conversation between music and preaching. If, as I am claiming, Begbie's work is best categorized as "theology through musicology," rather than "theology through music," then this distinction might also be useful in evaluating various approaches to the interdisciplinary dialogue between music and preaching outlined in this chapter. More specifically, Thomas Troeger's work is perhaps closest to the "preaching through (and with) music" approach, whereas Clayton Schmit's work, like Begbie's, is perhaps better understood as "homiletical theory through musicology." The latter approach is also perhaps the best categorization of the methodological basis underlying the musical homiletic developed in the following chapters.

FRAMING THE CONVERSATION: THREE
SHARED CHARACTERISTICS

As this chapter has demonstrated, methodology is of crucial importance in an interdisciplinary study such as this, as the method used for framing the conversation between the art of music and the art of preaching will determine in large part the insights subsequently generated by the conversation. Since all four methodologies used in the extant contributions examined in this chapter offer unique and indispensable insights to preachers who are seeking to develop their musical instincts, the musical homiletic developed over the next several chapters will attempt to chart a middle course among these various methodological options.[128]

What this will mean for the present study is that the primary exchange between music and preaching will occur through a sustained examination of three characteristics—*synchrony, repetition,* and *teleology*—that are shared between these two disciplines.[129] Special care will be taken to incorporate both metaphorical and literal perspectives, while also affording the art of

---

[128]In a significant sense, then, this project will seek to appropriate both Jana Childers's *shared characteristics* approach to preaching and the arts and Jeremy Begbie's *theology through music* approach to the study of doctrine. For more on Childers's *shared characteristics* methodology, see Childers, *Performing the Word*, 39-52. For more on Begbie's *theology through the arts* methodology, see Begbie, *Sounding the Depths*, 1-11.

[129]No doubt there are further characteristics that could be added to this study. However, given the theoretical, practical, and spiritual resonances that will emerge from these three characteristics alone, it is appropriate to limit the conversation in this way.

music a significant voice in the conversation through a detailed analysis of both the intrinsic and the emergent/extramusical properties of musical sounds. Throughout this project, the temptation toward instrumental reason will be resisted by concluding each of these chapters with an analysis of the theologically and spiritually formative potential of each characteristic. Insights from Begbie's *theology through the arts* project will provide crucial guidance in these concluding sections.

EXAMPLE: MUSIC IN PREACHING

The following excerpt provides an example of one of these four musical-homiletical methods, the "music in preaching" method.[130] Since none of the sermon excerpts included in subsequent chapters make use of this particular method, it is worth highlighting here. Notice the way Troeger draws specific attention to the musical qualities that Bach uses to "preach" the texts that Troeger himself also interprets linguistically. The music of Bach's cantata, as Troeger conceives it, provides in one sense another "text" on which his sermon is based, and in another sense another "sermon" that stands alongside his own interpretation of the Scripture readings from Isaiah 52:1-2, Revelation 19:6-8, and Matthew 22:1-14. This sermon was preached in the context of a full worship service "using congregational song, prayers, Scripture readings, and sacramental action," along with a performance of a full musical work, J. S. Bach's Cantata 180, "Schmücke dich, o liebe Seele (Deck Thyself, O Beloved Soul)."[131]

Troeger begins by illustrating the connection between clothing and issues of identity, behavior, and self-perception. He then continues:

> For most of human history the making of clothes was a labor-intensive activity. People did not shop in stores amid racks filled with ready-to-wear clothes. The biblical writers knew how demanding and time-consuming it was to make a garment. Therefore, when they wanted to convey the arduous work of living a life of integrity, they often turned to the metaphor of dressing. Isaiah says: "Awake, awake, put on your strength, O Zion! Put on your beautiful garments, O Jerusalem, the holy city." The author of Revelation envisions the church as

---

[130]Sermon Text Excerpt: Thomas Troeger, "Deck Thyself" in *Wonder Reborn*, 99.
[131]Troeger, *Wonder Reborn*, 94.

the bride of Christ to whom "'it has been granted to be clothed with fine linen, bright and pure'—for the fine linen is the righteous deeds of the saints." And the parable from today's gospel stresses the seriousness of being rightly attired. The king who has invited people to a wedding banquet for his son asks: "Friend, how did you get in here without a wedding robe?"

Bach builds the opening chorale[132] of today's cantata around the biblical metaphor of dressing ourselves in righteousness. As the choir sings "Adorn yourself, O dear soul," the accompanying instruments weave the finery with which the soul is to be attired.

To feel the wonder of the aria[133] that follows, imagine yourself all decked out for your first formal date, and finally the doorbell rings. Of course, in the time of the Bible and in the time of Bach there were no electric doorbells. Instead there was a knock at the door. Bach gives the knock to the flute, and a very insistent knock it is, repeated again and again as if we do not answer instantly. There is even a section in the aria where we get the impression of our being unable to respond: there are eighth-note rests in the musical phrases that accompany the words "Only partly broken words of gladness," suggesting how we are speechless with joy at the arrival of our beloved. This speechlessness finally gives way to a great sustained note and flourish on the word "utter," suggesting we have finally found our voice. There is insight here into the state of the human soul getting ready to welcome God. We attire ourselves in all that is most beautiful and gracious, but when God arrives we are at first speechless. Then when we finally find our tongue, our utterance is boundless.[134]

Troeger then goes on to provide musical-theological commentary on the remaining movements of the cantata (a total of seven) before offering this concluding word, which would then lead into a full performance of the cantata.

The entire spiritual process that the cantata has led us through is not just about the individual soul but about the soul of the community, about the soul of the congregation as a whole. Through the cantata God calls us to become a holy community, attired with the integrity and faithfulness that can transform a broken world. Listening to this cantata is like standing before the mirror in

---

[132]A "chorale" is a piece of vocal music written in four-part harmony—like a hymn tune, although in this case more musically complex than most congregational hymn tunes.

[133]An "aria" is a movement written for solo voice.

[134]Notice how Troeger comments on both the lyrics and the musical sounds of the composition, which demonstrates a confidence in the "witness" of the music itself, apart from (and in combination with) the text that is set to it.

which we check how we appear in some new clothes. The cantata reflects back to us the deepest anxieties and the greatest joys of the soul as we dress for royalty, as we prepare to welcome the holy one who stands at the door, the eternally hospitable host: Jesus, the bread of life.[135]

---

[135]Bach's cantata is then given "the final word," as the congregation attends to the subsequent musical performance with the preacher having primed them to listen in particular ways. The words of Scripture, the words of the preacher, and the text of the cantata are thus meant to resonate together through this musical performance in the context of a full worship service.

2

SHAPING COMMUNAL TIME

SYNCHRONY AND UNITY

ONE OF THE FIRST SKILLS any beginning music student needs to learn is how to count. The sooner a person develops a sense of musical timing, the sooner that person starts to sound like a proper musician. On the other hand, any music teacher can testify how difficult it can be to work with students who struggle to develop a sense of timing. It takes an abundance of patience to sit with a novice musician and teach them how to turn rhythmic notation into musical sounds in time.

Yet even accomplished musicians can sometimes get so used to performing solely within the technical confines of their particular instruments that they may struggle to integrate a sense of musical timing throughout their entire body. As a first-year undergraduate music student, I was required to take a course called "Eurythmics" (not to be confused with the 1980s British pop duo). The purpose of this course was to help undergraduate music majors develop a sense of rhythm in a holistic, bodily sense. I will never forget the class periods when we learned to keep a beat by bouncing a tennis ball or to sound triplet rhythms by skipping our feet.

This chapter will examine the gift God has given us in the musical-homiletical phenomenon of synchrony, paying special attention to the formative potential of shaping communal time through the embodiment of rhythmic instincts in the preached word.

SYNCHRONY IN MUSIC

The first of the three shared characteristics to be examined in the development of this musical homiletic is *synchrony*—a phenomenon that highlights the inescapable temporality of musical sounds, or even more generally, of sound itself. Both music and preaching make use of synchronous mechanisms in the shaping of communal time. Jeremy Begbie succinctly defines music as "the intentional production of temporally organized patterns of pitched sounds,"[1] and indeed, between the two of these sonic characteristics, temporal organization and pitch, it is the temporal organization of musical sounds that receives the most attention in Begbie's writing. In his magnum opus, *Theology, Music and Time*, Begbie summarizes the close relationship of music and temporality as follows: "Time is intrinsically bound up with music's sounds; musical sounds 'pull the strings' of the temporality 'in which' they occur."[2] "Music," writes Begbie, "is a temporal art through and through."[3] Thus, for Begbie, as for many music theorists, musicological analysis almost inevitably leads to—and overlaps with—a philosophical analysis of time itself.

Roger Scruton makes a similar claim about the intrinsic relationship between music and temporality in his massive work, *The Aesthetics of Music*, though he arrives at this claim by a much different route. Scruton begins his musical aesthetics not with an analysis of temporality, but rather of sound. Sound, or perhaps more precisely *sounds*, are secondary objects, he argues, making them neither qualities of things nor material objects. As such, sounds are "pure events": "Although the sound that I hear is produced by something, I am presented in hearing with the sound alone. The thing that produces the sound, even if it is 'something heard,' is not the intentional object of hearing, but only the cause of what I hear."[4]

If sounds themselves are to be classified as pure events, as Scruton contends, then it is inevitable that the temporality of music would become an irreducible dimension of its artistic ontology, since "music is an art of sound, and

---

[1] Jeremy Begbie, *Resounding Truth: Christian Wisdom in the World of Music* (Grand Rapids, MI: Baker Academic, 2007), 40. See also Begbie, *Theology, Music and Time* (Cambridge: Cambridge University Press, 2000), 9. While this definition focuses on the practice of *music-making*, it is important to note that Begbie identifies *music-making* as only one of two closely intertwined practices, the other being *music-hearing*. For further discussion of the interconnectedness of *music-making* and *music-hearing*, see Nicholas Wolterstorff, "The Work of Making a Work of Music," in *What Is Music? An Introduction to the Philosophy of Music*, ed. Philip Alperson (University Park, PA: Pennsylvania State University Press, 1987), 101-29.

[2] Begbie, *Theology, Music and Time*, 26.

[3] Begbie, *Theology, Music and Time*, 30.

[4] Roger Scruton, *The Aesthetics of Music* (Oxford: Oxford University Press, 1997), 11.

much that seems strange in music can be traced to the strangeness of the sound world itself."[5] "Sound events take time," he writes. "But being pure events, their temporal order is the *basic* order they exhibit."[6] Temporal organization, therefore, is a basic and intrinsic dimension of music as an art in sound.

However, given that temporal organization is so crucial to the ontology of music, it is somewhat surprising to discover the lack of philosophical and musicological attention afforded the phenomenon of synchrony, loosely defined as the bringing together of disparate individual temporalities into a single, coordinated temporal whole in the making and hearing of music.[7] Indeed, although Begbie examines at length the possibilities of music to help humankind live peaceably with the reality of time and to discover the goodness of time within God's creative purposes,[8] he only briefly notes some of the communal implications of the temporal organization of musical sounds.[9] Some authors, such as Christopher Small, have devoted significant attention to the sociological dimensions of music-making. However, much of this work has been done for deconstructive purposes, with Small's work in particular containing a strong ideological critique of modern Western musical practices.[10] Begbie rightly cautions that this line of critique "can veer perilously close

---

[5]Scruton, *Aesthetics of Music*, 16.

[6]Scruton, *Aesthetics of Music*, 12.

[7]This is distinguished from the more circumscribed phenomenon of *entrainment*, which refers to the ability "to extract a regular pulse from music and adjust some aspect of behavior to it." Synchrony might be thought of as a broader concept referring to the synchronizing of disparate temporalities, which may or may not involve observable manifestations of rhythmic entrainment. See Andrea Ravignani, Daniel L. Bowling, and W. Tecumseh Fitch, "Chorusing, Synchrony, and the Evolutionary Functions of Rhythm," *Frontiers in Psychology* 5 (October 10, 2014), http://dx.doi .org/10.3389/fpsyg.2014.01118.

[8]See especially *Theology, Music and Time*, chap. 4.

[9]There is, in fact, an extended discussion on the communal dimensions of music in *Resounding Truth*, 267-75, although this discussion focuses less on the unity that is created in the act of making music communally and more on the communal realities and responsibilities that impinge upon Christian musicians. For a much more theologically suggestive and scripturally insightful examination of the communal dimensions of music, or more particularly of singing, see Steven R. Guthrie, "The Wisdom of Song," in *Resonant Witness: Conversations between Music and Theology*, ed. Jeremy S. Begbie and Steven R. Guthrie (Grand Rapids, MI: Eerdmans, 2011), 382-407. Guthrie's contribution will be examined in greater depth below.

[10]Christopher Small, *Musicking: The Meanings of Performing and Listening* (Middletown, CT: Wesleyan University Press, 1998). Small's overall aim is a worthy one, in that he seeks to broaden the definition of music beyond Western classical music, and to widen the focus of musicology beyond the analysis of musical "works," abstracted from their performative context and conceived of as

to treating music-makers and music-hearers as little more than ciphers of group interests."[11] Yet there remains a dearth of alternative, positive accounts of the unifying effects of musical temporality among musicologists and philosophers of Western music.

In contrast, musical synchrony is a burgeoning topic of research in the natural and social sciences, particularly in the fields of evolutionary biology and psychology. For instance, an article in the journal *Human Nature* proposes that a possible adaptive advantage of music and dance, which might account for the emergence of these phenomena in human life, is the use of music as a coalition signaling system, a means of demonstrating the strength of a group's cohesion to those who are outside of the group.[12] This, the authors believe, accounts for rhythm and synchrony in music and dance better than other dominant evolutionary theories regarding the adaptive value of music.[13] Another article traces the growing body of scientific research that demonstrates the prosocial consequences of synchronous musical activity among both children and adults.[14] Nonetheless, even the authors of the latter piece acknowledge that the scientific study of musical phenomena has thus far favored isolated listeners and music-makers, with attention given to the neurological underpinnings of musical practices in individuals, for example, to the exclusion of the communal dimension of synchronous musical activity.

---

things in themselves. However, the deconstructionist implications of Small's framing question, "What's really going on here?" (see especially chap. 12), together with his open acknowledgment of his "dislike" of the rituals of the Western classical tradition (p. 213), leaves Small's work itself open to the very same deconstructive critiques that he levels at the scholars and purveyors of classical music.

[11]Begbie, *Theology, Music and Time*, 14n18. It should be noted that Begbie is not referencing Small specifically in this comment, but rather several other practitioners of the "New" musicology. However, it is reasonable to include Small's deconstructionist analysis in this group, for reasons specified in the preceding note. See also Small, *Musicking*, 220-21, in which Small concludes his study with an almost wholesale rejection of the entire corpus of Western classical music.

[12]Edward H. Hagen and Gregory A. Bryant, "Music and Dance as a Coalition Signaling System," *Human Nature* 14, no. 1 (March 2003): 21-51.

[13]The two other dominant evolutionary theories the authors examine are the sexual selection theory and the group cohesion theory. See Hagen and Bryant, "Music and Dance," 23-27. For an alternative evolutionary theory on the emergence of synchrony, see also Gary Tomlinson, *A Million Years of Music: The Emergence of Human Modernity* (New York: Zone Books, 2015). Tomlinson speculates on the emergence of musical synchrony in the context of the social synchronies that developed among the taskscapes of early hominins. See especially 275-78.

[14]Sandra E. Trehub, Judith Becker, and Iain Morley, "Cross-Cultural Perspectives on Music and Musicality," *Philosophical Transactions of the Royal Society B* 370, no. 1664 (February 2, 2015), http://dx.doi.org/10.1098/rstb.2014.0096.

One likely cause of this large-scale musicological neglect of the communal dimension is the preference of music theorists for analyzing form over function. As David Huron points out,

> Over the past half century, music theorists have largely worked on problems of musical "anatomy" (describing the structures of music) rather than problems of musical "physiology" (describing the purpose of these structures). In light of the difficulty of identifying function, many music theorists have accepted that describing structure is the intellectually more defensible occupation.[15]

While the analysis of musical structure (form) is, and should continue to be, an integral task of musicology, it must not be the sole focus. Indeed, Huron believes that "the tools of empirical research have advanced sufficiently that music theory can once again rekindle the dream of earlier generations of theorists—the goal of understanding how music works its magic."[16] Although Huron's empirical research remains largely focused on the brain (i.e., the cognitive experience of individual listeners), the aggregate data generated by his and others' experiments can yield patterns from which inferences can be drawn about groups of listeners who are enculturated into common musical traditions.

Another possible, yet closely related, reason for the paucity of scholarship regarding synchrony among musicologists is the predominant influence of the Western concert hall, the norms of which have significantly shaped the musical assumptions of both performers and listeners in the modern West, and have surely obscured the communal dimensions of synchrony among participants. "We learn to suppress [the inclination to move our bodies to music] in the Western concert hall," notes Kathleen Marie Higgins, "but many of us catch ourselves swaying a bit or pulsing a toe along with the music in spite of ourselves."[17] Indeed, the connection between the aural and the kinesthetic in our experience of both music-making and music-hearing is widely acknowledged, and it is a peculiar development within the past two centuries of Western concert hall etiquette to remain silent and still while listening to

---

[15]David Huron, *Sweet Anticipation: Music and the Psychology of Expectation* (Cambridge, MA: The MIT Press, 2006), 370.

[16]Huron, *Sweet Anticipation*, 371.

[17]Kathleen Marie Higgins, *The Music Between Us: Is Music a Universal Language?* (Chicago: The University of Chicago Press, 2012), 112.

a musical performance.[18] Inasmuch as the values of the Western concert hall have influenced the types of analysis undertaken by music scholarship, an inordinate degree of attention has been channeled toward individual composers and the internal form of musical works abstracted from their context.[19] The expansion of ethnomusicological awareness in recent decades provides a welcome corrective to this longstanding trend.[20]

Despite the paucity of scholarship related to synchrony, and regardless of the actual kinesthetic manifestations of music-makers and music-hearers—whether united in observable synchronous movement or suppressing their kinesthetic urges—a synchronous mechanism can nevertheless be identified in a variety of musical contexts. Roger Scruton offers an analogy by which to understand this principle, suggesting that Western musical practices have perhaps evolved in a parallel manner to the way in which Emile Durkheim imagines religious practices to have evolved. In the "elementary forms" of religious life, according to Durkheim's scheme, the tribe attains a sense of unity through forms of religious life that resemble a "collective dance, in which the tribe moves together, invoking the god who incarnates himself in the ritual—perhaps in the body of the priest or shaman."[21] But with the advent of writing and the development of sacred Scripture, the presence of God ceases to move directly through the collective ritual and the shaman. Rather than impersonating the deity, the priest now becomes a "mediator" of a more distant deity. The voice of God echoes from a more distant locale.[22]

---

[18]Small, *Musicking*, 43-44. Small links this to the Cartesian mind/body split that has plagued so much of modern Western culture (see pp. 51-52), which in this case has led to a musical culture in which listeners are merely spectators, not participants. "We have nothing to contribute but our attention to the spectacle that has been arranged for us." Small, *Musicking*, 44.

[19]One senses this tension running right through the heart of Begbie's work, in which a deliberate and sustained attempt is made to guard against decontextualization and abstraction (see especially Begbie, *Resounding Truth*, 39-40.), yet with vestiges of this musicological trajectory still found throughout his writing, inasmuch as individual composers, pieces of music, and philosophical reflections about the nature of sound remain the major foci of his analysis.

[20]See, for instance, Martin Clayton, Rebecca Sager, and Will Udo, "In Time with the Music: The Concept of Entrainment and Its Significance for Ethnomusicology," *European Meetings in Ethnomusicology* 11 (2005), http://oro.open.ac.uk/2661/. Within the field of worship studies, two recent articles by Nathan Myrick have examined the phenomenon of rhythm entrainment in congregational singing from an ethnomusicological perspective. See Nathan Myrick, "Relational Power, Music, and Identity: The Emotional Efficacy of Congregational Song," *Yale Journal of Music & Religion* 3, no. 1 (2017): 77-92, and Nathan Myrick, "Embodying the Spirit: Toward a Theology of Entrainment," *Liturgy* 33, no. 3 (2018): 29-36.

[21]Scruton, *Aesthetics of Music*, 439.

[22]Scruton, *Aesthetics of Music*, 439.

This, Scruton suggests, provides an analogy for the development of Western musical practices, as seen in two different musical contexts, a rock music concert and a classical orchestra concert:

> First is the rock concert, in which an audience moves excitedly in time to the rhythm, its eyes fixed upon the performers, who are the full and final object of attention, the living embodiment of the music's spirit. Second is the classical orchestra concert, in which the performers vanish behind their ritual dress, and only the conductor—himself in formal costume, and with his back to the audience—retains the charisma of his priestly office, while the audience sits motionless and expectant, wrapped in an awed silence, and focusing not on the performers, but on the music which makes use of them. The silence of the concert hall is a substantial silence, which lives and breathes with the music.[23]

Despite the differences in kinesthetic participation between these two listening cultures, a similar synchronous mechanism might be posited in both contexts. As Scruton suggests, the silence of the concert hall is a substantial silence. Although performers and listeners in some contexts are reluctant to give in to their kinesthetic urges and move with musical sounds, the power of music to move its listeners is widely observed and acknowledged across music of all genres. Rhythmic entrainment—moving one's body in time with the music—is a more obvious manifestation of listener engagement, but synchrony can and does occur even among silent and still listeners, who may nonetheless be deeply and emotionally engaged in what they are hearing.[24]

One might justifiably maintain, therefore, that similar synchronous mechanisms are at work in a variety of musical contexts, uniting the disparate temporalities of individual listeners into one unified temporal whole. Recent studies measuring changes in cardiovascular parameters (primarily blood pressure and pulse) among music listeners lend further support to the

---

[23]Scruton, *Aesthetics of Music*, 439-40.

[24]See, for instance, the discussion of music and emotion in Peter Kivy, "How Music Moves," in *What Is Music? An Introduction to the Philosophy of Music*, ed. Philip Alperson (University Park, PA: Pennsylvania State University Press, 1987), 149-63. See also Leonard B. Meyer, *Emotion and Meaning in Music* (Chicago: The University of Chicago Press, 1956). For a brief examination of the historic Christian ambivalence regarding music, the emotions, and the body, see Don E. Saliers, *Music and Theology* (Nashville, Abingdon Press, 2007), 14-18. See also Begbie, "Faithful Feelings: Music and Emotion in Worship," in *Resonant Witness: Conversations between Music and Theology* (Grand Rapids, MI: Eerdmans, 2011), 323-54.

hypothesis that synchronous mechanisms may be at work even in the absence of observed rhythmic entrainment.[25] This is not to suggest a false equivalence among various listening cultures, however, nor to erase any sociological consequences that may result from divergent listening practices among various listening cultures. Contrary to Scruton's subtle denigration of listening cultures in which overt kinesthetic engagement is the norm,[26] it may be, as Christopher Small argues, that the listening culture of the Western classical music hall, in which kinesthetic responses to hearing music are suppressed, will be judged in historical perspective to be emotionally and interpersonally damaging.[27] Nonetheless, it is reasonable to assume that a similar synchronous mechanism is at work, whether a listening culture is highly physically expressive and participative or highly physically restrained. This hypothesis will be revisited in the discussion of synchrony in preaching below. Proceeding on this assumption, however, focus will now shift to a closer examination of the specific means by which music organizes disparate temporalities and produces synchrony, namely, the phenomenon of rhythm.

RHYTHM AND MUSICAL TEMPORALITIES

"Just as rapid neuronal oscillations bind together different functional parts within the brain," writes Oliver Sacks, "so rhythm binds together the individual nervous systems of a human community."[28] But what exactly is this phenomenon called rhythm, which binds together the individual nervous

---

[25]For example, researchers from the University College London have found the heartbeats of audience members at a musical theatre show to respond in unison, "with their pulses speeding up and slowing down at the same rate." See "Audience Members' Hearts Beat Together at the Theatre" (November 17, 2017), https://www.ucl.ac.uk/pals/news/2017/nov/audience-members-hearts-beat -together-theatre. See also Hans-Joachim Trappe and Gabriele Voit, "The Cardiovascular Effects of Musical Genres: A Randomized Controlled Study on the Effect of Compositions by W. A. Mozart, J. Strauss, and ABBA," trans. Birte Twisselmann, *Deutsches Ärzteblatt* 113, no. 20 (May 2016): 347- 52, https://www.ncbi.nlm.nih.gov/pmc/articles/PMC4906829/.

[26]As seen in the quotation above, Scruton's adoption of Durkheim's religious classifications results in his use of the word "primitive" to describe kinesthetically engaged listening communities. Scruton, *Aesthetics of Music*, 439-40.

[27]A recent study of the social bonding effects of shared intentionality, expressed through rhythmic entrainment, seems to support this assessment. Researchers found that "shared intentionality combined with synchrony produced the highest level of cooperation and self-reported prosociality across all measures." See Paul Reddish, Ronald Fischer, and Joseph Bulbulia, "Let's Dance Together: Synchrony, Shared Intentionality and Cooperation," *PLoS One* 8, no. 8 (August 7, 2013): e71182, https://www.ncbi.nlm.nih.gov/pmc/articles/PMC3737148/.

[28]Oliver Sacks, *Musicophilia: Tales of Music and the Brain*, rev. ed. (New York: Vintage Books, 2008), 269.

systems of a human community? In music scholarship, rhythm is often used as a catchall term for the temporal dimension of music, the general "pattern of movement in time," as opposed to other dimensions of musical sounds not related to temporality, such as pitch, timbre, and volume.[29] Recalling Begbie's definition of music, "the *intentional* production of temporally organized patterns of pitched sounds,"[30] *rhythm* would refer to the temporal organization, rather than the tone(s) or pitch(es) produced (and perceived) in music. Whenever listeners encounter musical sounds, temporal organization is an integral dimension of what is perceived within the sound, and it is this perception of temporality that enables synchrony among the community of music-makers and music-hearers. Thus rhythm, in the broadest sense, simply refers to the temporal dimension of music.

But there is a second, narrower phenomenon to which the word rhythm might also refer: the specific temporal movement, or "pattern of attack," that is heard in the music. As Kernfeld explains, "a perceivable pattern of temporal space between attacks constitutes a rhythm."[31] In this sense, rhythm is distinguished from other aspects of temporal organization in music, such as meter, tempo, and beat.[32] The basic musical phenomenon of the beat and the various metrical configurations into which the beats are organized are therefore distinguished from the phenomenon of rhythm in this narrower sense, in that the beat and the meter are the larger framework of temporal organization within which rhythm takes shape.[33] Scruton summarizes this distinction well:

---

[29]Barry Kernfeld, "Rhythm," in *The New Harvard Dictionary of Music*, ed. Don Michael Randel (Cambridge, MA: Belknap Press, 1986), 700.

[30]Begbie, *Resounding Truth*, 40.

[31]Kernfeld, "Rhythm," 700. Huron takes issue with the scholarly emphasis on the "inter-onset interval," rather than the onset of the notes themselves, as the basic unit underlying temporal sequences. From a biological perspective, he considers the primacy of the inter-onset interval unlikely, arguing instead that "the ticks of the metronome truly are the stimuli." Huron, *Sweet Anticipation*, 199.

[32]The grouping of beats into hierarchical patterns of bars and phrases, etc., constitutes the phenomenon of *meter*, whereas the rate at which the beat occurs constitutes the *tempo*. The regularly recurring pulse of the music is the *beat* itself. Incidentally, all three of these phenomena can be discerned in the practice of conducting: the *beat* is signaled by each individual gesture of the conductor, whereas the *tempo* is signified by the rate at which the gestures occur and the *meter* is conveyed by the spatial pattern into which the gestures are organized.

[33]See Victor Zuckerkandl, *Sound and Symbol: Music and the External World*, trans. Willard R. Trask (Princeton, NJ: Princeton University Press, 1956), 157-60.

"Beat" denotes a pattern of time-values and accents, while "rhythm" denotes
the movement that can be heard in that pattern, and which may be influenced
by harmony and melody so as to reach across metrical closures and establish
contrary motions of its own. A piece of music may have a strong beat but little
or no rhythm, and some of the most rhythmical pieces in our tradition are
characterized by a light beat and a refusal to emphasize the bar line.[34]

Thus the phenomenon of rhythm in music, whether understood in the wider
or the narrower sense, comprises a complex array of mechanisms for the
organization of temporality in a piece of music, and as a result, for the creation
of synchrony among music-makers and music-hearers.[35]

Although not all musical traditions and genres evince a hierarchical metrical structure, one common rhythmic mechanism that aids listener understanding and fosters synchrony is the phenomenon of the downbeat, the first
beat of every bar, which tends to be the metrically strongest beat in every bar.
In his illuminating study on music and the psychology of expectation, David
Huron analyzes the cause of the pleasurable feeling evoked by the perception
of the downbeat.[36] The pleasure we experience when listening to music in
general, Huron contends, can be attributed to either the positive emotional
reward of successfully predicting a future sound event or the contrastive
emotional valence (the thrill) that occurs when an auditory surprise, an
incorrect prediction, is retroactively appraised as a positive experience.[37] In
other words, while the general goal of all music listeners is to correctly predict
future sound events, there is a different type of pleasure that comes from being
surprised (i.e., from realizing one has predicted the sound event incorrectly)

---

[34]Roger Scruton, *Understanding Music: Philosophy and Interpretation* (New York: Bloomsbury,
2009), 65.

[35]It should be noted here that although this brief explanation of rhythm and meter assumes Western
tonal music as its immediate context, the Western practice of organizing beats into regularly divis-
ible metric structures is not shared across all musical cultures. As Scruton notes,

Not all music has meter and not every meter is like the meters familiar in Western music,
which govern the divisions and subdivisions that correspond to time-signature and bar-line.
There are musical traditions that derive metrical patterns by adding note-values and not, as
we do, by dividing larger units symmetrically. In classical Arab music, for example, rhythmic
cycles are composed of times units added together to make often asymmetrical patterns,
which do not permit whole-number division. (Scruton, *Understanding Music*, 59)

[36]Huron, *Sweet Anticipation*, 184-85.

[37]Huron, *Sweet Anticipation*, chap. 2 and throughout.

yet still assessing the experience positively, similar to the way listeners derive pleasure from being surprised by a joke.[38]

All musical understanding, Huron argues, comes from a process of statistical learning. Through this process, listeners unconsciously acquire informal "rules of thumb" as they engage with musical sounds. This same process, according to Huron, underlies the formal theoretical rules that are codified by musicologists and learned by advanced students of music. Through regular exposure to certain patterns of organized sounds, musical understanding is developed, similar to the manner in which linguistic understanding is developed. This is what enables listeners to make correct (or incorrect) predictions. The phenomenon of the downbeat, then, and the pleasure associated with its occurrence, is generated through enculturation into a musical tradition in which listeners have learned over time that there is a high probability that certain sound events will occur at certain precise moments in time as the music unfolds.[39] The highest probable moment for the onset of a tone in any bar is the downbeat; thus the downbeat has emerged as one of the most readily perceivable rhythmic phenomena in Western music.

Huron further notes that the same predictive mechanism that enables the perception of the downbeat within individual measures is also operative at higher metrical levels. As Huron demonstrates through statistical analysis, an even higher probability exists that the onset of a note will occur on the downbeat of a metrically strong measure than on the downbeat of a metrically weak measure (i.e., the downbeat of a hyperbar, a group of four or eight bars).[40] Thus even groups of measures display a strong-weak-medium-weak pattern similar to the pattern by which beats within individual measures are organized.[41] The perception of these regular patterns of temporal organization is what enables synchrony to occur, as the community of music-makers and music-hearers becomes oriented to a predictable, recurring rhythmic scheme bearing common characteristics, such as the metrical primacy of the downbeat.

---

[38]Huron, *Sweet Anticipation*, 184-85.

[39]Huron, *Sweet Anticipation*, 184.

[40]Huron, *Sweet Anticipation*, 178-80.

[41]Huron, *Sweet Anticipation*, 178-80. Huron demonstrates this phenomenon through a statistical analysis of a Haydn string quartet in which, fascinatingly, the hypermetric structure evinces the same strong-weak-medium-weak pattern that is commonly found throughout the beat structure of individual measures in Haydn's music, and indeed throughout Western tonal music.

Thus, according to Huron, the pleasure of making music is created through both the pleasure of predictive success and the pleasure of surprise, as expectations are either confirmed or thwarted in the creation of musical sounds.

Indeed, as Huron also shows, the latter of these mechanisms—the pleasurable thwarting of temporal expectations—is what lies behind another common rhythmic phenomenon, syncopation. In contrast to the phenomenon of the downbeat, in which listening pleasure is derived from the successful prediction of a sound event, the phenomenon of syncopation is enabled by the creation of a delightful rhythmic surprise. Contrastive valence is created by the listener's incorrect expectation that a tone will occur on the beat, a metrically strong position. Instead, in the case of syncopation, the onset of the sound event is displaced. In broad terms, syncopation can simply refer to the frustration of musical norms, and may involve not only rhythmic, but also harmonic and tonal elements.[42] The most common form of specifically rhythmic syncopation occurs when the onset of tones occurs off the beat.[43]

As an example, in 4/4 (common) time, if an eighth note occurs on the second half of the fourth beat, listeners expect the next note to occur on the next beat, the downbeat, since it is the next strong metrical position and the eighth note seems to lead into the downbeat. However, if there were to be a rest on the downbeat (as in fig. 2.1), or if the eighth note were tied to another eighth note and held across the bar line (as in fig. 2.2), the phenomenon of syncopation would be created.

Figure 2.1. Syncopation with rest

It is important to note, however, that although the phenomenon of syncopation involves the thwarting

Figure 2.2. Syncopation with tie

of expectations, a generally stable metric structure is necessary in order for the experience of syncopation to create contrastive valence among listeners.

---

[42]See Huron, *Sweet Anticipation*, 294-303.

[43]Nate Sloan and Charlie Harding attribute the success of Carly Rae Jepson's 2012 #1 hit "Call Me Maybe" to the skilled use of rhythmic syncopation, combined with an "avoidance-of-the-home-chord" technique, which may both be considered types of syncopation in a broad sense. See Nathaniel Sloan and Charles Harding, *Switched on Pop: How Popular Music Works, and Why it Matters* (New York: Oxford University Press, 2020), 1-3. See also chapter 9, on the skilled use of rhythmic syncopation in Kendrick Lamar's song "Swimming Pools (Drank)."

As Huron explains, "Syncopation only *challenges* metric perceptions; it never annihilates meter. In order for syncopation to exist, it is essential to maintain normal (unsyncopated) metric expectations. Syncopated schemas piggyback on unsyncopated ones. The meter provides the schema against which *when*-expectations are formed. Meter and pulse are preserved."[44] Thus, although the phenomena of the downbeat and of syncopation make use of two different psychological effects, both rely on a similar principle— the organization of musical sound events into the hierarchical rhythmic structure of meter.

SYNCHRONY AND TEMPORAL ORGANIZATION IN PREACHING

This brief overview of musical synchrony and some of the rhythmic phenomena that enable music-makers and music-hearers to perceive temporal organization in music—and moreover, to derive pleasure from it and to unite their own individual temporalities to it—must now yield to an examination of synchrony in preaching. As noted above, the musical homiletic developed in this project will loosely pair three shared characteristics between music and preaching with three sermonic "tasks" or instincts. The shared characteristic of synchrony, which comprises the focus of this chapter, will be examined here in relation to the art of preaching, with special attention given to the creation and maintenance of synchrony throughout the preaching event.

The African American context. Perhaps a fruitful place to begin an examination of the establishment of synchrony in preaching would be the African American preaching tradition, which is well known for its communal, participatory nature, with congregation members often becoming engaged in an audible "call and response" rhythm with the preacher throughout the sermon.[45] Indeed, the audible engagement of one's hearers in the Black preaching tradition is sometimes a cause for envy by homileticians outside the

---

[44]Huron, *Sweet Anticipation*, 303. See also Scruton, *Aesthetics of Music*, 29-30.

[45]The descriptive terms "African American" and "Black" will be used interchangeably throughout, reflecting their interchangeable usage throughout the homiletical literature. On the possibility and legitimacy of isolating the Black preaching tradition as a discrete area of homiletical study, see Cleophus LaRue, "Two Ships Passing in the Night," in *What's the Matter with Preaching Today?*, ed. Mike Graves (Louisville, KY: Westminster John Knox, 2004), 137-39.

tradition.[46] Moreover, as noted in the previous chapter, the close connection between the Black preaching tradition and the emergence of the African American spirituals is undoubtedly a strong factor in the persistence of the communal, musical nature of Black preaching. As Luke Powery notes, "African American sermons have historically been known to be musical because music and speech are inseparable as African traditions treat songs like speech and speech like songs."[47]

Jon Michael Spencer provides a more detailed description of the connection between Black preaching and the spirituals:

> Although it is likely that, apart from worship, slave preachers worked at composing pleasing combinations of tune and text to later teach their spirituals to their congregations, it is probably that the more frequent development was from extemporaneous sermonizing which crescendoed *poco a poco* to intoned utterance. This melodious declamation, delineated into quasi-metrical phrases with formulaic cadence, was customarily enhanced by intervening tonal response from the congregation.[48]

With such a vital connection between preaching and congregational song in the African American ecclesial context, it is not surprising to find Black preachers clearly embodying the goal of establishing communal synchrony among congregations through the use of rhythmic speech patterns, nor is it surprising that congregations in the African American ecclesial context would evince a more tangible sense of unity through oral and kinesthetic participation in the preached word.

Evans Crawford describes this interactive dynamic between preacher and congregation as "the hum," which stems from a "homiletical musicality" in which preachers use "timing, pauses, inflection, pace, and the other musical qualities of speech to engage all that the listener is in the act of proclamation."[49] As Spencer notes, "Rhythm is the element that gives black preaching locomotion

---

[46]LaRue catalogs at least eight statements from prominent White homileticians regarding the comparative vitality of the Black preaching tradition. LaRue, "Two Ships," 127-28.

[47]Luke A. Powery, *Dem Dry Bones: Preaching, Death, and Hope* (Minneapolis: Fortress, 2012), 23.

[48]Jon Michael Spencer, *Sacred Symphony: The Chanted Sermon of the Black Preacher* (Westport, CT: Greenwood Press, 1987), xiii.

[49]Evans E. Crawford, with Thomas H. Troeger, *The Hum: Call and Response in African American Preaching* (Nashville: Abingdon Press, 1995), 16. See also Bruce A. Rosenberg, *Can These Bones Live? The Art of the American Folk Preacher*, rev. ed. (Chicago: University of Illinois Press, 1988), 56-57.

and momentum. Without it preaching would not only be static, it would hardly have an audience."[50] Multiple rhythmic techniques may be employed in the Black preaching tradition, according to Spencer, perhaps to "compensate for the sometimes static recitative-like melody" of the preacher's speech pattern.[51] William Turner reports one particular technique, in which preachers would create a rhythmic feel through the expansion of syllables, with "several tones corresponding to one syllable, as the preacher pressed to feel the motions of words that transmit the vitality and life of the communication."[52] As preachers established metric speech patterns, the "inner cultural codes" of the congregation "evoked sounds and gestures that amounted to a call-and-response. The congregation became far more than an audience: they were participants in an unfolding drama."[53]

Of particular importance in historic Black preaching is the establishment of a metric pattern in the sermon introduction. According to Turner, the use of rhythmic pauses and a slower opening cadence served as one way for preachers in the African American tradition to "[close] the discursive distance between the preacher and the congregation."[54] The beginning of a typical sermon in the Black church context, recalls Turner, was slow, "almost to the point of being torturous. Pauses and silences punctuated the measured cadence."[55] Crawford identifies a similar phenomenon, with Howard Thurman epitomizing for him the power of a measured, deliberate pause at the outset of the preaching event: "Nobody made use of the pause like Howard Thurman. Students who have traveled hundreds of miles to hear him speak

---

[50]Spencer, *Sacred Symphony*, 3.

[51]Spencer, *Sacred Symphony*, 3.

[52]William C. Turner, "The Musicality of Black Preaching: Performing the Word," in *Performance in Preaching: Bringing the Sermon to Life*, ed. Jana Childers and Clayton J. Schmit (Grand Rapids, MI: Baker Academic, 2008), 191. See also Spencer, *Sacred Symphony*, 3-5. For a musically transcribed example of this phenomenon, see Rosenberg, *Can These Bones Live?*, 60.

[53]Turner, "Musicality," 191-92. Rosenberg also describes this dynamic well (although it should be noted that his study of the chanted American folk sermon is not limited to the African American context):

What strangers to chanted sermons find most striking is that during most of the performance, and especially during the chanted portions, the congregation is actively involved in the service. They hum, sing aloud, yell, and join in the sermon as they choose, and almost always their participation is rhythmic. The quality of the congregation appears to have a great effect upon sermons, influencing the preachers' timing, their involvement in the delivery, and sometimes even the length of performances. (Rosenberg, *Can These Bones Live?*, 56)

[54]Turner, "Musicality," 191.

[55]Turner, "Musicality," 191.

have been known to call him great just for rising, standing at the pulpit or podium, rubbing his hands over his face, and looking skyward before uttering his first word."[56]

The intensity of the sermon would begin to build from there. Turner reports that a common pattern among African American preachers of a previous generation was to "start low, go slow, climb higher, strike fire, then sit down in the storm."[57] Preachers would build on and play off of the rhythmic patterns they had established in the introduction. The climax of the sermon, reports Spencer, would often become "extra-rhythmic," prompting outbursts of applause.[58] Given this high level of homiletical musicality in the African American ecclesial context, with special attention afforded to the rhythmic and metric features that enable the congregation to orally and kinesthetically participate, synchrony almost inevitably becomes a prominent and immediately manifest feature of the preaching event.[59]

Crucially, however, both Crawford and Turner emphasize that these musical elements, or what Crawford has termed "holiness in timing,"[60] are more than mere technique or manufactured emotionalism; rather, these reflect both the preacher's and the congregation's immersion in the life of the Spirit:

> The motion of life in the musical tone struck in preaching is like the dance in the heart of the preacher, evoking a dance in the heart of the hearer. These motions are described no better than in the words of worshipers who speak of how the Spirit "runs from heart to heart and breast to breast." The moment is no less than mystical participation in the deep, preconscious, atavistic, liminal spaces where spiritual community is formed.[61]

Indeed, this is the deep resonance of Luke Powery's use of the term "spiritual preaching."[62] Although the intoned, rhythmic speech that is characteristic

---

[56]Crawford, *The Hum*, 26.
[57]Turner, "Musicality," 191.
[58]Spencer, *Sacred Symphony*, 3.
[59]To be precise, the call-and-response pattern evident in much of the Black preaching tradition is probably more accurately described as *antiphony*, rather than *synchrony*, because it is an alternating pattern of oration, rather than a simultaneous action. The general term *synchrony* is being retained here, however, as a description of an overall metric scheme within which both parties resound their parts. See Rosenberg, *Can These Bones Live?*, 131.
[60]Crawford, *The Hum*, 17.
[61]Turner, "Musicality," 207. See also Crawford, *The Hum*, 55-56.
[62]Powery, *Dem Dry Bones*, 51 and throughout.

of much historic and contemporary African American preaching (which many "spiritual preachers" have explicitly understood as their distinguishing mark)[63] could be explained in simple sociological terms, there is a deeper theological significance to this practice. The deep theological conviction underscored by the presence of musical elements in the Black preaching tradition is the presence of the Holy Spirit, bringing the dead to life, and uniting the community in hope.[64] As Powery writes, "the significance of sound in African American preaching traditions implies a welcome of the presence of the Spirit."[65]

Henry Mitchell, whose scholarship first highlighted the distinctive contribution of Black preaching in the North American homiletical academy, similarly notes the significance of verbal participation among African American worshipers during the preaching of the sermon: "The Black worshipper does not merely acknowledge the Word delivered by the preacher; he talks back! Sometimes the Black worshipper may shout. The day is not far past, if indeed it has passed at all, when the Black worshipper would consider a worship service a failure if there were no shouting."[66]

Yet, he cautions, the emphasis is not on shouting for shouting's sake. "The measure of authenticity . . . would have to be not how much shouting is done, but out of what wellsprings of spiritual motivation it comes."[67] Black congregations, Mitchell maintains, are remarkably adept at sensing a "put-on," and they will suppress such insincere behavior. Only truly Spirit-filled sound is encouraged.

Thus, in the African American preaching tradition, the establishment of an immediate, tangible sense of synchrony between preacher and congregation is not simply a distinctive yet ultimately meaningless cultural norm that derives from a historical oddity. Rather, it is essential to Black preachers' and Black congregations' self-understanding as communities filled with the Spirit. This connection between being united in song—or, in the case of the African American sermon, being united in a synchronous musically charged

---

[63]Powery, *Dem Dry Bones*, 24-25.
[64]Powery, *Dem Dry Bones*, 55-57.
[65]Powery, *Dem Dry Bones*, 55.
[66]Henry H. Mitchell, *Black Preaching* (Philadelphia: J. B. Lippincott, 1970), 44.
[67]Mitchell, *Black Preaching*, 44.

proclamatory experience—and being filled with the Spirit will be explored in greater depth below, with special reference to the work of Stephen Guthrie and Jeremy Begbie. However, at this point it should suffice to note the connection between synchronous sonic expression and the theological theme of the Holy Spirit's presence and movement.

The White mainline context. If the norm in traditional Black preaching contexts is for preachers to create synchronous rhythmic interaction with the congregation through the establishment of metric speech patterns, what might the norm be in the historically dominant ecclesial culture in North America, the White Protestant mainline? Recalling the discussion above, in which a similar synchronous mechanism was posited in both the rock concert and the classical orchestra concert despite the vastly divergent kinesthetic engagement of listeners in each context, a parallel might be drawn in the homiletical context. Although listeners in many Black church traditions are stereotypically much more active and vocal in their participation during the sermon, whereas listeners in predominantly White congregations are stereotypically more silent and still, a similar level of synchronous engagement might be posited among the congregation in both settings.

Indeed, Evans Crawford allows for such a scenario in his own development of the concept of "participant proclamation." "The presence of oral response," he cautions, "does not *automatically* mean the congregation is participating in proclamation."[68] Various listeners in widely varying contexts may be engaging similarly well in the temporal movement of the preached word, although some listeners may be of the "talk-back" variety, he explains, whereas others may hail from the "'feel-back' school of response." "The silent attentiveness of their faces, rather than words, reflects [the] acute listening" of the latter type of listeners.[69] A laudable feature of Crawford's work is his refusal to prematurely disparage the perceived level of engagement of those who fail to orally and kinesthetically manifest their participation. The faces of many silent listeners, he believes, display their intense engagement with the sermon.

Nonetheless, there is a general distinction to be noted between the cultural norms regarding listener participation in historically Black congregations

---

[68]Crawford, *The Hum*, 39.
[69]Crawford, *The Hum*, 40.

and historically White congregations, and this inevitably affects the methods by which preachers themselves approach the creation of synchrony among the congregation. Indeed, it seems a positive development in the last several decades that, due to the influence of the New Homiletic, preachers in White mainline congregations are even considering the importance of creating communal synchrony in the first place. This renewed focus is most clearly represented in the "paradigm shift" away from deductive, didactic styles of preaching toward more inductive, narrative forms.[70] Homileticians in the White mainline tradition are increasingly attending to listeners' temporal experiences during the sermon, rather than simply aiming for the "reception" of a cognitively focused, deductively oriented "message."[71] As a result, the shape of preaching in the White mainline context is rapidly changing.

Yet, undoubtedly due to persistent differences in cultural norms regarding listener participation, methodological differences still emerge between preachers in the White mainline context and preachers in the African American context as to the creation of synchrony. Whereas preachers in the Black preaching tradition have tended to create synchrony through the rhythmic and metric patterns they create with performance and pronunciation techniques, preachers in the White mainline tradition have focused more on creating synchrony by infusing the content of the sermon itself with a greater sense of movement. The key is not to elevate one "listening culture" above the other, but rather to attend to, and work within, the listening culture in which one is preaching.

This emphasis on creating a sense of "movement" in sermon content in the White mainline context has come about largely as a reaction against the structure of "traditional" preaching models.[72] One of the most common complaints

---

[70]O. Wesley Allen Jr. identifies this shift (which he terms a "homiletical revolution") as one of the three distinctive features of the New Homiletic. See O. Wesley Allen Jr., "Introduction: The Pillars of the New Homiletic," in *The Renewed Homiletic*, ed. O. Wesley Allen Jr. (Minneapolis: Fortress, 2010), 8.

[71]Indeed, Eugene Lowry's entire career has been devoted to the emphasis of temporal models over spatial models in preaching. See, for instance, his most recent monograph, *The Homiletical Beat: Why All Sermons Are Narrative* (Nashville: Abingdon Press, 2012).

[72]Wesley Allen traces the history of the "traditional" sermon model to two sources, the late medieval *university sermon* and the early modern *Puritan plain style*. "These two homiletical forms," writes Allen, "have dominated most of preaching in the West for the last four or five centuries." Allen, *Renewed Homiletic*, 3.

about "old style" sermons in the White preaching tradition is that they did not "go anywhere." Rather, traditional sermons often began by stating the main point (i.e., the conclusion) first, and then only subsequently developing the particular subpoints.[73] But this technique, it is averred, amounts to spoiling the end of a story or trying to tell a joke after the "punch line" has already been ruined.[74] A general lack of movement in this traditional style was often indicated, according to Eugene Lowry, by a preponderance of "*therefores, oughts, shoulds,* and *musts*"—motivational words added to the sermon in a futile attempt to breathe life into an otherwise flat, unmoving experience.[75]

For this reason, a major thrust in the homiletical literature coming out of the White mainline context over the past several decades (and the almost singular focus of the New Homiletic) has been the development of a methodology focused on shaping sermon content to create a greater sense of movement in the experience of listeners. The inductive and narrative forms have emerged as perhaps the most widely used and thoroughly developed methods for achieving this effect. A brief examination of the work of three of the five "pillars of the New Homiletic,"[76] David Buttrick, Fred Craddock, and Eugene Lowry, will demonstrate some of the ways homileticians in the White mainline preaching tradition have focused on the temporal organization of sermon content as a means of establishing synchrony between preacher and congregation.

The first exemplar of this focus on the movement of content is Fred Craddock, whose groundbreaking book *As One Without Authority* has occupied a privileged place in the mainline homiletical literature for four decades. The primary aim of this iconic text is to present an alternative to the "most unnatural mode of communication"[77] found in traditional, deductively organized sermons, in which a thesis is stated, and then broken down into "points and

---

[73]Fred B. Craddock, *As One Without Authority*, rev. ed. (St. Louis: Chalice Press, 2001), 45-46.

[74]Craddock, *As One Without Authority*, 52. It should be noted, however, that this characterization of traditional sermon models has been critiqued on many fronts as a kind of "straw man" argument. See, for instance, LaRue, "Two Ships." LaRue's critique will receive further attention below.

[75]Lowry, *The Homiletical Beat*, 22 (italics original). For a fascinating psychological theory regarding the causes of "the petrified and predictable sermon where nothing is allowed to happen," see Robert C. Dykstra, *Discovering a Sermon: Personal Pastoral Preaching* (St. Louis: Chalice Press, 2001), especially 26-28.

[76]O. Wesley Allen Jr., *The Renewed Homiletic*, 1-2.

[77]Craddock, *As One Without Authority*, 46.

subtheses, explaining and illustrating these points, and applying them to the particular situations of the hearers."[78] A major problem with this traditional structure, according to Craddock, is its implicit authoritarianism; the hearers have nothing to contribute, except as passive recipients of a prepackaged message.[79]

In contrast, inductive movement, in which "thought moves from the particulars of experience that have a familiar ring in the listener's ear to a general truth or conclusion," is a much more communally oriented method for organizing the content of the sermon, argues Craddock.[80] Listeners are welcomed into the movement of the sermon itself: "If done well, one often need not make the applications of the conclusion to the lives of the hearers. If *they* have made the trip, it is *their* conclusion, and the implication for their own situations is not only clear but personally inescapable."[81] Through the deft organization of the sermon content, with thought patterns moving inductively rather than deductively, the congregation becomes more than simply the "destination of the sermon," but rather the cocreators of its conclusions. The listeners themselves are the ones who complete the sermon.[82]

Craddock's clear assumption here is that the primary way in which the congregation will participate in the preaching moment is not through oral and kinesthetic involvement, but rather through active cognitive engagement with the sermon content (which may or may not involve oral or kinesthetic manifestations). Rhythm, meter, and movement are envisioned in the content itself, not in the performance: "Anyone who would preach effectively will have as a primary methodological concern the matter of movement. . . . Movement is of fundamental importance not simply because the speaker wants to 'get somewhere' in the presentation but because the movement itself

---

[78]Craddock, *As One Without Authority*, 45.

[79]Craddock, *As One Without Authority*, 46-47 and throughout. This assertion can be challenged, of course, for its unnecessary devaluation of the listener's contribution regardless of sermon structure.

[80]Craddock, *As One Without Authority*, 47.

[81]Craddock, *As One Without Authority*, 48-49.

[82]Craddock, *As One Without Authority*, 53. Of course, the characterization of inductive movement as therefore more "communal" than traditional sermon models can also be challenged, insofar as the desire for individuals to draw their own conclusions to the sermon could be viewed as a much more *individualistic*, rather than communal, approach to sermon design.

is to be an experience of the community in sharing the Word."[83] Delivery is important as well,[84] but this is not the primary means whereby the preacher creates movement that welcomes listeners into the experience. For Craddock, the primary means whereby a connection is established and communal synchrony is created is through the inductive method of organizing thought patterns. Listeners are united in a common experience as they connect with the content as it unfolds.

A similar emphasis is found in one of the homileticians who most explicitly and extensively draws on the musical metaphor, Eugene Lowry. As noted in the previous chapter, the most prominent theme in Lowry's career has almost certainly been the advancement of a temporal, as opposed to a spatial, understanding of the organization of sermon content.[85] This is what is meant by Lowry's use of the term *narrative*, and his subsequent assertion that all sermons are narrative. Narrative preaching, Lowry insists, is more than telling stories or being story-driven; it is, rather, the prioritization of time over space in preachers' working models of what a sermon is.[86] In fact, Lowry is at such pains to emphasize temporal movement over spatial arrangement that he noticeably avoids using words with possible spatial connotations, such as *arrangement, outline,* or *structure.*[87]

Yet this prioritization of *time* over *space* in sermon form does not occasion an extensive analysis of the temporal aspects of homiletical performance

---

[83]Craddock, *As One Without Authority*, 45.

[84]Craddock, *Preaching*, rev. ed. (Nashville: Abingdon Press, 2010), 210-22.

[85]This theme is prominent in many of Lowry's works, including *The Homiletical Plot: The Sermon as Narrative Art Form*, expanded ed. (Louisville, KY: Westminster John Knox, 2001), *The Sermon: Dancing on the Edge of Mystery* (Nashville: Abingdon Press, 1997), *The Homiletical Beat*, and most especially, *Doing Time in the Pulpit*.

[86]Lowry, *Homiletical Beat*, 7. Lowry is incredulous at the misunderstandings that have resulted from the conflation of the concepts of narrative and story. See *Homiletical Beat*, 11-18. His use of the word *narrative*, he explains, denotes a more general concept of temporal sequence, which may include, but is not limited to, the concepts of story or storytelling.

[87]If the use of such words is unavoidable, Lowry will often attach a temporal modifier, even if this makes for such clumsy phrases as "ordered forms of moving time." Lowry, *Homiletical Beat*, 30. On close examination, this dogged avoidance of words that might have spatial connotations seems both unnecessary and practically impossible. A more helpful solution to this dilemma would be the acknowledgment that, even in the case of music, despite its intrinsic temporal nature, a "quasi-spatial order" does emerge: "When listening to music we attend to sequences, simultaneities and complexes. But we hear distance, movement, space, closure. Those spatial concepts do not literally apply to the sounds that we hear. Rather they describe what we hear *in* sequential sounds, when we hear them as music." Scruton, *Understanding Music*, 30.

per se,[88] but rather a focus on creating movement within the content itself, as in Craddock's work. This preference for the temporality of content over the temporality of performance is seen clearly in Lowry's recent defense of the term *narrative*:

> When I use the term *narrative sermon* or *narrative preaching* normatively, I refer to the arrangement of ideas that takes the form of a homiletical plot. . . . [A parable of Jesus] is easily formed into a narrative sermon. One can also take a text that is not itself in narrative form and yet strategically move it into effective narrative homiletical shape—a plot form. I am talking about the arrangement of ideas that happens by means of the human voice, moment-by-moment-by-moment.[89]

Despite the reference to the human voice as the means of delivery, the emphasis clearly remains on the cognitive content of the sermon itself, the "arrangement of ideas," and not necessarily on the sociological reality of what is occurring among the congregation on noncognitive levels as the sermon content is delivered.

The contrast between the contextual expectation of oral/kinesthetic listener participation, as found in the African American call-and-response tradition or Evans Crawford's concept of "the hum," and the silent/cognitive listener participation assumed in the White mainline context, is even more clearly demonstrated in Eugene Lowry's elucidation of the musicality of preaching. "One could speak of the basic *musicality* of any sermon," writes Lowry.[90] But rather than referring to the musical qualities of the preacher's speech patterns, as does Turner in his account of the "musicality" of Black preaching, Lowry draws an analogy between the ordering of certain tones in the melody of a song and the ordering of ideas in a sermon. The tune to any well-known piece of music would be unrecognizable if the notes were played out of order, Lowry argues, since "content and form are inseparable."[91] Similarly, the order in which the ideas of a sermon are plotted is inseparable from the message of

---

[88]For a helpful examination of the temporal dimension of performance in preaching, see Paul Scott Wilson, "Preaching, Performance, and the Life and Death of 'Now,'" in *Performance in Preaching: Bringing the Sermon to Life*, ed. Jana Childers and Clayton J. Schmit (Grand Rapids, MI: Baker Academic, 2008), 37-52.
[89]Lowry, *Homiletical Beat*, 17.
[90]Lowry, *The Sermon*, 55.
[91]Lowry, *The Sermon*, 56.

the sermon itself. The methodological contrast between the Black preaching tradition and the White mainline tradition is further evidenced to the extent that Lowry focuses on melody and harmony (i.e., the sequential ordering of notes and chords) in his development of the musical metaphor,[92] whereas Turner focuses on rhythm and meter. In other words, Lowry focuses on shaping temporality more in the act of sermon composition than in the act of performance.

This is not to suggest that Lowry is unconcerned with listener participation, however. In fact, his stated aim is to take listeners on a journey from "itch" to "scratch," to create movement that flows from *tension* to *resolution*, similar to the experience of listening to a classical symphonic work or a jazz tune.[93] Thus he believes preachers should take major responsibility for engaging listeners with the theme of the sermon: "What has been our sermonic itch must become theirs—and within a matter of two or three minutes—else their attention will move to other matters."[94] The technique of "upsetting the equilibrium" or "creating conflict" at the outset of the sermon—a hallmark of the *Lowry Loop* narrative technique—assumes that the responsibility of creating movement lies almost exclusively with preachers in the plotting of ideas, just as playwrights, television writers, and novelists arrange dialogue and events in such a way to engage their audience with the plot sequence.[95] The goal is to create an *experience* in which listeners desire to come along with the preacher on a journey from tension to resolution.

For Lowry, the ultimate emphasis is on the strategic announcement of the gospel. If strategies of tension and resolution are utilized effectively in preaching, similar to the way they are used in music, the experience of the gospel becomes even more powerful than if the good news were prematurely

---

[92]See, for example, Lowry, *Homiletical Plot*, 9-11, 52, 65-73.

[93]Lowry, *The Sermon*, 18-20, and throughout.

[94]Lowry, *Homiletical Plot*, 29.

[95]The distinction between performance-oriented and content-oriented temporal organization need not be conceived as a strict dichotomy, of course. Nor would Lowry likely endorse such a dichotomy. The scriptwriting of Aaron Sorkin, for example, necessitates correct performance in order for the content to "work." In a 2012 interview with Terry Gross on the radio program *Fresh Air*, Sorkin spoke about the "musical" quality to which his dialogue aspires, and how he auditions actors differently than other directors do, because they need to have an ear for the music of the script. Aaron Sorkin, "Aaron Sorkin: The Writer Behind 'The Newsroom,'" interview by Terry Gross, WHYY, Monday, July 16, 2012, https://www.npr.org/programs/fresh-air/2012/07/16/156841284/.

announced at the outset of the sermon and then deductively explored through points and subpoints. Rather, Lowry argues, "Timing based on the creation of proper context is the key. As a matter of fact, the gospel as preached is a relatively uncomplicated matter. Whether it is credible or not is dependent upon the context in which it is set."[96] Listener participation is paramount for Lowry. However, the "context" in which the gospel is set refers to the development of the sermon content that leads up to the announcement of the good news, with the assumption that listeners' attention—and hence communal synchrony—must be gained through an intriguing arrangement of ideas, rather than a proper assessment of the performance factors that might enable greater synchrony among listeners within a given sociological, relational, ecclesial, and liturgical context.[97]

A similar technique for creating communal synchrony by attending to the temporal dimension of sermon content is found in a third "pillar of the New Homiletic," David Buttrick. In his massive study, *Homiletic: Moves and Structures*, Buttrick conceives of sermon content as a series of moves—"modules of language" that are designed to form in the understanding of the congregation's "shared consciousness."[98] Prime concern is given to the temporal requirements of communal consciousness, the time it takes for ideas to form in the consciousness of a gathered congregation, which, according to Buttrick, is greater than the time it takes for ideas to form in the minds of individuals.[99] As he explains, "Preaching mediates some structured understanding in consciousness to a congregation. Therefore, preaching is speaking related to *understanding*. The language of preaching will tend to imitate phases of understanding in consciousness."[100] A major concern of Buttrick's homiletical theory, therefore, is the development of "moves" that are appropriately calibrated to produce the desired effect among the congregation.[101]

---

[96]Lowry, *Homiletical Plot*, 76.

[97]For a systematic approach to the assessment of contextual factors in preaching, and the strategic creation of sermon content based on these observations, see James R. Nieman, *Knowing the Context: Frames, Tools, and Signs for Preaching* (Minneapolis: Fortress, 2008).

[98]David Buttrick, *Homiletic: Moves and Structures* (Philadelphia: Fortress, 1987), 24.

[99]Buttrick, *Homiletic*, 24-28.

[100]Buttrick, *Homiletic*, 320.

[101]It is worth noting that Buttrick's theological analysis of what a congregation is—what he calls the *being-saved community*—informs his understanding of the concept of *consciousness*. Thus a purely secular analysis of consciousness would not seem to suffice in his homiletical theory. See, e.g., Buttrick, *Homiletic*, 254.

This concern is illustrated well in Buttrick's counsel regarding sermon introductions. The purpose of an introduction, Buttrick argues, is to focus the congregation toward a particular subject matter, a particular "field of meaning."[102] It is crucial, however, not to "tip one's hand." The preacher should not give away too much about where the sermon is going ahead of time. Instead, introductions should "bring into consciousness the 'scene' of the sermon."[103] Furthermore, the length is significant. Sermon introductions must be neither too long nor too short: "As a general guideline, introductions may run between seven and twelve sentences in length."[104] Given the time it takes for congregations simply to adjust to a preacher's syntax, appropriate time must be given for the subject matter to form in communal consciousness, yet without belaboring the point.[105] Finally, Buttrick counsels, in order for introductions to be effective, "the end of the introduction and the start of a first move must be clearly separated . . . so that no matter how long the pause that follows, people will be ready to start a first move."[106] The remainder of *Homiletic* explores various strategies for plotting "homiletical moves" through the rest of the sermon.

Thus for Buttrick, as for Craddock and Lowry, a sense of movement is created through sermon content as disparate listeners become united around a single focus and are led through a developing series of thought patterns. Listener participation seems to be envisioned here primarily as a cognitive activity; thus the flow of ideas becomes a major concern. For this reason, compositional technique emerges as the primary focus of the homiletical theory of these three men. Buttrick is unquestionably the most prescriptive in matters of compositional style,[107] though all three of these pillars of the New Homiletic have developed theories that are heavily weighted toward the arrangement of content. Nevertheless, a similar concern for synchrony as

---

[102]Buttrick, *Homiletic*, 84.

[103]Buttrick, *Homiletic*, 86.

[104]Buttrick, *Homiletic*, 86.

[105]Buttrick, *Homiletic*, 86. It is important to note here that Buttrick's status as a researcher has been widely called into question, due to his overreliance on unsubstantiated claims regarding the necessities of communal consciousness. See David Rietveld, "A Survey of the Phenomenological Research of Listening to Preaching," *Homiletic* 38, no. 2 (2013): 30-31.

[106]Buttrick, *Homiletic*, 87-88.

[107]For instance, an entire chapter in *Homiletic* provides technical advice regarding conjoining moves. See chap. 5, "Conjoining Moves," 69-79.

was observed in the Black preaching tradition can arguably be found in the White mainline tradition as well, though listener participation in the movement of the sermon is assumed to be more silent and cerebral, rather than oral and kinesthetic. In the White mainline context, the preacher is seen as somewhat akin to a composer in the Western classical tradition, creating synchrony among listeners not through manifest rhythmic entrainment, but rather through engagement with the movement and development of the musical "ideas" presented.[108]

SUMMARY OBSERVATIONS: SYNCHRONY IN MUSIC AND PREACHING

Having surveyed some of the rhythmic and metric strategies that enable the phenomenon of synchrony in music and some of the homiletical strategies that enable the creation of synchrony in both the Black preaching tradition and the White mainline context, some evaluative comments are now in order. As noted above, one of the most powerful and distinctive phenomena produced by the art of music is synchrony, in which disparate individual temporalities are united in a common temporal experience. Often, but not always, this phenomenon is manifest in kinesthetic movement that matches the metric structure of the music. Rhythm and meter, as David Huron demonstrates, are the structural features of music that enable listeners to form when-related expectations regarding musical sounds. Common rhythmic and metric patterns become more and more recognizable and understandable to listeners through the process of statistical learning that occurs when listeners are enculturated into a particular sonic environment.[109] In an especially fascinating demonstration of this process, Joseph Daniele and Aniruddh Patel have even discovered a similarity between the typical speech-rhythms of a given language and the most common rhythmic structures found in the music of that culture.[110] Synchrony occurs as listeners become oriented to, and "move" together with, a recognizable temporal structure established through

---

[108]For a composer's perspective on how to engage with "musical ideas" in works within the Western classical tradition, see Aaron Copland, *What to Listen for in Music*, rev. ed. (New York: New American Library, 2009).

[109]See especially Huron, *Sweet Anticipation*, chap. 10, "Expectation in Time," 175-202.

[110]See Aniruddh D. Patel, *Music, Language, and the Brain* (Oxford: Oxford University Press, 2008), 161-68. See also Huron, *Sweet Anticipation*, 188-90.

sound, and the process of statistical learning and enculturation allows many distinct rhythmic and metric features to develop and flourish among various listening cultures.

Similarly, in the art of preaching, at least two distinct methods can be discerned in the homiletical literature for creating synchrony among listeners, with each method corresponding to a distinct listening culture among North American congregations. In the African American ecclesial context, in which a higher degree of oral and kinesthetic participation is historically normative among listeners, preachers are more accustomed to establishing synchrony by means of rhythmic and metric speech patterns, in which listeners are invited into "the hum," a call-and-response pattern of oral participation in the preached word. In the White mainline context, in which listeners are historically more silent and still during the sermon, preachers are more accustomed to creating synchrony by attending to movement within the sermon content itself. In both contexts, a similar phenomenon of synchrony, in which disparate temporalities are united within a common temporal framework, is assumed to exist, even though this phenomenon is certainly manifest in different ways within different contexts. The key, especially for preachers within various contexts, is not to judge one listening culture as preferable to the other, but rather to be aware of these differences in listening cultures and to adjust as necessary.

Based on these observations and building on the metaphorical connection between music and preaching, some further theoretical speculation is also possible. David Huron notes the extraordinary speed with which music listeners are able "to detect schematic-appropriate cues and switch schemas as necessary."[111] In one experiment, "ordinary listeners' abilities to recognize broad stylistic categories [were shown to be] nearly at ceiling" after only one second of exposure.[112] Analogously, listeners of sermons might reasonably be expected to be able to distinguish between different styles of preaching based on the rhythmic and tonal dimensions of the speech alone. In other words, the speech cadence of various preachers, in itself, is a key indicator of the assumed listening cultures in which the preaching is taking place, and

---

[111]Huron, *Sweet Anticipation*, 207.
[112]Huron, *Sweet Anticipation*, 207. The categories referred to include "jazz, rock, blues, country & western, and classical, among others."

the preacher's preferred means (if any) of creating synchrony among listeners—whether by engendering oral/kinesthetic participation in the preaching moment or by creating a movement of ideas.

This matter is complex, of course, as listeners may not always be fully aware of a preacher's reasons for using a certain technique for the creation of synchrony. It may be, for example, that a preacher would prefer to build synchrony with more oral/kinesthetic participation than is common among a given listening culture, but the preacher has been compelled to adjust over time. Or the preacher may have an entirely different goal in mind during the preaching event and may therefore not be well attuned to the question of synchrony at all. For any number of reasons, there may be a mismatch between the listening culture and the preacher in this matter, and there might be some discord felt as a result.

Nonetheless, if we are able to posit a match between preacher and listener as it relates to different listening schemas that exist among different listening cultures, further implications for the practice of preaching might be noted. One possible implication has to do with the level of predictability that may be present in a number of different aspects of musicality. Huron shows that, as a rule, greater predictability in one aspect of musical sound will be offset by less predictability in another aspect, presumably in order that an optimal level of listener arousal might be retained, with listeners neither becoming bored nor failing to comprehend what they are hearing. For instance, one study found greater variety (and thus less predictability) within the chord progressions of pop music, in comparison to classical music. However, pop music was also found to be more rhythmically and harmonically repetitive than classical music, thus compensating for the lower degree of predictability in one aspect of the music with a higher degree of predictability in other aspects.[113]

Analogously, the greater rhythmic and metric variety of speech patterns in African American preaching—during sermon introductions, for instance— might be expected to necessitate a slower unfolding of sermon content. Conversely, the focus of White mainline homileticians on creating movement in sermon content (thus more variation and less predictability) might be shown to correlate with less rhythmic and metric variation within the speech

---

[113]Huron, *Sweet Anticipation*, 252-53.

performances themselves in White mainline sermons. At the very least, preachers in every setting must be aware of the "aural demands" they are placing on listeners with regard to the level of predictability that is present in various dimensions of their preaching, and they must be prepared to make some adjustments—whether in the realm of content or delivery—in order that listeners might be able to synchronize their individual temporalities with the temporality of the sermon.

From these speculations, however, one further, more fundamental issue emerges for homiletical theory: the extent to which preachers' sociological and theological understanding of their listeners affects their method. Of the three pillars of the New Homiletic examined above, David Buttrick is the only homiletician to have developed his theory with a specific theological view of the congregation in mind—that of the being-saved community. Even so, Buttrick retains a noticeable bias regarding communal temporal norms, occasioning his highly specific stylistic prescriptions for the "appropriate" length of individual "moves" within the sermon. Even the argument for the use of moves itself derives from a specific cultural understanding of the use of time and what is required to create movement within communal consciousness.[114]

In his essay, "Two Ships Passing in the Night," Cleophus LaRue describes the disconnect that is often felt between the African American listening culture and the White mainline listening culture, and the impact these cultural differences have had on the homiletical theories that have arisen from either one context or the other. As an example, LaRue reports that while many in the homiletical academy were decrying the traditional three-point sermon after the appearance of Craddock's inductive homiletical method, the three-point sermon remained alive and well in the Black church, "clothed in imagination, humor, playful engagement, running narrative, picturesque speech, and audible participation on the part of the congregation."[115] Likewise, Buttrick's counsel regarding the length of sermon introductions does not easily

---

[114]For an engaging, nontechnical sociological account of cultural differences related to time and temporality, see Robert Levine, *A Geography of Time: The Temporal Misadventures of a Social Psychologist, or How Every Culture Keeps Time Just a Little Bit Differently* (New York: Basic Books, 1997). Studies regarding sociological differences in the perception, measurement, and use of time might help homileticians temper their prescriptions on what is "necessary" in the timing of various moves in their sermons.

[115]LaRue, "Two Ships," 131.

translate into the Black preaching tradition: "In black churches it is under-stood that the preacher is going to take his or her time in the introduction of the sermon," writes LaRue.[116] In fact, "Take your time, preacher" is, according to LaRue, "the most common refrain heard in the congregation at the begin-ning of the sermon."[117] Thus, "hard-and-fast rules about length, timing, and retaining elements of surprise" are less helpful in the Black church context, since such rules "are not strictly enforced" within this listening culture.[118]

However, as noted above, although these differences in temporal under-standings and listening practices could perhaps be studied from a purely sociological viewpoint, the rhythmic and metric performance techniques by which preachers have historically created synchrony in the Black preach-ing tradition are not ultimately to be understood simply in relation to the liveliness of the sermon and the level of listener engagement, devoid of further theological significance. Rather, as Crawford, Turner, and Powery emphasize, in the Black ecclesial context, these "musical" features of preach-ing have been integrally related to the presence of the Holy Spirit among the community. Musicality in preaching serves as a sign of the spiritual realities that are at work both in and through the preacher's own person and among the gathered congregation.

This, of course, is not meant to imply the opposite claim: that the absence of musicality in preaching is a sign of the Holy Spirit's absence. Rather, the lesson to be drawn here is that musicality in the African American preaching tradition carries a richer spiritual significance than many who are outside of the tradition may be inclined to acknowledge. Whereas Craddock, Lowry, and Buttrick seem to picture the listening community as a somewhat skepti-cal group (of autonomous individuals, for Lowry and Craddock) who may perhaps be lured into a sudden experience of the gospel through a skillfully crafted sermon, the homileticians writing in the African American tradition assume a communal context in which both the preacher and the congrega-tion seem more prepared to cultivate a participatory proclamation of the gospel that serves as a sign of the Spirit's indwelling of the church. The final section of this chapter will now further explore the theological dimensions

---

[116]LaRue, "Two Ships," 132.
[117]LaRue, "Two Ships," 133.
[118]LaRue, "Two Ships," 132.

of synchrony with particular reference to the unity of the church in the power of the Holy Spirit.

SYNCHRONY AND UNITY IN THE HOLY SPIRIT

Might the creation of synchrony—whether through the act of congregational singing, preaching, or some other instance of rhythmic entrainment—be one way in which the church manifests its unity in the Spirit? This fascinating suggestion has been developed with respect to communal music-making by Steven Guthrie in his intriguing essay, "The Wisdom of Song."[119] Making music together, or more specifically "the activity of singing," argues Guthrie, "is both an enactment and an exposition of the church's unity."[120]

The scriptural basis for the connection between music and church unity is found in the injunction in the book of Ephesians to "sing psalms and hymns and spiritual songs among yourselves, singing and making melody to the Lord in your hearts" (Eph 5:19).[121] This command, Guthrie shows, appears in a list of several commands, which are all subsumed under the larger command to "be filled with the Spirit" (5:18). Although many commentators have treated the injunction to "sing and make melody in your hearts" as a "stray remark," Guthrie argues convincingly that in context it is grammatically connected to the command to "be filled with the Spirit," serving in fact as one specific instance of what it means to be filled with the Spirit.[122] Of the five participles that elaborate the larger command of being filled with the Spirit, Guthrie notes, "three of these have to do with music: *speaking* to one another *in songs, hymns, and spiritual songs; singing;* and *making music*."[123] In the ecclesial context, therefore, singing and making music together can be a powerful indicator of the indwelling of the Holy Spirit.

Furthermore, the attempt by some commentators to interpret this command as referring solely to singing in worship is not sustainable, Guthrie

---

[119]Steven R. Guthrie, "The Wisdom of Song," in *Resonant Witness: Conversations between Music and Theology*, ed. Jeremy S. Begbie and Steven R. Guthrie (Grand Rapids, MI: Eerdmans, 2011), 382-407. Guthrie develops a similar argument within a larger treatment of the Holy Spirit's dynamic work through the arts in *Creator Spirit: The Holy Spirit and the Art of Becoming Human* (Grand Rapids, MI: Baker Academic, 2011). See chap. 4.

[120]Guthrie, "Wisdom of Song," 385. See also Guthrie, *Creator Spirit*, 81.

[121]A parallel, shortened form of this command is also found in Colossians 3:16.

[122]Guthrie, "Wisdom of Song," 387.

[123]Guthrie, "Wisdom of Song," 387-88 (italics original); Guthrie, *Creator Spirit*, 79.

argues, for it appears that in this passage singing and making music serves a didactic, pedagogical function as much as a liturgical function.[124] The "songs, hymns, and spiritual songs" referred to in the first participial phrase are meant to be addressed not to God but to *one another*.[125] Thus it appears that "Paul's commendation of song is connected to one of the other principal concerns of the letter [of Ephesians]: wisdom."[126] As Guthrie summarizes this wider concern of Ephesians:

> In their epistolary context, the songs, hymns, and spiritual songs of verse 19 are connected with the long string of commands found in chapters 4 and 5: to learn the truth, to be wise, to know what is right. Paul says in effect:
> —*Put away ignorance* . . .
> —*Let no one deceive you* . . .
> —*Know the truth* . . .
> —*Be wise* . . .
> —*Sing!*[127]

Singing and making music, then, is "a means of teaching and admonishing, that the Christian may attain wisdom," which is connected to the command to be filled with the Spirit, since "in the theology of Ephesians it is the Holy Spirit who is particularly associated with giving knowledge and understanding, and revealing the wisdom of God."[128] Singing to one another and making music together thus becomes one way that the Spirit of God reveals wisdom to the church.

But, Guthrie continues, the wisdom that is revealed has a more specific referent, namely, the unity of the church: "The multi-ethnic church of Jesus Christ in all its diverse unity *is* the 'wisdom of God' revealed by the Spirit."[129] Through Jesus, God has abolished the hostility not only between God and humanity, but also between Jew and Gentile. In place of old divisions, a "New Humanity," a reconciled community, has been created (Eph 2:14-16). Since humans are created to be God's image bearers, not only individually but also

---

[124]Guthrie, "Wisdom of Song," 389.
[125]Guthrie, "Wisdom of Song," 388.
[126]Guthrie, "Wisdom of Song," 389.
[127]Guthrie, "Wisdom of Song," 390.
[128]Guthrie, "Wisdom of Song," 390.
[129]Guthrie, "Wisdom of Song," 390.

communally, "then the divisions and hatred among humanity are nothing less than a destruction of the image of God."[130] As the church "puts on" Christ, the perfect image of God, it is remade in the image of Christ and "restored to humanity's rightful role as God's image bearer and the declaration of his glory."[131] Thus, in the context of Ephesians, the connection between wisdom and unity proves to be reciprocal. Wisdom leads to community, as believers come to know the love of God for them and to share that love with one another. But then the unity of the church itself also becomes a "theological statement," as it "shows forth the shape of the triune life—a community of self-giving love and differentiated unity."[132]

The command to sing, therefore, is bound up with both of these reciprocally reinforcing themes, wisdom and unity, with both of these connections having even further ramifications. As to the first connection, singing contributes to wisdom in that it "[deepens an] awareness that may or may not become fully (verbally) articulate; an awareness that arises from *sharing in the practices of the community*."[133] Through the core practices of the church, the Holy Spirit mediates this "participatory knowledge" of God. Thus, writes Guthrie, singing "provides the prosody of the church's proclamation."[134] As to the second connection, the singing of the church further becomes an enactment of the church's unity, the "voice of the New Humanity."[135] Far from being simply "a *metaphor* of the socially and ethnically diverse church," this congregational song "*is* this gathered body; or at least, this body's voice, this body made audible."[136] The church's song serves as one way the Holy Spirit manifests the unity of the reconciled community both to its members and to the world. The song of the church is the voice of the unified body of Christ.[137]

Revisiting the earlier exploration of synchrony in preaching, then, the intuition in the Black preaching tradition to connect the synchronous "hum"

---

[130]Guthrie, "Wisdom of Song," 393.

[131]Guthrie, "Wisdom of Song," 394.

[132]Guthrie, "Wisdom of Song," 395. See also Guthrie, *Creator Spirit,* 82-86.

[133]Guthrie, "Wisdom of Song," 395.

[134]Guthrie, "Wisdom of Song," 397.

[135]Guthrie, "Wisdom of Song," 397.

[136]Guthrie, "Wisdom of Song," 398.

[137]Guthrie adds three further sections detailing the specific shape of the church's unity that is manifest in song: *differentiated unity, freedom in submission,* and *sensitivity to and awareness of others.* See Guthrie, "Wisdom of Song," 400-403.

between preacher and congregation with the presence and power of the Holy Spirit proves insightful, and indeed must be understood as more than simply a cultural and historical oddity. Rather, when explored in relation to the scriptural connection between the church's communal song and its unity in the Holy Spirit, the audible synchrony that is established in African American churches through the preacher's use of rhythmic and metric speech patterns to create a call-and-response pattern is seen to be full of theological significance. Creating synchrony in preaching, therefore, becomes more than simply a method for holding the congregation's attention, but rather a means of generating "participatory knowledge" of—or even further, the very manifestation of—the church's unity in the Holy Spirit. Whether through an expressive oral/kinesthetic participation style or through a more limited, silent style of engagement, when preachers seek to engender synchrony among their congregation, they might understand themselves as not simply seeking greater listener engagement, but as seeking rather to manifest through the practice of preaching the unifying wisdom that comes from the Holy Spirit's indwelling of the church.

Of course, as Guthrie reminds us, it is not music itself (or, in this case, a musical homiletic itself) that brings this about. "Music cannot summon up from within itself the power to 'break down the dividing walls' and 'abolish the hostility between us' (see Eph. 2:14). This is the work of God."[138] Nonetheless, when preachers are attuned to this musical-homiletical dynamic of synchrony, a powerfully formative communal dynamic can develop—a communal dynamic which is nothing less than a glimpse of the "remaking of human community," an incarnation and announcement of the New Humanity formed in Christ.[139] Through the power of the Holy Spirit, communal song—and by extension, a synchronically-attuned sermon—can become "a shared and participatory experience that in turn gives rise to a sounding emblem of the community."[140]

One final observation regarding music and the nature of sound in the writing of Jeremy Begbie extends the theological significance of synchrony in preaching even further. In his essay, "Room of One's Own? Music, Space,

---

[138]Guthrie, *Creator Spirit*, 91.
[139]Guthrie, *Creator Spirit*, 92.
[140]Guthrie, *Creator Spirit*, 92.

and Freedom," Begbie notes the extent to which modern thought patterns have been influenced by an implicit visual-spatial model, which has then presented conceptual problems for certain theological themes, especially the quintessentially modern theme of freedom. Begbie seeks to remedy this situation with a musical model that corrects some of the theological errors to which visual-spatial conceptual models have led.[141] "The perception of musical sounds holds considerable potential," Begbie argues, for "getting outside of" visual-spatial conceptualities, the "pictures" that have, in the words of Ludwig Wittgenstein, "held us captive."[142]

The problem, Begbie explains, is that in visual-spatial perception, two objects cannot simultaneously occupy the same space. Thus the relationship between two objects vying for the same space inevitably becomes a "zero-sum" relationship.[143] When "the space of visual perception" is assumed to be "space as it 'really is,'" an unhelpful zero-sum assumption creeps into, for instance, our conception of the relationship between divine and human freedom: "For God to be in my space means that I will be either displaced or diminished in some manner. The more God's power is affirmed, the more human agency is rendered inconsequential. The more of God, the less of us (and vice versa)."[144]

The consequences of this line of reasoning can be devastating, especially in our understanding of the divine-human relationship. The historic struggles over doctrines of salvation are but one example of what can happen when a "zero-sum scheme" remains unchallenged: on the one extreme, God's grace develops into "an untrammelled, unrestricted divine causality," and on the other extreme, the human "decision" develops into "an entirely unprompted, self-generated response to God (an expression of 'my personal space') such that divine agency becomes effectively dispensable."[145] Numerous resultant efforts to either "divide things up" between these two extremes, or else develop some sort of synthesis, have yielded mixed results. "If we move from the visible to the audible, however, a rather different world unfolds," in which the zero-sum relationships of visual-spatial conceptualities are no longer assumed.[146]

---

[141]Jeremy Begbie, "Room of One's Own? Music, Space, and Freedom," in Jeremy Begbie, *Music, Modernity, and God: Essays in Listening* (New York: Oxford University Press, 2013), 141-75.
[142]Begbie, "Room of One's Own?," 142-43.
[143]Begbie, "Room of One's Own?," 143.
[144]Begbie, "Room of One's Own?," 147.
[145]Begbie, "Room of One's Own?," 149.
[146]Begbie, "Room of One's Own?," 155.

Begbie offers a musical example to illustrate how a "move from the visual to the audible" helps us reconceive the theme of freedom:

I play a note on the piano. The tone I hear fills the whole of my aural field, my heard space. It does not occupy a bounded location. It "saturates our hearing." It is "everywhere" in that space; there is nothing "outside" it, no spatial zone where the sound is not. I then play a second higher tone along with the first. This second sound fills the entirety of the *same* (heard) space; yet I hear it as distinct, irreducibly different. In this aural environment, two different entities, it would seem, can be in the same space at the same time. And they are not each in a place that we can describe as "here" rather than "there." Each seems to be "everywhere."[147]

These distinctive features of musical space, Begbie suggests, might not be simply amusing oddities, but might in fact "[enable] the perception of aspects of the physical world's space that are opaque to visual-spatial models."[148]

Drawing on the work of Victor Zuckerkandl, Begbie notes the "interpenetration" that is possible in musical sounds, in which tones can "sound through" one another, occupying the same sonic space, being *in* one another while still "being heard *as* two distinct tones."[149] This creates a spatial order not marked by mutual exclusion or displacement, but rather by interpenetration.[150] Through the phenomenon of sympathetic resonance, by which, for instance, a string on a piano will cause the string an octave above it to resonate without the second string being struck, a "resonant order" is opened up, a spatial order not marked by "mutual diminution," but rather by mutual reinforcement.[151]

This sonic-spatial order, Begbie argues, offers a viable alternative to the predominantly visual-spatial conceptualities that have held us captive in relation to certain key theological themes. Particularly relevant in the present exploration of synchrony in music and preaching are the relational themes Begbie highlights—including not only the relationship between divine and human agency noted above but also the shape of the corporate life of the church. If, building on a sonic-spatial conceptuality, human freedom is

---

[147]Begbie, "Room of One's Own?," 155.
[148]Begbie, "Room of One's Own?," 158.
[149]Begbie, "Room of One's Own?," 159.
[150]Begbie, "Room of One's Own?," 159.
[151]Begbie, "Room of One's Own?," 161.

conceived as "being enabled by God to participate, through the resonating agency of the Spirit, in God's own resonance," then the church's corporate freedom might also be conceived as a scenario in which "we are freed *by* the other *for* the other, and in this manner, find (against our expectations and self-willed desires) our God-intended resonant space."[152]

Citing Paul's understanding of the church as "both one and many," Begbie proposes further implications for how these insights regarding the order of sonic space might enhance our understanding of interpersonal agency within the church:

> [The church is not] a mosaic of bounded places in which the whole is simply the sum of the parts, still less an aggregation of interest groups self-protected against the encroachment of others, nor—the chronic tendency of many Western churches—a homogenous mass in which all diversity has been effectively wiped out in the name of "oneness," but a diverse body of mutually resonating members, in which, through an excentric dynamic set in motion by the Spirit, particularity is established, sustained, and enabled to flourish just *as* persons are united in fellowship.[153]

All of this, Begbie maintains, is made possible through a reflection on the nature of sound itself and, more particularly, the experience of music that helps to open up aspects of sonic space in which communal resonance and synchrony might occur.[154]

Begbie's reflections on the theological potential of music and sound thus suggest an even greater theological significance to the task of establishing synchrony in preaching. If the act of becoming united in synchronic sonic resonance might serve not only as an enactment of the church's unity in the Holy Spirit, but also as an experience of mutually reinforcing empowerment as the church learns to resonate with the Spirit's own resonant agency, then a musical homiletic that attends to synchronic resonance among the congregation might also become a powerful means of building and enacting a Spirit-empowered unity in which individuals are set free, paradoxically,

---

[152]Begbie, "Room of One's Own?," 166.
[153]Begbie, "Room of One's Own?," 168.
[154] For a multidimensional, "ecological" exploration of the theme of resonance in Christian music-making, see Mark Porter, *Ecologies of Resonance in Christian Musicking* (New York: Oxford University Press, 2020), especially chap. 1.

through the act of being joined as one.[155] Thus the aspects of homiletical theory related to synchrony among practitioners from within not only the African American and White mainline Protestant contexts, but also throughout the diverse cultures and subcultures of the worldwide church, might be understood within this larger theological frame.

CONCLUSION: ATTENDING TO SYNCHRONY IN PREACHING

All spoken language has rhythmic and tonal content, even if that rhythmic and tonal content is ignored, obscured, or otherwise underutilized. Given this reality, all preaching may be understood as inevitably involving certain metric features, as the tempo of a sermon combines with its rhythmic and tonal qualities in the homiletical moment. Preachers who desire to utilize musical instincts to create synchrony among their listeners, therefore, might begin by developing a greater awareness of the temporal dynamic of their words, seeking to embody a musician-like poise in the shaping of time through the sermon content and delivery. This music-like shaping of time can be achieved through the literal musicality of a preacher's speech or through the strategic unfolding of sermon content, or likely some combination of both.

As this chapter has demonstrated, however, preachers do not speak into a vacuum. Every homiletical act takes place within a context that has been shaped by certain personalities and traditions over time, such that a "listening culture" must be assumed to exist in every context—even in a newly planted church. Preachers therefore must learn to recognize the norms and expectations of the listening culture in which they are speaking, and seek appropriate ways to bring together the musicality of their own voice, the norms of the homiletical tradition(s) with which they most closely identify, and the expectations of the local listening culture, in order to cultivate the phenomenon of synchrony more intentionally.

This does not mean, of course, that preachers should be encouraged to develop an inauthentic voice in order to satisfy the "itching ears" of one's listeners, nor does it assume that preachers have no ability to shape the listening

---

[155]Begbie and Guthrie both emphasize a model of unity in which individuals are differentiated, particular, empowered, and free, not *at the expense of* participation in group resonance and synchrony but rather *precisely through the act of* becoming united in Spirit-shaped communal life. See Begbie, "Room of One's Own?," 165-68, and Guthrie, "Wisdom of Song," 398-403.

culture of a given church over time. In fact, as subsequent chapters will further elaborate, the musical homiletic proposed here assumes the ability of preachers to shape the listening habits of their congregation, which in turn assumes preachers' ability to play a role in the Holy Spirit's work of character formation in the community. Thus it is crucial for preachers to remain connected to the deeper spiritual significance of synchrony. The leveraging of homiletical temporality to create synchrony among one's listeners is not merely for the sake of increasing listener engagement or satisfaction, although there is certainly some value in these goals as well. The ultimate goal of attending to synchrony in preaching, however, is nothing less than the building up and binding together of the body of Christ, using this musical instinct to rehabituate the church into its corporate identity as the New Humanity, the body of Christ, the family of God—the community that is brought together in Christ and filled with the Holy Spirit in order to witness to the reality of God's coming kingdom.

SYNCHRONY IN PRACTICE

The following excerpt provides an example of a sort of "middle ground" approach to the creation of synchrony in preaching.[156] Gardner Taylor's delivery was well known to make use of rhythmic and tonal qualities in order to unite his listeners in a call and response, but he also displayed a skillful use of sermon content to create synchrony among his more silent listeners. He did this primarily through pleasing turns of phrase and intriguing, narrative-like flows. In this way, Taylor truly exemplifies what Jared Alcántara calls "crossover preaching," a style of preaching that displays deep intercultural competence.[157] Although a full demonstration of synchrony in preaching would require listening to a performed sermon, the effect can still be grasped if the reader pays careful attention to the rhythm, pacing, and flow of the text.

After reading the Scripture text, Taylor begins:

> You must not realize it, but you are out every day to find out what life is all about. Every person, whether the case is stated or left in silence, is trying to

---

[156]Sermon text excerpt from Gardner Taylor, "Struggling but Not Losing," on 2 Corinthians 4:8-10 in *The Words of Gardner Taylor*, vol. 3, 182-87.

[157]Jared E. Alcántara, *Crossover Preaching: Intercultural-Improvisational Homiletics in Conversation with Gardner C. Taylor* (Downers Grove, IL: IVP Academic, 2015).

find out what this life is all about. We look for clues as to the nature of life; we search for some sign of a pattern; we believe that there is a design.[158]

I heard my father long ago preach a sermon on "The Riddle of Life." In it he reflected upon what he called the "fascinating legend of the Sphinx at Thebes." In that legend the creature with a lion's body and human head terrorized the people of the city of Thebes by demanding the answer to a riddle taught her by the muses. Each time the riddle was answered incorrectly, the cruel Sphinx would devour a human soul. At last, Oedipus gave the correct answer. He was throned by a grateful citizenry, and the Sphinx thereupon killed herself. So the riddle was answered in an old and fascinating legend, but in some way or another in the days of our years the riddle is put to us in the events of our existence. What is life all about? What is its nature? Does it have a pattern? Can you solve its riddle? Are you able to see a design, a meaning?[159]

Taylor goes on to suggest that life's meaning is best understood when it is viewed as a struggle, and he illustrates many aspects of the struggle of life for his listeners. He identifies Paul as a man who knows well what it means to suffer and struggle for Jesus' sake, and quoting Paul, he begins to "crescendo" toward the resolution:

Now listen to how Paul talked about suffering and struggling but not losing. The difference between winning and losing in his life was Jesus Christ. It was the gospel which put joy bells ringing in his heart and singing in his soul, the love of Jesus which shed abroad bright sunshine in his spirit. "We have this treasure in earthen vessels"—Paul was saying that he was not much, but he had a great possession. He was very weak, but he had a friend who was very strong. "We have this treasure in earthen vessels. . . . We are troubled on every side"—all

---

[158]From the very first words of the sermon, the listener is drawn in by a strong claim of what everyone's daily life goal is. Moreover, to accompany this bold opening claim and the swift movement of content it creates, the listeners' disparate life experiences are classified together in this unifying experience of the human condition. This is an example of creating synchrony through the movement of the content, which when combined with rhythmic/metric features of the spoken word, lends itself well to a multidimensional synchrony among the gathered community.

[159]Here again, by expounding on an ancient legend that Taylor heard his father preach on, a sense of shared human experience is created. His statement of the contemporary relevance of the legend—the unsolved riddle of life's purpose—propels the sermon forward. The questions with which he ends this section become the questions the preacher and congregation are now seeking to answer. A "musician-like" poise, with a vocal tone that "savors" the sound of the words used, combines well with swift movement of the content. For more on Taylor's high valuation of the "currency" of words, see Jared E. Alcántara, *Learning from a Legend: What Gardner C. Taylor Can Teach Us about Preaching* (Eugene, OR: Cascade Books, 2016), 61-67.

around there is a hard struggle—"troubled on every side, yet not distressed; we are perplexed," puzzled, confused, sometimes, "but not in despair; persecuted but not forsaken; cast down, but not destroyed," struggling but not losing. There is no place for defeat in God's plan.

Taylor then weaves together several more Scripture verses that speak to victory and hope, and offers this conclusion:

God is going to win, and we who enlist in his army are going to win because we are his, and he is ours. When our warfare is over, we shall claim the triumph, and we shall go stately stepping to the great coronation, waving palms of victory in our hands and shouting, "We have overcome the wicked one." We shall march on through floods and flames, through sufferings and sorrows, until the great victory banquet of the Lamb. We shall come up from every side, from the north, south, east, and west carrying our crosses, bearing our burdens, weeping in our tears, suffering our sorrows, limping with our hurts, and nursing our wounds. When the journey is past, we shall live, love, learn, and labor in that sunlit land where the flowers never fade, the day never dies, and the song never stills.[160]

---

[160]Here Taylor builds momentum and sustains it through the end, piling biblical image upon biblical image, phrase upon phrase. The victory he proclaims is therefore not just spoken of; it is felt on a visceral level through the language and tone he uses. This is by no means a cheap victory, however, as Taylor acknowledges the burdens and tears and wounds the people are bringing with them to the Lamb's banquet. Nonetheless, Taylor concludes on a peaceful and triumphant note— a serene vision of eternal life in God's peaceable kingdom.

3

SANCTIFICATION THROUGH HEARING

REPETITION AND PATIENCE

WHEN I WAS YOUNG, I had a neighborhood friend whose father was a Baptist pastor. From time to time in the course of our play, my friend would parody his father's preaching, saying something like, "And my father was up there preaching, 'Jesus died on the cross for our sins.'" I remember thinking at the time that my friend must get pretty bored hearing that same formulaic message over and over again. But when I thought back on that experience years later, I envied my friend a bit in that regard. After all, I had grown up attending worship every Sunday as he had, but in my mainline Protestant church no preacher had ever repeated such a simple gospel declaration with such regularity as to be vulnerable to being parodied by their child for it. What did that say about the preaching I sat under in my formative years?

This raises an important question for all preachers to ask themselves: What core theological convictions and impulses am I so convinced of, so captured by, that I would open myself up to the charge of redundancy and the possibility of parody? If someone were to parody my preaching, what tones and phrases would they use?

This chapter will examine the musical-homiletical characteristic of repetition, paying special attention to the formative potential of repeated theological themes and impulses in preaching and ministry.

REPETITION IN MUSIC

The second shared characteristic to be examined in this musical-homiletical conversation is *repetition*. If music is indeed "a temporal art through and through," then the means of creating temporal structure in music is the use of repetition. As Huron has argued, the human brain rewards the successful prediction of stimuli, which includes the prediction of both *when* a certain stimulus will occur and *what* exactly the stimulus will be when it does occur. The pleasure associated with listening to music might thus be attributed to the listener's (largely subconscious) formation of schematic filters through which the successful prediction of auditory stimuli might be achieved.[1] Repetition is what enables these large-scale schematic structures to emerge in music, with *meter* emerging as the auditory schema for *when-related* predictions and *tonality* emerging as the auditory schema for *what-related* predictions.[2] Thus repetition becomes a central characteristic of the art of music, both as a readily perceptible feature of musical sounds and as the means by which schematic musical structures are created.

Repetition may in fact be one of the key characteristics distinguishing music from other arts. As Begbie writes, "Every piece of music, to some extent, integrates 'sameness' with 'difference.' . . . What is striking about music is that relations of sameness would appear to play a more crucial role than relations of difference. . . . Music tends toward the pole of absolute sameness."[3] Even though repetition does in fact play a major role in other art forms, such as tapestry or architecture, a key difference remains in that "in these cases we have the simultaneous presence of many similar or identical elements."[4] Admittedly, the *perception* of repetition in other art forms may not be simultaneous, but "the enjoyment depends in large part on being able to set part against part, to wander back and forth, to compare."[5] In music,

---

[1]David Huron, *Sweet Anticipation: Music and the Psychology of Expectation* (Cambridge, MA: The MIT Press, 2006), 131-40.

[2]See Huron, *Sweet Anticipation*, chaps. 10 and 9, respectively.

[3]Jeremy Begbie, *Theology, Music and Time* (Cambridge: Cambridge University Press, 2000), 156. Referencing the work of Richard Middleton, Begbie contrasts the two poles along the spectrum of musical structural types: the "monadic" pole, "most nearly approached by silence or by a single, unchanging, unending sound," and the "infinite set" pole, "most nearly approached by pieces whose aim is that nothing be heard twice." He acknowledges, however, that "absolute monadic sameness and absolute non-recurring difference are . . . impossible to achieve. Further, sameness and difference are mutually dependent and can only be mediated through each other." See also Richard Middleton, "'Play It Again Sam': Some Notes on the Productivity of Repetition in Popular Music," *Popular Music: A Year Book* 3 (1983): 235-70.

[4]Begbie, *Theology, Music and Time*, 158.

[5]Begbie, *Theology, Music and Time*, 158.

however, we have no such freedom to compare repetitive elements outside of the "prescribed, irreversible, unbroken sequence" in which the elements are presented to us.[6]

Of course, even the kind of sequential, nonsimultaneous repetition that is characteristic of music can also play a crucial role in other art forms, such as literature, film, poetry, and theater. However, the degree of repetition in music undoubtedly surpasses that of other arts in all but the most extreme examples. As Begbie notes, "In a typical eighteenth-century symphony it is common for the entire first section of a movement (lasting, say, five minutes) to be repeated note for note. It is very rare for a novel, poem or play to do anything like this."[7] The highly repetitive nature of music is furthermore what distinguishes music from language on a more fundamental level. "Notwithstanding the likenesses between music and language," Begbie writes, "we should not be blind to the marked differences. And [repetition] is one of them."[8] Language, in broad terms, builds its structure primarily on relations of difference and contrast, whereas music builds its structure primarily on relations of sameness and attraction.[9] Thus music might be characterized as exhibiting a "bias" toward repetition.

Victor Zuckerkandl refers to repetition as "a sort of natural state of music," which he believes is evidenced in "primitive" musical cultures.[10] However, if repetition is in fact the "natural" state of music, then "the 'exceptional case' would be not repetition but nonrepetition, something new."[11] For music to "say something new," it has to break through "the magic circle of enforced repetition."[12] "Every new tonal statement," according to Zuckerkandl, is thus "made *against* the will of an ever-present urge for repetition," which is, he argues, "an urge fed by time itself."[13] If time had its own way, music, as the shaping of time through the medium of sound, would never say anything new: "As time projects wave after wave, the tones are to do nothing but

---

[6]Begbie, *Theology, Music and Time*, 158.

[7]Begbie, *Theology, Music and Time*, 158.

[8]Begbie, *Theology, Music and Time*, 158.

[9]Begbie, *Theology, Music and Time*, 158-59. See also Elizabeth Hellmuth Margulis, *On Repeat: How Music Plays the Mind* (New York: Oxford University Press, 2014), 15.

[10]Victor Zuckerkandl, *Sound and Symbol: Music and the External World*, trans. Willard R. Trask (Princeton, NJ: Princeton University Press, 1956), 219.

[11]Zuckerkandl, *Sound and Symbol*, 219.

[12]Zuckerkandl, *Sound and Symbol*, 219.

[13]Zuckerkandl, *Sound and Symbol*, 219.

reproduce wave after wave in their material."[14] The creativity of the musician is needed, therefore, to actively engage this "natural state," resisting the lure of unending sameness with the introduction of variety and difference.

Repetition and tonality. Begbie undertakes a relatively thorough examination of musical repetition in *Theology, Music and Time*, which will be explored further below. Yet because his primary interests in that volume involve the relationships of various musical phenomena to the theology of time, the key insights he pursues regarding repetition are ultimately focused on meter. In establishing such a focus, Begbie leaves unexplored another (or, rather, *the* other) fundamental musical phenomenon generated through repetition, the phenomenon of tonality. However, the connection between repetition and tonality has been thoroughly explored in the work of David Huron, and the results are quite suggestive.

As noted in the previous chapter, Huron's empirical study attempts to discover the psychological principles of expectation by which music engages its listeners. Thus his work is properly understood as an extension of the theory of emotion and meaning in music that was developed by Leonard Meyer six decades ago.[15] The main thesis of Meyer's theory is that the pleasure of listening to music can be attributed to either the successful prediction of a future sound event (including both the *what* and the *when* of musical sounds) or the appraisal of an incorrect prediction (i.e., a musical surprise) as innocuous. Furthermore, as Huron argues extensively, in order to aid in prediction, listeners undergo a process of statistical learning similar to the process that enables language acquisition, in which the most frequently occurring sound events are encoded into listening schemas that enable comprehension.[16]

In music, according to Huron, there are two major classes of schematic structures "whose predictability create opportunities for both the pleasure

---

[14]Zuckerkandl, *Sound and Symbol*, 219.

[15]Leonard B. Meyer, *Emotion and Meaning in Music* (Chicago: The University of Chicago Press, 1956). As Meyer summarizes his own argument, "Embodied musical meaning is, in short, a product of expectation. If, on the basis of past experience, a present stimulus leads us to expect a more or less definite consequent musical event, then that stimulus has meaning." Meyer, *Emotion*, 35. See also Eric Clarke's review of Huron's *Sweet Anticipation* in *Music Analysis* 27, no. 2-3 (2008): 389-92.

[16]Huron, *Sweet Anticipation*, 59-64. Researchers refer to the process of statistical learning and schematic formation as "neural Darwinism." According to this model, "the auditory system is spontaneously capable of generating several representations from which the less successful can be eliminated." See Huron, *Sweet Anticipation*, 107-10.

arising from accurate prediction and the contrastive valence arising from innocuous surprises."[17] These two classes of schematic structures are meter and tonality. Having already explored meter to some extent in the previous chapter, and with a brief return to the topic of meter yet to come in reference to Begbie's analysis of musical repetition, the following section will therefore examine more closely the repetitive processes through which the phenomenon of musical tonality emerges, with particular reference to David Huron's empirical musicological analysis.

Contrary to the popular saying "familiarity breeds contempt," an oft-noted finding not only in musicological research but also in other areas of research is that familiarity in fact lends itself to an increase in pleasure. This phenomenon, called the exposure effect (or sometimes the mere exposure effect), has been replicated over two hundred times in various experiments, according to Huron.[18] The *exposure effect* is seen in people's preference for familiar foods, smells, faces, words, photographs, objects, and even nonsense words, and it is operative even apart from conscious recognition—that is, in the "fast" brain rather than the "slow" brain.[19] In fact, the effect is most apparent "when the slower (cortical) brain is taken out of the loop—that is, when conscious mental processing is disrupted or distracted."[20] Thus the preference for the familiar occurs as a "fast, reflex-like" process.[21]

However, it is not simply familiarity *as such* that aids enjoyment, according to Huron. Rather, it is the successful prediction of future events that makes frequently occurring sounds pleasurable. As he explains, "There is nothing inherently pleasant about the pitch G4. But if a listener predicted the occurrence of G4, then the tone itself is likely to be experienced as pleasant."[22] If this theory is correct, then "the pleasure of the exposure effect is not a phenomenon of 'mere exposure' or 'familiarity.' It is accurate prediction that is rewarded—and then misattributed to the stimulus."[23] Thus, Huron suggests, the "exposure effect" might more accurately be called the "prediction effect."[24]

---

[17]Huron, *Sweet Anticipation*, 141.
[18]Huron, *Sweet Anticipation*, 131.
[19]Huron, *Sweet Anticipation*, 132.
[20]Huron, *Sweet Anticipation*, 133.
[21]Huron, *Sweet Anticipation*, 133.
[22]Huron, *Sweet Anticipation*, 138.
[23]Huron, *Sweet Anticipation*, 138-39.
[24]Huron, *Sweet Anticipation*, 139.

The phenomenon of tonality can be understood, therefore, as a listening schema that enables successful pitch-related predictions (i.e., *what*-related, as opposed to *when*-related predictions), thus aiding comprehension and enhancing pleasure. When a certain sound or combination of sounds is recognized as a pitch or a chord, listeners who have been enculturated into a particular musical tradition will begin to make both conscious and unconscious aural predictions from within the mental schemas that they have developed through their exposure to recurring sound patterns. According to Huron, the process of learning through repetition underlying the perception of both meter and tonality occurs in accordance with the "Hick-Hyman law" of statistical learning, in which perception is shown to be "more efficient for expected stimuli than for unexpected stimuli."[25]

An extreme example of the process of statistical learning that underlies the phenomenon of tonality is the ability of some musicians to correctly identify the name of any given pitch without external reference. This "seemingly magical" ability, called perfect pitch or absolute pitch (AP), is as rare as it is intriguing.[26] "Wake up an AP possessor in the middle of the night, play an isolated tone, and the AP musician will accurately identify the pitch."[27] Since the names of tones are culture-specific, it is clear that this ability is acquired through learning. "But the evidence for learning runs much deeper," Huron explains. "Japanese researcher Ken'ichi Miyazaki has shown that people who have absolute pitch are faster at identifying some pitches than others."[28] Specifically, pitches corresponding to the white keys on a standard keyboard were found to be more quickly identified than pitches corresponding to the black keys. When Huron and one of his students, in response to this finding, tallied the rate of occurrence of "white notes" and "black notes" in a large sample of music, they confirmed their suspicion that white notes were indeed more common than black notes, and certain black notes were more common than others.[29] They also found that "the relationship between

---

[25]Huron, *Sweet Anticipation*, 64.

[26]Huron reports that "fewer than one person in a thousand" possesses absolute pitch. Huron, *Sweet Anticipation*, 64.

[27]Huron, *Sweet Anticipation*, 64.

[28]Huron, *Sweet Anticipation*, 64.

[29]"Pitches like C# and F# occur more frequently than pitches like D# and G#." Huron, *Sweet Anticipation*, 64.

speed of identification and frequency of occurrence is consistent with the Hick-Hyman law," implying that absolute pitch "is learned through simple exposure, and that AP possessors learn best those sounds that occur most frequently in the sound environment."[30]

Further support for the speculation that absolute pitch is learned through exposure to recurrent sounds is found in the research showing dramatic differences between Chinese and American musicians in the rate of absolute pitch possession. A 2006 study showed that "for students who had begun musical training between ages 4 and 5, approximately 60% of Chinese musicians showed AP, compared to 14% of the English speakers."[31] The most likely cause of this gap is the types of languages spoken among each group of musicians, as Mandarin is a tone language, whereas English is not. Such a wide difference in AP possession between musicians who speak a tone language and musicians who do not speak a tone language suggests that "developing a framework for the categorical interpretation of pitch in speech facilitates the acquisition of musical pitch categories."[32] It may even be that the Chinese musicians were raised in an environment in which the tonal content of the language itself approached a sort of "linguistic" absolute pitch.[33]

Whatever the explanation might be, a clear finding of the extensive research surrounding absolute pitch is that the acquisition of this ability requires a stable pitch environment in early childhood.[34] However, Huron explains, if a child experiences an auditory environment with a high degree of pitch variability,

---

[30]Huron, *Sweet Anticipation*, 64.

[31]Aniruddh D. Patel, *Music, Language, and the Brain* (Oxford: Oxford University Press, 2008), 48. The testing took place among "a large number of musicians in the Central Conservatory of Music in Beijing and in the Eastman School of Music in New York. . . . Participants were given a musical AP test involving naming the pitch class of isolated tones spanning a 3-octave range." Patel, *Music*, 47-48.

[32]Patel, *Music, Language, and the Brain*, 48. "Independent of the putative link between tone languages and musical absolute pitch, it may be that learning a tone language shapes the perception of non-linguistic pitch more generally," Patel explains. Either way, there is a strong connection between the semantic function of tones in a spoken language and the acquisition of absolute pitch in music.

[33]Patel, *Music, Language, and the Brain*, 47. Patel cautions that the idea of absolute pitch in speech, originating from a 2004 study by Deutsch et al., is proving quite controversial and cannot be conclusively determined. However, the suggestion made by Deutsch and colleagues that "tone-language speakers have a precise and stable absolute pitch template that they use for speech purposes," which is "acquired as a normal part of early development, in the same way that infants acquire other aspects of their native phonology," is quite suggestive. See Patel's discussion of linguistic absolute pitch in *Music, Language, and the Brain*, 46-47.

[34]Huron, *Sweet Anticipation*, 111. See also his summary discussion on p. 364.

"any latent perfect pitch capacity is likely to atrophy."[35] In other words, the cognitive representation and recognition of musical tones is made possible by the stable, repeated sounding of various pitches, which are then associated with certain pitch names. Even for musicians who do not possess absolute pitch, other abilities that may prove no less useful are acquired in the same manner—through the frequent repetition of various tones within a certain tonal context. For example, instead of acquiring the ability to name tones without external reference, musicians who do not possess absolute pitch may instead acquire the ability to reliably name the intervals between tones. In fact, the former ability seems to impede the latter.[36] The acquisition of various tonally related aural skills, therefore, requires a more or less "stable" sound environment, an auditory context with a high degree of pitch-related repetition.

Tonal centers and tonal systems. The extreme example of absolute pitch demonstrates the fundamental level on which the phenomenon of tonality is created through the repetition of pitched sounds within a given tonal system. A more common definition of tonality, however, refers not simply to this "deep" level on which tonality is created, but also to the melodic and harmonic patterns that, through repetition, form the tonal "center" within any given piece of music. As Mark DeVoto explains, in Western music, tonality refers to "the organized relationships of tones with reference to a definite center, the tonic, and generally to a community of pitch classes, called a scale, of which the tonic is the principal tone."[37] Though there are many possible ways of organizing a system of tonality,

> the system of tonality (sometimes termed the tonal system) in use in Western music since about the end of the 17th century embraces twelve major and twelve minor keys, the scales that these keys define, and the subsystem of triads and harmonic functions delimited in turn by those scales, together with the possibility of interchange of keys. A piece embodying this system is said to be tonal.[38]

---

[35]Huron, *Sweet Anticipation*, 111.

[36]Huron, *Sweet Anticipation*, 111-12. As Huron notes, "For many AP-possessors, the ability to identify pitches impedes their ability to learn intervals by ear. Rather than identifying intervals from the relative distance separating the tones, AP-possessors often rely on deriving intervals from pitch names. [Ken'ichi] Miyazaki's work suggests that many possessors of AP have no native mental representations for intervals." Huron, *Sweet Anticipation*, 112.

[37]Mark DeVoto, "Tonality," in *The New Harvard Dictionary of Music*, ed. Don Michael Randel (Cambridge, MA: Belknap Press, 1986), 862.

[38]DeVoto, "Tonality," 862.

The phenomenon of musical tonality, therefore, relies on the creation of pitch-related expectations through repetition on both the "deep" and the "surface" levels.

Huron refers to three levels of listener expectation created through repetition, which may be charted along a spectrum ranging from "deep" to "surface." These three levels are the schematic, the veridical, and the dynamic levels, respectively.[39] Schematic expectations are formed over time through exposure to a wide range of examples within a given tonal system. "Schemas exist to help us deal with situations that are novel yet also broadly familiar," allowing listeners to process sounds more quickly. "In music, schemas represent common enculturated aspects of musical organization."[40] Veridical expectations, on the other hand, are formed by repeated exposure to the specific melodic, harmonic, and rhythmic patterns that comprise a particular work.[41] Veridical expectations are what enable listeners to distinguish one work from another, to recall what comes next on repeated hearings, and to identify a "wrong" note when it occurs.[42] Veridical memories of certain tonal and metric patterns are what enable many people to have "perfect" expectations for some of the most well-known pieces of music, such as the song "Happy Birthday" or their country's national anthem.[43]

In addition to the deep schematic level and the intermediate veridical level, expectations are also formed through repetition on the immediate surface level, which Huron refers to as the *dynamic* level. These are expectations formed after "very brief periods" of exposure to a new stimulus, with repetitive patterns being encoded into short-term memory. It is through repetition on this level that listeners are able to perceive the tonal center of a piece of

---

[39]Huron, *Sweet Anticipation*, 221-31. Huron credits the psychologist Jamshed Bharucha with the origination of the term "veridical expectation."

[40]Huron, *Sweet Anticipation*, 225.

[41]Huron, *Sweet Anticipation*, 224-25.

[42]Huron, *Sweet Anticipation*, 234-35. Interestingly, Huron notes that in improvised music, such as jazz, it is possible to incorporate a "wrong" note into a performance through the performer's repetition of the error in such a way that a note which, in the listener's schematic and/or veridical expectations, has a "low probability of occurrence," and thus sounds jarring at first, will begin to sound like it belongs in the piece as it recurs throughout the performance. This technique of incorporating "wrong" notes into a performed work, however, is only possible in improvised music, not in the "set" compositions of Western classical music. Huron, *Sweet Anticipation*, 234-35. See also Begbie, *Theology, Music and Time*, 229.

[43]Huron, *Sweet Anticipation*, 222.

music, the tonic (which, of course, may refer to a single melodic tone or to a harmonic chord). The perception of the tonic serves as the primary aid to pitch-related dynamic predictions as a listener encounters a musical work for the first time. "As the events of a musical work unfold, the work itself engenders expectations that influence how the remainder of the work is experienced."[44] Thus, in every musical event, tonality operates by means of repetition on these three concurrent levels: the schematic level, on which the fundamental tonal system is created and a general sense of understanding and anticipation is enabled, and the veridical and dynamic levels,[45] on which expectations and memories are formed with regard to the more specific harmonic and melodic patterns within a work itself as it is being performed and recalled.

These multiple levels are even further connected, however, as all schematic expectations must begin as dynamic expectations, and it is only through repeated exposure that tonal patterns transition to the level of veridical expectation and are eventually incorporated into listeners' schematic expectations, allowing greater comprehension and nuance to be gradually and incrementally developed.

> Commonly, listeners will form a broad category of "otherness" into which all deviant stimuli are, by default, indiscriminately assigned. . . . A typical Western-enculturated listener may have a handful of non-Western schematic categories available—such as Chinese music, Australian didgeridoo, and west African drumming. But for the inexperienced listener, much of the remaining world of music is clumped into a single "exotic" category.[46]

Even within the large-scale schema of Western tonal harmony, experienced listeners are able to distinguish and categorize specific works of music within a wide range of generic and subgeneric schemas, with greater exposure leading to greater nuance:

> Any taxonomy for genre is a combination of the actual music and the listener's unique listening experience. . . . In general, people make more refined

---

[44]Huron, *Sweet Anticipation*, 227.
[45]Since *veridical* and *dynamic* repetition are both related to repetitive patterns within specific works of music, these two categories will henceforth be combined into one single level—the level of "surface" or "immediate" repetition, as opposed to "deep" or "schematic" repetition—in order to facilitate analytical clarity.
[46]Huron, *Sweet Anticipation*, 215.

distinctions for music that is central to their taste, and then use cruder classifications for music that is peripheral to their interests. For example, while
a jazz fan will distinguish a large number of varieties of jazz, other musical
styles may be given broad classifications (e.g., country and western, classical,
pop) with little internal differentiation. Characterizations depend on a person's listening experience.[47]

The crucial point is that repetition is the operative mechanism in the emergence of a range of tonal phenomena. Not only is repetition the means by
which a large-scale tonal system is created; it is also the means by which generic
and subgeneric distinctions are developed within that system and the means
by which the specific melodic, harmonic, rhythmic, and metric features of a
musical work are able to emerge as distinctive to an individual work.

Tonality thus requires the concurrent operation of various levels of pitch-
related memory, and repetition is what helps "cement patterns into memory."
This, claims Huron, is what accounts for the ubiquity of repetition in music.[48]
In an intriguing study, Huron and a colleague, Joy Ollen, discovered that in
a wide crosscultural sample of fifty musical works,[49] "94 percent of all musical passages longer than a few seconds in duration are repeated at some point
in the work," and even this figure, Huron believes, may underestimate the
amount of repetition actually present in the music, since "repetition need
not be verbatim in order to convey useful predictive patterns."[50] Through
repetition, music passes almost involuntarily from short-term memory into
intermediate-term memory, and eventually into long-term memory.[51]

"It is perhaps no surprise," Huron writes, "that a musical motive is both
(1) the shortest distinct unit of repetition in a work, and (2) the most memorable feature or characteristic of a work."[52] Repeated and combined, motives

---

[47]Huron, *Sweet Anticipation*, 214.
[48]Huron, *Sweet Anticipation*, 228.
[49]Included in Huron and Ollen's sample were "Calypso, Inuit throat singing, Japanese New Age,
    Estonian bagpipe music, Punjabi pop, fifteenth-century Chinese *guqin*, Norwegian polka, a Navaho
    war dance, bluegrass, Macedonian singing, Ghanaian drumming, Spanish flamenco, Kalimantan
    ritual music, Hawaiian slack key guitar, Gypsy music, and thirty-five other works from similarly
    varied cultural sources." Huron, *Sweet Anticipation*, 228-29.
[50]Huron, *Sweet Anticipation*, 229.
[51]Huron, *Sweet Anticipation*, 229-30.
[52]Huron, *Sweet Anticipation*, 229. For a more comprehensive examination of musical motif and
    melody, further developing into harmony and polyphony, see Roger Scruton, *The Aesthetics of
    Music* (Oxford: Oxford University Press, 1997), 39-73.

become melodies, and melodies interact with chords and harmonic counter-points to form the larger tonal signature of a work of music.[53] Short-term, episodic memories of motives and phrases within a piece of music eventually become encoded into longer-term veridical memories of the piece itself, which are further enabled by—and also help to refine and enhance—the semantic memory systems of large-scale listening schemas. On both the small and the large scales, then, repetition helps to "cement" these patterns into listeners' memories.

Repetition, newness, and the metrical matrix. However, if repetition is such a central characteristic of music—if music "tends toward the pole of absolute sameness"—an important question arises: How does music remain interesting? As Begbie inquires, "How, then, is it that music can operate with such a high degree of repetition, that it can 'turn about and recoil' upon itself without inducing paralyzing boredom?"[54] The answer, according to Begbie, is multifaceted. On the most basic level, the art of music simply would not exist without a high degree of repetition, since it lacks the ability to consistently and precisely denote extramusical phenomena.[55] Since music cannot reliably signify anything outside of itself, "repetition becomes vital for imprinting the characteristic shape of music's features in the memory."[56] Repetition is necessary in order for music to acquire a sense of coherence and intelligibility.

Yet beyond the need for a basic sense of coherence and intelligibility, Begbie continues, "the deeper and more pressing issue is: how can so much repetition be interesting?"[57] Two answers become immediately apparent. The first is the "variation of musical parameters." As Begbie explains in relation to a particular composition of Beethoven's:

> As the section unfolds, the rhythm of the repeated motif remains constant, but
> the shape of the melody alters slightly, the timbre changes through varied

---

[53]For a critique of the reification of musical "works," see Christopher Small, *Musicking: The Meanings of Performing and Listening* (Middletown, CT: Wesleyan University Press, 1998), 3-12, and throughout. See also Jeremy Begbie, *Resounding Truth: Christian Wisdom in the World of Music* (Grand Rapids, MI: Baker Academic, 2007), 39-40.

[54]Begbie, *Theology, Music and Time*, 159.

[55]Begbie, *Theology, Music and Time*, 160.

[56]Begbie, *Theology, Music and Time*, 160. See also Middleton, "Play It Again Sam," 236. As demonstrated above, this is Huron's explanation for the ubiquity of repetition in music as well.

[57]Begbie, *Theology, Music and Time*, 160.

orchestration, the background harmony shifts, the volume swells and dies. This is a very common procedure in music: one parameter stays constant, the others are modified. And even when such modifications are not written down, often a performer will vary repeated material by ornamenting it, "stretching" it in time, and so forth.[58]

Similarly, the previous chapter noted Huron's finding that greater repetition (and therefore greater predictability) in one parameter of a piece of music is typically offset by greater variation (and therefore less predictability) in another.[59]

The second answer to the question of how repetition can remain interesting is the observation that "the 'environment' of a repeated unit is always different."[60] If, for example, a phrase is repeated several times in a row, each particular repetition will nonetheless sound different according to its arrangement in relation to the others. "The sounds may be duplicated but the music *as heard* is not."[61] Though this may account for some instances of musical repetition, perhaps especially "remote" repetition, Begbie finds this explanation less than satisfying in general, especially as it relates to multiple, "immediate" repetitions: "It is hardly convincing to say that in a string of identical motifs, the fifth will hold our interest because it is surrounded by the fourth and sixth as distinct from, say, the third which is surrounded by the second and fourth!"[62]

While both of these suggested explanations "may account for part of the interest in musical repetition," Begbie believes that "they are partial and secondary, and overlook a more fundamental factor": the situation of each of the repeated elements within the overall matrix of metrical waves that are generated within a piece of music.[63] This "metrical matrix," the contours of which Begbie explores in the first several chapters of *Theology, Music and Time*, is perhaps the best explanation, in Begbie's opinion, of the ability of repeated elements to avoid the induction of boredom in listeners.

---

[58]Begbie, *Theology, Music and Time*, 160. On performance techniques that lessen precise repetition (and therefore predictability), see also Huron, *Sweet Anticipation*, 314-18.

[59]Huron, *Sweet Anticipation*, 252-53. See also Middleton, "Play It Again Sam," 237-38.

[60]Begbie, *Theology, Music and Time*, 160.

[61]Begbie, *Theology, Music and Time*, 161.

[62]Begbie, *Theology, Music and Time*, 161.

[63]Begbie, *Theology, Music and Time*, 161.

Meter, to reiterate, is the deep rhythmic structure of a piece of music, the underlying (or perhaps overarching) temporal pattern within which tones and rhythms take shape. Meter is "a configuration of beats,"[64] which is not heard directly, but is rather extrapolated "by means of mental processing of musical information," including surface rhythms.[65] Similar to the various concurrent levels on which tonality has been shown to operate, the "metrical matrix" also comprises many levels at once, as successive layers of metrical waves are generated, one on top of the other, throughout the course of a piece of music. As Begbie explains,

> Meter does not work on one level alone. The successive downbeats of each bar are themselves differently accented. Together they constitute another wave at another level, itself a wave of equilibrium, tension, and resolution. . . . The same dynamic is repeated at a further level: the downbeats of hyperbars become new beats in another metrical wave (a higher hyperbar). And so on. The process is extended in still higher hyperbars, the lower waves giving rise to ever higher waves.[66]

This generative process, resulting in the "metrical matrix" is illustrated in figure 3.1.

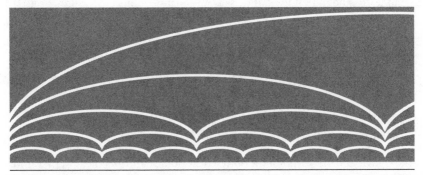

Figure 3.1. The metrical matrix, based on Jeremy Begbie, *Theology, Music and Time* (Cambridge: Cambridge University Press, 2000), 161.

---

[64]Begbie, *Theology, Music and Time*, 39.
[65]Jonathan D. Kramer, *The Time of Music: New Meanings, New Temporalities, New Listening Strategies* (New York: Schirmer Books, 1988), 97. Begbie rightly emphasizes that although "meter is sensed with peculiar directedness through rhythm, it can be articulated by any parameter of music—including pitch change, tone, duration, harmonic change, textural change, the entrance of a new voice, change of tempo, new register, contour change and dynamics. In fact, all parameters of music potentially contribute to the delineation of metric accents, and thus to metrical waves." Begbie, *Theology, Music and Time*, 41. See also Kramer, *Time of Music*, 108-20.
[66]Begbie, *Theology, Music and Time*, 41-42.

The metrical matrix thus provides a complex temporal context, "a multi-layered texture of superordinate and subordinate waves"[67] in which a high degree of repetition can nonetheless retain a sense of continued newness as "each [repeated element] occurs in relation to a different configuration of metrical tensions and resolutions."[68] If one were to draw vertical lines through the graph at various points representing various iterations of a repeated element in a given piece of music, one would notice that individual iterations intersect the various metrical layers at different points in the layers' respective "journeys of tension and resolution," giving each repeated element "a different dynamic quality."[69] "This," argues Begbie, "is where the fundamental novelty lies within tonal music," as "two occurrences of the same motif can be sensed as different because each relates to a different combination of metrical tensions and resolutions."[70]

Zuckerkandl is almost poetic in his description of this phenomenon:

> Tones may repeat themselves; time cannot repeat itself. It is only because time does not repeat itself that so much repetition is possible here; or vice versa, that so much repetition does not become meaningless is only to be understood if time does not repeat itself, if there is no equality of times. Measures, beats, groups of measures may be exactly alike so far as tonal content is concerned, but since they must occur at different times they can never be mere repetition; they are necessarily different, as the phases of a wave or the degrees of intensification are different. The repetition of a tonal statement never simply says the same thing over again; it accomplishes its particular share in the metric process, whether as the fulfillment of a demand for symmetrical complementation or as a link in the chain of intensification.[71]

The metrical matrix, maintain both Zuckerkandl and Begbie,[72] is therefore what gives musical repetition its fundamental dynamic quality. While the other explanations for musical repetition are viable—namely, that repetition is necessary to make music intelligible, that repetition occurs to greater or lesser degrees within a variety of concurrent parameters, and that the context

---

[67]Begbie, *Theology, Music and Time*, 43.
[68]Begbie, *Theology, Music and Time*, 161.
[69]Begbie, *Theology, Music and Time*, 161.
[70]Begbie, *Theology, Music and Time*, 162.
[71]Zuckerkandl, *Sound and Symbol*, 219.
[72]Begbie follows Zuckerkandl's thought quite closely in *Theology, Music and Time*. See pp. 37-51.

of each repeated element is always different—these explanations are not sufficient apart from a broader consideration of the layers upon layers of tension and resolution that comprise the metrical matrix of a piece of music.

REPETITION IN PREACHING

Having noted many of the most prominent features of—and questions related to—the phenomenon of repetition in music, the discussion will now turn to the use of repetition in preaching. Just as the creation and maintenance of synchrony in preaching became the first major instinct in this musical homiletic, the skillful use of repetition in preaching now becomes the second. Perhaps not surprisingly, many of the features of the phenomenon of repetition in music explored above may in fact provide a useful frame for an analysis of the phenomenon of repetition in preaching as well.

In the homiletical literature, the phenomenon of repetition, if mentioned at all, is typically subsumed under the category of rhetoric, with little significance attached to it beyond its persuasive power and aesthetic appeal. For instance, Clayton Schmit identifies repetition as one of sixty figures of speech with which preachers might become acquainted as they enlarge their poetic "toolbag" in order to amplify the evocative power of language in preaching.[73] "Repetition comes in many forms," according to Schmit, among which are "accumulatio, diacope, and symploce."[74] Moreover, what makes repetition powerful is its insistence: "repeated words, phrases, and structures strike our ears and hammer our perceptions until we cannot escape their persistent message."[75]

Interestingly, the basic rhetorical function of repetition in preaching proves similar to the basic tonal and metric functions of repetition in music. As in musical repetition, homiletical repetition is especially helpful in cementing the spoken word into memory, according to Schmit. He cites

---

[73]Clayton J. Schmit, *Too Deep for Words: A Theology of Liturgical Expression* (Louisville, KY: Westminster John Knox, 2002), 96-114. To be sure, aesthetic appeal is not advised *for its own sake* in Schmit's writing. Quite the opposite, Schmit develops "a theology of liturgical expression" that encourages aesthetic excellence "for the people's sake and for the sake of their faith." Schmit, *Too Deep for Words*, 66. He borrows a phrase from Jerry Evenrud to encapsulate his approach: "Art for faith's sake." See especially chap. 1 in *Too Deep for Words*.

[74]Schmit, *Too Deep for Words*, 103. Schmit references Arthur Quinn, *Figures of Speech: 60 Ways to Turn a Phrase* (Salt Lake City: Gibbs M. Smith, 1985), as the source of these terms, which are not explained individually in Schmit's text.

[75]Schmit, *Too Deep for Words*, 103.

James Kilpatrick's statement that, whereas "the mind boggles" to imagine
the number of public speeches a journalist might hear over a lifetime, "only
a handful are truly memorable, and in each of them, we hear the device of
repetition."[76] Moreover, similar to the way in which a tonal center—a tonic—
is established in a piece of music through repetition, Schmit counsels that
the purpose of repetition in preaching is "to give rhetorical shape to discourse
and to keep the audience near the center of the [preacher's] message."[77]

There are several types of repetition preachers may use in order to enhance
a sermon's rhetorical strength, Schmit continues. Anaphora involves the
repetition of words at the beginning of phrases or sentences. Repetend is "the
irregular repetition of a word, phrase, or image throughout a discourse."[78]
Two structural repetitive devices that preachers might also use are refrain and
recapitulation.[79] Repetition might even be disguised: antithesis involves
"repetition by negation." "Rather than saying something and then repeating
it in other words, you both deny its contrary and assert it."[80] Antithesis provides "an alternative to simple repetition and has the benefit of lending a
definitive thrust to an assertion."[81] A final form of repetition, which H. Grady
Davis identifies as an essential element of "writing for the ear," is restatement,
the repetition of an idea in other words. "The ear is far more tolerant than
the eye of reiteration, so long as it is not deadly repetition."[82] Thus a short,
pithy sentence or phrase restating the point of a given section can also be a
powerful rhetorical tool for preachers.[83]

---

[76]Schmit, *Too Deep for Words*, 103-4. Quotation from James Kilpatrick, *The Writer's Art* (Kansas City: Andrews and McMeel, 1984), 101.

[77]Schmit, *Too Deep for Words*, 104.

[78]Schmit, *Too Deep for Words*, 104.

[79]Schmit, *Too Deep for Words*, 104. As an example of *refrain*, Schmit cites the first chapter of Genesis: "And there was evening and there was morning, the first (second, third, etc.) day." He references musical form to explain recapitulation: "A theme is stated (A), is developed (B), and is stated again or recapitulated (A)." The ABA form, Schmit claims, is found in sermons "that begin with a story or image as a way to introduce the sermon topic, then develop the theme in the body of the sermon, and bring closure by returning in the conclusion to the opening scene or image." Schmit, *Too Deep for Words*, 104.

[80]Quinn, *Figures of Speech*, 67, quoted in Schmit, *Too Deep for Words*, 104.

[81]Schmit, *Too Deep for Words*, 104. An example of antithesis cited by Schmit is John 1:3, "All things came into being through him, and without him not one thing came into being." Schmit, *Too Deep for Words*, 105.

[82]H. Grady Davis, *Design for Preaching* (Philadelphia: Fortress, 1958), 280.

[83]Davis, *Design for Preaching*, 280.

Perhaps not surprisingly, the intoned sermon of much African American and American folk preaching, as analyzed by Jon Michael Spencer and Bruce Rosenberg and explored in the previous chapter for its rhythmic and metric features, also utilizes a high degree of linguistic and structural repetition.[84] As Jon Michael Spencer notes regarding the African American formulaic unit,

> As a preacher is intoning and ultimately engaged in the spontaneous formation of a spiritual, there are three compositional choices to be made which determine form. Given a word, phrase, or sentence, the preacher can repeat it, vary it, contrast it, or extend it. . . . There are further options when a word, phrase, or sentence is repeated verbatim. . . . Upon repetition, the preacher can stress the same syllables and words or emphasize other syllables and words, deliver the material with the same rhythmic pattern or superpose a different pattern, and, lastly, sing the text to the same tune, vary it, or intone a new tune.[85]

Consistent with the aims of his research project, Spencer subsequently provides several examples of preached sermons that contain such a high degree of repetition that they naturally transition into sung spirituals, the form of which is often determined by the type of repetition employed by the preacher.[86]

Similarly, in his analysis of the American folk sermon, Bruce Rosenberg acknowledges that the primary mark of the oral compositional techniques used in this style of preaching is repetition. However, he cautions, "there is no universality of opinion about those aspects of the formula [i.e., the basic unit of repetitive material] that must be repeated in order to qualify; metrical, syntactical, semantic elements have all been considered, but these phenomena vary among oral narrative traditions."[87] Despite a lack of scholarly agreement on those aspects of oral performance that qualify as "repetitive," Rosenberg believes that repetition is ubiquitous in oral preaching traditions because it aids memory, thus serving a similar function as repetition in music.[88]

Moreover, like Huron, Rosenberg posits a reassessment of the so-called "exposure effect" that causes pleasure to be derived from listening to repetitive material in preaching:

---

[84]See especially Jon Michael Spencer, *Sacred Symphony: The Chanted Sermon of the Black Preacher* (Westport, CT: Greenwood Press, 1987), 11-15, and Bruce A. Rosenberg, *Can These Bones Live? The Art of the American Folk Preacher*, rev. ed. (Chicago: University of Illinois Press, 1988), 74-80.

[85]Spencer, *Sacred Symphony*, 12.

[86]Spencer, *Sacred Symphony*, 12-14.

[87]Rosenberg, *Can These Bones Live?*, 83.

[88]Rosenberg, *Can These Bones Live?*, 83.

Too much has been made of the aural audience's liking for familiar language (and language patterns) because of its comforting qualities; it is more likely that aural participants in oral narrative performances like formulas and familiarity with the plot because they enable them to participate more than passively. They are not active performers, but neither are they as merely receptive as modern hushed audiences at a poetry reading.[89]

One wonders if Rosenberg would agree with Huron's proposal that the "exposure effect" should perhaps be renamed the "prediction effect," inasmuch as repetitive material in both preaching and music might be thought of as being pleasurable to listeners not simply because it is familiar, and thus comforting, but rather because greater familiarity leads to greater predictability and thus enables greater listener participation and satisfaction.[90]

However, though many authors in the homiletical literature have focused on only one type of repetition, which might be referred to as *dynamic* or *veridical*—the type of linguistic repetition that occurs within individual sermons themselves, creating a certain amount of coherence and predictability[91] —there is a deeper level of repetition that can also be identified in preaching. As is the case with repetition in music, there are various levels of repetition in preaching, which serve different functions. Dynamic or veridical repetition in preaching might be thought of as creating a rhetorical or thematic "center" within a particular sermon, akin to the "tonic" that is created through repetition in a given piece of music. However, using the larger understanding of tonality given to us by Huron—as pitch-related patterns generated through repetitive mechanisms operating on at least two concurrent levels, the dynamic/veridical and the schematic—we might also analyze repetition in preaching as forming larger-scale schematic patterns, as certain theological concepts and hermeneutical frames recur over time in the preaching that occurs in a particular context or is performed by a particular preacher.

One homiletician who has advocated strongly for this understanding of schematic repetition in preaching is William Willimon. In an essay titled "Play It Again, Sam," Willimon writes of the "glorious, holy moment in preaching,

---

[89]Rosenberg, *Can These Bones Live?*, 83.

[90]Notice the overlap here between repetition and synchrony, especially with the emphasis in both phenomena on listener participation.

[91]This might also be referred to as *immediate* repetition.

when the congregation remembers its story, the story that has nurtured it through thick and thin, the story that convenes us in the first place."[92] In Willimon's opinion, the primary means by which the congregation encounters and remembers "the story that has nurtured it through thick and thin" is through the faithful preaching of the Word of God. Preachers may exercise their own creativity and develop their own recurrent thematic emphases, to be sure, but first and foremost, preachers are accountable to the tradition that has been handed down to them. Thus, for Willimon, "we preach *what we have been told to preach*."[93] The large-scale schematic patterns that ought to characterize the preaching of any particular individual must therefore be recognizable as faithful repetitions and extensions of the church's long theological tradition of interpreting Scripture, rather than simply the preacher's own invention. "Our preaching," Willimon writes,

> is not our little, personal crusade, the latest thing to emerge from the denomination's head office. Our preaching is informed, formed by the saints. Each Sunday, in submitting ourselves to Scripture, in listening to God's Word in Scripture more than we listen to ourselves, we are demonstrating that we Christians think, not for ourselves, but with the saints.[94]

The large-scale schema Willimon envisions in Christian preaching emerges through the repetition, the continuation, of the church's story, which is handed on to us by the saints through the theological traditions of the church. Faithful preaching thus becomes an extension of, a repetition of, the church's historical schematic patterns.[95]

Here Willimon seems to be adopting a similar approach to that of Karl Barth, whose homiletical model Willimon summarizes as follows: "Preaching arises from scripture, repeats scripture, and follows the 'distinctive movement' of the text."[96] Or again: "Preaching is biblical when it is grateful, joyful, playful submission to and repetition of the biblical text that is a faithful exposition

---

[92]William H. Willimon, "Play It Again, Sam," in *Preaching Master Class: Lessons from Will Willimon's Five-Minute Preaching Workshop*, ed. Noel A. Snyder (Eugene, OR: Cascade, 2010), 29.

[93]Willimon, "Formed by the Saints," in *Preaching Master Class: Lessons from Will Willimon's Five-Minute Preaching Workshop*, ed. Noel A. Snyder (Eugene, OR: Cascade, 2010), 101.

[94]Willimon, "Formed by the Saints," 101.

[95]For a more thorough treatment of this theme, see also William H. Willimon, *Undone by Easter: Keeping Preaching Fresh* (Nashville: Abingdon Press, 2009), chap. 3.

[96]William H. Willimon, *Conversations with Barth on Preaching* (Nashville: Abingdon Press, 2006), 25.

of what God says and is saying."[97] Barth was apparently so confident of God's continued use of "biblically derived theological language" to create faith in the hearts and minds of listeners that, according to Willimon, "Barth could advise us preachers that all we must do is hear, then repeat, without ornament or anxiety, the Word of God, and thereby others will be given the grace to trust this word in life and in death."[98] Thus for Barth, and to a large extent for Willimon, following Barth, the large-scale schemas that arise through repetition over time in preaching will ideally be derived from the repetitive schemas that are found within the pages of Scripture itself, as preaching will aspire to be an unadorned repetition of what Scripture itself says.[99]

"Whether [Barth] is being precritical or postcritical" in adopting a homiletical model that idealizes the repetition of Scripture in such a way, Willimon "cannot say for sure."[100] But there is no doubt that such a position involves a certain naïveté.[101] Whether such a naïveté is viewed as an asset or a liability probably depends on the theological sympathies of individual preachers and homileticians. But without a doubt, the idea that large-scale schematic patterns in preaching would or should arise from the simple repetition of biblical language avoids (perhaps intentionally) many crucial epistemological and hermeneutical questions that are raised in and through the practice of preaching itself.[102]

---

[97]Willimon, *Conversations with Barth*, 26.

[98]Willimon, *Conversations with Barth*, 108.

[99]For further analysis of the role of repetition in the development of long-term conceptual "schemata," see Jeffrey D. Arthurs, *Preaching as Reminding: Stirring Memory in an Age of Forgetfulness* (Downers Grove, IL: IVP Academic, 2017), 30-35. Of course, Arthurs does not advocate the "unadorned repetition" that Barth seems to advocate, but his project does support the more general thrust of Willimon's and Barth's counsel: that preachers' primary task is to stir the memory of the biblical story among God's people.

[100]Willimon, *Conversations with Barth*, 24.

[101]As Willimon writes,

I love the way that Barth continues to be shocked, surprised, and filled with wonderment at biblical texts, all the way to the end of his life. In seminary courses in biblical interpretation we usually think of hermeneutics as a matter of acquiring increasing interpretive sophistication. However, Barth's childlike naïveté enables him to see and hear things that we more serious adults miss. (Willimon, *Conversations with Barth*, 24)

Scott Hoezee captures this same sentiment as he counsels preachers, "Don't ever lose your ability to be surprised by the Bible." Scott Hoezee, *Why We Listen to Sermons* (Grand Rapids, MI: Calvin College Press, 2019), 63.

[102]Willimon is not unaware of these critical questions, of course, and includes many lengthy sections on epistemology and hermeneutics in his writing. See, e.g., Willimon, *Conversations with Barth*, 49-65, 86-90, 134-38. Furthermore, drawing upon the work of Søren Kierkegaard, Willimon

Every honest, self-reflective preacher, including Willimon, must acknowledge that certain theological schemas and hermeneutical lenses are both necessary and unavoidable in the act of interpretation. As Thomas Long comments, with reference to the Barthian "herald" model of preaching,

> Preaching does not occur in thin air but always happens on a specific occasion and with particular people in a given cultural setting. These circumstances necessarily affect both the content and style of preaching, but if we think of preaching as announcing some rarefied biblical message untouched by the situation at hand, we risk preaching in ways that simply cannot be heard.[103]

A better approach, it seems, would be for preachers to attempt to become more aware of, and thus more responsible for, the pervasive theological and hermeneutical schemas that are evident over time in their own preaching.

In *Claiming Theology in the Pulpit*, Burton Z. Cooper and John S. McClure encourage such an approach, proposing a method by which preachers may become more theologically self-aware. Having analyzed one's theological profile using a tool they created, Cooper and McClure then propose several steps to aid preachers in "claiming" their dominant theological frames more confidently and forthrightly in the pulpit.[104] However, it seems unclear the extent to which preachers using Cooper and McClure's approach should try to derive their schemas themselves from Scripture or simply applying preconceived schemas to particular texts more confidently. If the latter characterization is accurate, then perhaps Barth's emphasis on the repetition of scriptural language as the source of the theological concepts and hermeneutical frames of preaching would provide a much-needed theological baseline.

Between these two extremes—on the one hand an understanding of preaching as involving an unadorned repetition of the biblical text, and on the other hand a homiletical theory that acknowledges the preconceived schemas through which preachers unavoidably interpret Scripture yet fails to allow for the repeated study of Scripture itself to shape, refine, and critique

---

cleverly demonstrates the necessity of repetition for the acquisition of knowledge itself. See Willimon, *Undone by Easter*, 59-63.

[103]Thomas G. Long, *The Witness of Preaching*, 2nd ed. (Louisville, KY: Westminster John Knox, 2005), 26.

[104]Burton Z. Cooper and John S. McClure, *Claiming Theology in the Pulpit* (Louisville, KY: Westminster John Knox, 2003).

those schemas—a mediating position is found in the homiletical theory of Paul Scott Wilson. Especially in his *four pages* model, Wilson seeks to provide a flexible yet unmistakably gospel-centered schema by which to ensure that the long-term repetitive patterns of preachers remain focused on the good news of God's redemptive action in the world.[105]

In the preface to the revised edition of his homiletical textbook, *The Practice of Preaching*, Wilson identifies the major concern that lies behind the development of his homiletical method, especially as it contrasts with the methods that have been developed by the pillars and inheritors of the New Homiletic:

> The previous edition was designed to help any student to become a card-carrying member of the New Homiletic (or whatever term was being used then to classify the homiletical revolution since the 1950s). I still treasure those revolutionary learnings and I uphold them here, yet I have become aware also of their limitations. Sermons in the New Homiletic became more biblical, more in touch with the contemporary world, more imagistic. They taught in ways that did not just address the mind but allowed listeners to experience what was said; they had greater variety in form and allowed for diversity in the congregation. They were more artistic. But were they more faithful? Did the teachings of the New Homiletic enable better proclamation of the gospel?[106]

Were they more faithful? Did they enable better proclamation of the gospel? These questions, according to Wilson, must remain central in the identification, analysis, and promotion of large-scale schematic patterns in preaching. As Wilson further explains, "Up to the time of probing the above question, I assumed that biblical sermons preached the gospel just as a matter of course. Now I am no longer confident. Some do, but many, perhaps most, do not."[107] What is needed, Wilson believes, is for homiletics "to re-examine its approach, . . . and this examination needs to be centered on the nature of the gospel."[108] Thus it seems that Wilson distances himself both from the Barthian-inspired simple-repetition-of-the-text model and also from the

---

[105]Paul Scott Wilson, *The Four Pages of the Sermon: A Guide to Biblical Preaching* (Nashville: Abingdon Press, 1999).

[106]Paul Scott Wilson, *The Practice of Preaching*, rev. ed. (Nashville: Abingdon Press, 2007), xii.

[107]Wilson, *Practice of Preaching*, xii.

[108]Wilson, *Practice of Preaching*, xii.

many models derived from the New Homiletic, to the extent that both (or all) of these options fail to identify the gospel as the most important schematic pattern through which Christian preachers must always interpret and preach the biblical text.[109]

One of Wilson's most memorable and enduring assertions is that a more faithful proclamation of the gospel is enabled when preachers are intentional about crafting themes with God as the subject of active verbs.[110] Faithful preaching, claims Wilson, must be marked by a long-term pattern of witnessing to God's redemptive work in the world. Indeed, the main purpose of Wilson's *Four Pages of the Sermon* is to provide an easily understandable and repeatable model by which sermons may reliably retain a focus on divine action.[111] To summarize, the schema Wilson proposes by which sermons are to remain centered on the gospel involves the identification of four recurrent scriptural and theological themes (i.e., four *pages*): (1) trouble in the Bible, (2) trouble in the world, (3) God's action in the Bible, and (4) God's action in the world. The regular application of this pattern is advocated as a simple means of ensuring that God's action retains a central place in preaching.

Yet even beyond sermon composition, Wilson further advises that his *four pages* model may also be used as an evaluative tool of long-term homiletical patterns: "As preachers, we should be able to go back over recent sermons and determine quickly what page or pages need more attention."[112] Preachers may find, for instance, that they repeatedly afford much more attention to trouble in the world or trouble in the text than they do to God's action in the world or in the text. The *four pages* model of composition and analysis thus becomes Wilson's chief proposal for remedying the "apparent absence of God" in much contemporary homiletics.[113] Preachers, Wilson claims, should be

---

[109]For further support of a gospel hermeneutic in preaching, see Richard Lischer, *A Theology of Preaching: The Dynamics of the Gospel*, rev. ed. (Eugene, OR: Wipf and Stock, 1992), esp. chap. 3.

[110]Wilson, *Practice of Preaching*, 45-53.

[111]Mary Hulst similarly advises, "The words we use when we preach about God teach our hearers how they are to speak about God. Our *God language* shapes their God language." Mary Hulst, *A Little Handbook for Preachers: Ten Practical Ways to a Better Sermon by Sunday* (Downers Grove, IL: InterVarsity Press, 2016), 39. Drawing upon the language of Scripture, as well as historic creeds and confessions, Hulst further emphasizes the need for faithful and robust trinitarian language, encouraging an appropriate precision about the words preachers associate with each member of the Trinity. Hulst, *Little Handbook*, 44-46.

[112]Wilson, *Four Pages*, 17.

[113]Wilson, *Four Pages*, 15.

able to evaluate blocks of their own sermon content according to these "four biblical and theological functions," and faithful preaching of the gospel will be marked by the presence of these four emphases in "roughly equal duration."[114] The proclamation of the gospel—of God's redemptive action in the world— therefore serves for Wilson as something akin to a large-scale tonal system, created through the consistent repetition of certain "biblical and theological functions" over a long period of time. Perhaps individual sermons might even be thought to acquire their specific thematic "tonal centers" within this larger theological schema, this "system of tonality" established through long-term repetition of the distinctive shape of the gospel.

SUMMARY: REPETITION IN MUSIC AND PREACHING

As the above discussion has shown, the phenomenon of repetition in music provides a most suggestive metaphorical frame for an analysis of repetition in preaching, with many striking similarities becoming immediately apparent. Some evaluative comments on these similarities are now appropriate.

Similar to the role of pitch-related repetition in music, linguistic repetition in preaching might be thought of as comprising at least two concurrent operative processes: the dynamic/veridical and the schematic. Dynamic and veridical memories and expectations are formed as repetitive language creates a "tonal center" within individual sermons, whereas schematic memories and expectations are formed over time through recurrent theological frames that settle in the long-term, unconscious memories of listeners, fostering certain patterns of theological understanding through which listeners may hear and understand the language of preaching, thus resembling a "system of tonality" that enables listeners to hear, understand, and remember particular pitch-related patterns in music.[115] The empirical analysis of David Huron demonstrating the statistical learning processes through which the *Gestalt* phenomenon of tonality is created proves crucial in the development of a more thorough understanding of the role of repetition in music.[116] Thus,

---

[114]Wilson, *Four Pages*, 17.

[115]Clayton J. Schmit, "What Comes Next? Performing and Proclaiming the Word," in *Performance in Preaching*, ed. Jana Childers and Clayton J. Schmit (Grand Rapids, MI: Baker Academic, 2008), 185-87.

[116]Although Scruton has developed his entire musical aesthetics around the *Gestalt* phenomenon of *tone*, believing it to be the foundational phenomenon of all music, and even comparing "the

in order for musical repetition to provide a helpful metaphorical frame for the analysis of repetition in preaching, the large-scale view of tonality Huron gives us—as a phenomenon that emerges by means of statistical learning through the repetition of pitch-related patterns, encompassing dynamic, veridical, and schematic memories and expectations—is necessary.

However, it is possible for this metaphorical comparison to be misapplied in some instances, as perhaps may happen if one were to apply Wilson's four pages analysis too rigidly in an evaluation of the relative strength of certain schematic elements in one's preaching. This, in fact, is Eugene Lowry's critique of Wilson's homiletical prescriptions. Referencing another of Wilson's works, Lowry writes,

> I disagree with Paul Scott Wilson, who wants us to divide the sermon into two halves—with "a fifty-fifty balance between law and gospel." I certainly understand his concern that people carry with them from the worship service the resolution born of grace. *But quantity of words is not the appropriate measure.* The quality of impact, the suddenness of perception, and the power of decisive insight are central.[117]

Reading this critique carefully, it seems as if Lowry notes a general agreement with Wilson on the importance of the proclamation of the gospel, yet interestingly, disagrees with Wilson on the means of assessment. "Quantity of words," contends Lowry, is not necessarily an appropriate measure of a faithful gospel emphasis.

Tracing the disagreement between Lowry and Wilson on whether or not the quantity of words that focus on God's saving action might serve as an

---

transformation from sound to tone" to "the transformation of a sound into a word," it is Huron's empirical work that has most thoroughly explored the repetitive mechanisms by which the *Gestalt* of musical tonality is possible. See Scruton, *Aesthetics of Music*, 17-18. On the practice of hearing sounds as tones that constitutes the phenomenon of tonality, see also Francis Sparshott, "Aesthetics of Music—Limits and Grounds," in *What Is Music? An Introduction to the Philosophy of Music*, ed. Philip Alperson (University Park, PA: Penn State University Press, 1987), 33-98. Sparshott summarizes tonality as follows:

> A tone is such a sound segment as is regularly assigned to a music. It must then belong to a system of such sounds and must be recognizable as occupying a determinate place in the system. It must then be repeatable. It must then have audible properties that relate it systematically to other sound segments. Such properties are duration, loudness, pitch and timbre or tone-color. ... In practice, pride of place among such differentiae is occupied by pitch. (Sparshott, "Aesthetics," 46)

[117]Eugene L. Lowry, *The Sermon: Dancing the Edge of Mystery* (Nashville: Abingdon Press, 1997), 78 (emphasis added). The work Lowry cites here is Paul Scott Wilson, *Imagination of the Heart* (Nashville: Abingdon Press, 1988), 108.

appropriate measure of the faithful proclamation of the gospel, Richard Eslinger counsels individual preachers to use their own discernment about how their respective contexts might best be served in the selection of one or the other methodological option. Wilson's four pages model will serve one well, Eslinger believes, if one finds the need for a fifty-fifty balance of law and gospel to maintain a sufficient repetitive emphasis on God's action, whereas Lowry's model might serve one well if one finds the need for strategic delay and a "sudden shift" to enable a more powerful announcement of the gospel to occur later on in the sermon.[118] Yet Eslinger himself refrains from further specifying any basis on which preachers might make such determinations.

Perhaps this is an instance, therefore, in which the principles of statistical learning explored by Huron with reference to tonality are not fully adequate to resolve this debate. In this case, the insights of Begbie and Zuckerkandl regarding the metrical context of musical repetition might also provide a helpful metaphorical resource. As Begbie and Zuckerkandl point out, musical sounds typically involve a high degree of interpenetration, operating on many levels at once. Through a complex mix of repetitive rhythmic and harmonic patterns, an ascending hierarchy of metrical "waves" of tension and resolution are generated throughout a piece of music. This, then, is perhaps the best explanation for the ability of music to "tend toward the pole of absolute sameness" without resulting in monotony. But to measure the impact of any given musical motif, this would mean that due attention must be given not only to the sheer duration of the element, but also its placement within the ascending hierarchy of metrical waves. In this sense, contrary to Wilson's suggestion, Lowry is perhaps justified in his insistence that the sheer repetitive quantity of a given element does not ensure its overall impact or memorability.

An illustration from Begbie's *Theology, Music and Time* provides an example of this dynamic. "One of the intriguing things about listening to a piece

---

[118]Richard L. Eslinger, "Tracking the Homiletical Plot," in *What's the Shape of Narrative Preaching? Essays in Honor of Eugene L. Lowry*, ed. Mike Graves and David L. Schlafer (St. Louis: Chalice Press, 2008), 79. Here Eslinger also includes another citation of Wilson's strong opposition to Lowry's method of strategic delay: "When God suddenly comes into focus at the end of a sermon the gospel is not brought home and applied to the listener's life or the world. Considerable sermon time is needed to make the gospel concrete and to allow people to experience what God is accomplishing in and through them and others." Paul Scott Wilson, *Preaching and Homiletical Theory* (St. Louis: Chalice Press, 2004), 90. Quoted in Eslinger, "Tracking the Homiletical Plot," 78.

of music for the first time," Begbie writes, "is that one never knows how many upper metrical waves are being generated. There is always, potentially, a higher wave."[119] Moreover, even in Western tonal music—so often maligned for its obsession with finality and closure—there is an often-overlooked feature of musical cadences that prompts a reconsideration of the true nature of their supposed closure:

> *Cadences* are normally *metrically weak* even though they may be (and usually are) *rhythmically strong.* They normally occur on the weak beat of a metrical wave—the beat which leads forward to the first beat of the next bar or hyperbar. If we move up to the highest metrical level (the level of the piece as a whole) in many musical forms we discover that the final cadence of the piece is likewise metrically weak even though rhythmically strong. . . . In cases such as these, *metrically speaking, the piece never finishes.*[120]

Harmonically, Begbie notes, "a cadence is a *closure,*" but metrically, "it typically occurs *prior to closure* and *demands (metric) resolution.*"[121] This rarely acknowledged feature of cadences creates a phenomenon in which the music "'stretches forward' for further resolution," thus retaining an "incomplete character, an 'opening out.'"[122] As Begbie summarizes it, "We are given a tension which is not fully resolved, or which is only dissipated in the silence which follows the piece. The music is projected beyond the final cadence into the ensuing silence. Promise 'breaks out' of sound."[123] "The wave," he concludes, "is not closed."[124] This phenomenon is illustrated in figure 3.2.

| EXPOSITION and DEVELOPMENT | RECAPITULATION | CLOSE |

Figure 3.2. Final cadence in sonata form, based on Jeremy Begbie, *Theology, Music and Time* (Cambridge: Cambridge University Press, 2000), 126.

---

[119]Begbie, *Theology, Music and Time,* 123. See also Margulis, *On Repeat,* 35.

[120]Begbie, *Theology, Music and Time,* 125 (emphasis original).

[121]Begbie, *Theology, Music and Time,* 126 (emphasis original).

[122]Begbie, *Theology, Music and Time,* 126.

[123]Begbie, *Theology, Music and Time,* 126. See also Margulis, *On Repeat,* 33.

[124]Begbie, *Theology, Music and Time,* 126.

Building on this example, Lowry may be justified in maintaining that, due to the placement of a certain phrase within the "metrical matrix" of the sermon as a whole—or perhaps even more broadly, within the "metrical matrix" of the worship service as a whole—listeners may be primed to experience the strength of the language affirming God's redemptive action as being greater than the strength of the language acknowledging trouble in the world. Depending on the placement within the overall temporal (or "metrical") matrix, which is generated by a complex mix of repetitive patterns and associations, naming the action of God might possess more weight in its performative context than a retrospective analysis of the quantity of words used might suggest.

Further support for this suggestion is seen in Huron's surprising finding that in Western tonal music, the dominant fifth chord (V) is in fact more prevalent than the tonic (I). However, it is the tonic, not the dominant, that produces more pleasure in the ears of listeners, more of a feeling of closure and stability. Why would this be? If "mere exposure" caused the pleasure of hearing a given element, "then we would expect the dominant pitch to evoke more pleasure than the tonic."[125] However, the occurrence of the tonic chord *in the context of a musical cadence* is "quite simply the most predictable pitch-related musical stimuli."[126] It may be that within preaching a similar schematic mechanism is at play, in which the theological and hermeneutical schemas that listeners have developed over time cause them to expect that the announcement of God's saving action must inevitably follow the acknowledgment of the heartbreaking reality of sin and brokenness in the world—or in Wilson's language, the "trouble" we observe in Scripture and in the world must be followed by an affirmation of God's grace in Scripture and in the world.[127]

In this way, then, both Wilson and Lowry seem to have important insights regarding the homiletical implications of schematic patterns in gospel-centered preaching. Surely an honest assessment of the repetitive patterns in one's own preaching over time must take account of the frequency with which the affirmation of God's saving action occurs, as Wilson contends. But should

---

[125]Huron, *Sweet Anticipation*, 164.
[126]Huron, *Sweet Anticipation*, 165.
[127]See also Clayton Schmit, "What Comes Next?," 185. This theme will receive significantly more attention in the following chapter.

this aspect of one's preaching be found to receive less emphasis in terms of sheer quantity, a quantitative deficiency alone may not necessarily indicate a schematic weakness, as Lowry contends. It may be that, though occurring slightly less frequently in terms of pure repetition, the regular placement of the theme of God's redemptive action within a strategically strong position in the overall "metrical matrix" of one's preaching may nonetheless lend a greater schematic strength and pleasantness in the hearing of one's listeners than the sheer numerical quantity of this theme might otherwise indicate.[128] In this way, then, a meaningful analysis of the repetitive patterns found in preaching might involve not only the mere quantitative tallying of certain schematic themes but also a more nuanced qualitative or contextual analysis regarding which themes follow upon which in the larger "homiletical metrical matrix" that is generated in individual sermons.[129]

REPETITION AND PATIENCE

As the above discussion demonstrates, analyzing the phenomenon of repetition in preaching exposes certain theological themes that are far deeper than the mere desire for rhetorical effectiveness without respect to content. Wilson, Lowry, and Schmit all retain a strong concern for the primacy of *the gospel* among the many possible schematic patterns that might be created through both "surface" and "deep" repetition in preaching. However, there is an even further theological dimension that may be explored with regard to repetition in preaching. In the writing of Willimon especially, the phenomenon of

---

[128] As Begbie summarizes it, "Repetition is a kind of 'natural state' of music because the very equality of repetitive units brings out with special clarity the inequality (wave patterns) of successive bars and hyperbars, the manifold differences within the metrical matrix. Music depends on repetition—in some form—to highlight the endlessly different hierarchy of metrical waves." Begbie, *Theology, Music and Time*, 164.

[129] A caution should be noted here in favor of Wilson's overall admonition that "the apparent lack of God" in contemporary homiletics must be remedied. To be sure, although the tonic chord may not statistically be the most prevalent chord in Western tonal music, it is nonetheless the *second most prevalent*, and its occurrence in cadential contexts, as Huron notes, is in fact the most predictable pitch-related stimulus in Western tonal music. Analogously, whereas a slight quantitative deficiency in the prevalence of naming God's action in one's preaching might not prove detrimental to the overall aim of the faithful proclamation of the gospel, a more serious quantitative deficiency would surely indicate a schematic theological issue. In this way, then, Wilson's general point surely holds. However, Lowry himself seems to agree with this general point, arguing in favor of a gospel emphasis in preaching, but simply disagreeing about the means of assessing the presence of such an emphasis.

repetition is connected to a concern for *faithfulness*, specifically to the scriptural text and to the theological traditions of the church. A virtue closely related to faithfulness—but connoting an even stronger disposition of steadfastness and contentment regarding time and temporality—is patience. The final section of this chapter will further examine the skillful use of repetition in preaching—the second musical-homiletical instinct—not only as a means of developing a gospel-centered theological schema within a particular homiletical context, but also as a means of forming a certain kind of steadfast patience among one's hearers.

As was mentioned above in relation to Begbie's understanding of repetition, one of the primary effects of repetition in music is the foregrounding of the dynamics of time itself. "There is, in a sense, no such thing as redundancy in music," writes Begbie, because of the dynamic positioning of individual musical elements within a complex hierarchy of metrical waves.[130] However, "in order that these differences in dynamic quality can be sensed, wave patterns have to be brought into relief, 'etched' by sound."[131] Thus there must be "variation in some parameter of the music in order that the ever-different wave patterns can be heard."[132] Yet these variations within repetitive patterns occur not simply for the sake of "staving off boredom," but rather in order that "the patterns of tension and release in metrical waves" might be brought to our ear.[133] Consequently, "a fascinating irony" emerges: "The tones do not alter for the sake of variety, that is in order to give the same thing an *appearance* of being different; on the contrary, *because what is apparently the same is basically always different*, the tones do not always want to remain the same."[134] The skillful use of repetition in both music and preaching (which also inevitably includes some measure of variety) might thus be conceived as a means by which attention is drawn to the unfolding dynamics of time itself, "the ever-different metrical network" within which individual elements of a piece of music or a sermon are heard.[135]

---

[130]Begbie, *Theology, Music and Time*, 162.
[131]Begbie, *Theology, Music and Time*, 162.
[132]Begbie, *Theology, Music and Time*, 162.
[133]Begbie, *Theology, Music and Time*, 162.
[134]Begbie, *Theology, Music and Time*, 162 (emphasis original).
[135]On the connection between repetition and shifting attention among varying hierarchic metric levels, see also Elizabeth Hellmuth Margulis, "Musical Repetition Detection Across Multiple Exposures," *Music Perception: An Interdisciplinary Journal* 29, no. 4 (April 2012), 377-85.

If used effectively, then, repetition in both music and preaching has the potential to become "a conduit of the Spirit's transformative power"[136] by "rehabituating" both the preacher and the congregation into a certain kind of patience, a certain contentedness within the world of created temporality. As Begbie explains, in a postmodern culture that is permeated by "a certain malaise with regard to time," the repetitive processes of music might provide a temporal experience that is life-giving, an experience of time in which a sense of newness endures.[137] Within this context, the virtue of learning to wait for things to unfold can be modeled and encouraged.

Perhaps counterintuitively, music and preaching achieve this effect precisely in how they take time to happen. As Begbie writes,

> music challenges the assumption that because something takes time to be what it is, it is thereby of deficient value or goodness compared to that which is not subject to created time. It is part of the being of creation (and its constituent elements) to be temporal. The created world takes time to be. Music presents us with a concrete demonstration of the inseparability of time and created reality, of the truth that it need not be seen as a vice of creation that it can only reach its fulfillment, its perfection through time. It shows us in an intense way that "taking time" can be good, profitable and enriching.[138]

In a hyperconnected world of "information overload," with our attention constantly being drawn from one soundbite to the next,[139] the skillful use of repetitive processes in music and preaching has the possibility to become a means by which a certain posture of contentedness within created temporality—"a waiting which need not be empty or resigned but felicitous and abundant"—is formed.[140] This is the virtue of patience.

---

[136]James K. A. Smith, *Imagining the Kingdom: How Worship Works* (Grand Rapids, MI: Baker Academic, 2013), 15.

[137]Begbie, *Theology, Music and Time*, 73-75, 97.

[138]Begbie, *Theology, Music and Time*, 86.

[139]See Neil Postman's prophetic critique of the "Now … This" worldview in *Amusing Ourselves to Death: Public Discourse in the Age of Show Business*, 20th anniv. ed. (New York: Penguin Books, 1985).

[140]Begbie, *Theology, Music and Time*, 87. Begbie further emphasizes,

> Music itself is not the bearer of detachable commodities, timeless truths or abstract principles or visions. … And yet, even without a neatly packaged reward or "take-away" value, the waiting which music demands, by catching us up in its inter-relations, is experienced as anything but pointless or vain. Music can teach us a kind of patience which stretches and enlarges, deepens us in the very waiting.

Notably, however, the language of "timeless truths," "abstract principles," and "neatly packaged" takeaways is touted in some circles as a central purpose of preaching.

Following Begbie's logic, the use of repetitive processes in preaching to develop the virtue of patience among one's hearers might then be even further connected to the more general pastoral concern for Christian formation, in which the development of a mature Christian identity never happens instantaneously, but rather unavoidably occurs over a (long) period of time. As Begbie writes,

> The process of salvation can be conceived along just these lines, as an ongoing healing of our time through participation in the temporality established in Jesus Christ. . . . Far from abstracting us *out of* time, the vision opened up by music in this way is one in which to be "saved" is, among other things, to be given new resources for living "peaceably" *with* time. . . . In contrast to conceptions of human personhood which trade on notions of quasi-timeless "essences," the importance of time and narrative for the formation of identity has been underlined and explored extensively [in recent decades].[141]

Not only in the practice of preaching particularly, but also in the practice of pastoral ministry more generally, repetition might thus be utilized not simply as an aid to memory and retention, but even further, as an aid to developing the patience needed to wait for God's purposes to unfold. "But if we hope for what we do not see, we wait for it with patience" (Rom 8:25). Repetition brings to listeners' conscious awareness the dynamics of time itself, and in so doing it "challenges the assumption that because something takes time to be what it is, it is thereby of deficient value or goodness."[142]

Understood in this context, the use of repetition in preaching might be further connected to a related pastoral concern, the resistance of idolatry. In this case, one of the idolatries that repetition helps guard against is the idolatry of instantaneousness—the worship of the clock—which manifests itself, among other things, in the contemporary expectation that preaching should deal in pithy soundbites, "timeless truths," "helpful hints," or even abstract "biblical principles," as that phrase is sometimes understood.[143] The development of a mature Christian character, which includes the development of an ever-greater understanding of the "mysteries of God," simply and unavoidably

---

[141]Begbie, *Theology, Music and Time*, 150-52.

[142]Begbie, *Theology, Music and Time*, 86.

[143]Compare Jesus' pedagogical/homiletical method in Matthew 13:10-13.

takes time, and therefore the virtue of patience is necessary in order to resist the desire for instantaneous growth.

Repetition in preaching can bring to listeners' awareness the simple reality that just as the sermon itself takes time to unfold, just as the truth of the gospel takes time to sink deeply into the human heart, so also do God's purposes in the world—and God's purposes in a given individual's life—take time to unfold. What Begbie affirms in the case of music might be affirmed in the case of preaching as well: "Music asks for my patience, my trust that there is something worth waiting for."[144] Just as God is patient toward humankind, graciously allowing us time to come to repentance (2 Pet 3:9), so also can the practice of preaching model a certain human patience toward God—waiting in patient trust for God's purposes to unfold, even while we cry out, "How long?"

When patience takes root and the idolatry of instantaneousness is resisted, the experience of salvation might then be experienced not as a process of being rescued from time, but rather as "[being] given new resources to live peaceably with time."[145] This is not to imply that time somehow inevitably "heals all wounds" for those who are patient, or that the experience of waiting patiently for something to occur is equated with a certain stoicism (which would thus delegitimize the practice of lament), but rather simply that "there is a patience proper to Christian faith in which *something new is learned* of incalculable *value*, which cannot be learned in any other way."[146] Seen in this light, repetition in preaching might become a small but significant pastoral tool for modeling and encouraging the kind of patient, attentive disposition that is necessary for the development of a faithful and mature Christian character.

This final point—the development of a mature Christian character, and the time it takes for that development to occur—should not be underestimated. As Jeffrey Arthurs maintains, repetition in preaching is necessary because the cultivation of memory itself is understood by Scripture to be a serious spiritual matter. Forgetfulness, in scriptural terms, is not due simply

---

[144]Begbie, *Theology, Music and Time*, 87.

[145]Begbie, *Theology, Music and Time*, 151-52.

[146]Begbie, *Theology, Music and Time*, 105. "Music introduces us to just this kind of dynamic, this enriching meantime, in which we are made to cultivate a kind of patience which subverts the belief that delay must inevitably be void or harmful ('negatively problematic'). It can do so with a distinct potency, given, as we have seen, its intense involvement with a temporal dynamic that interweaves the temporal modes in a multi-leveled matrix."

to human frailty but also to human fallenness. Forgetting is not just "lack of mental recall" but rather a parallel concept to "forsaking" and "rejecting" (cf. Hosea 4:6-7).[147] The development of patience—or of any virtue, for that matter—requires a deep rootedness in the story of God's covenant faithfulness, such that over time God's story—the story of Scripture—is the only story that God's people come to accept as a given. All other stories must come to be interpreted in light of this story.[148] Such rootedness, argues Arthurs, requires preachers who are committed to embodying the role of "the Lord's remembrancers," developing patience among God's people by "reminding them of the great truths of the faith," not through the nagging repetition of "threadbare platitudes" but rather through the faithful and steadfast rehearsal of God's story, using a variety of methods within a variety of contexts, both in individual sermons and over the course of a preacher's long-term ministry.[149]

CONCLUSION: ATTENDING TO REPETITION IN PREACHING

Preaching is an oral/aural art by nature, and thus it requires the repetition of words, phrases, themes, and concepts in order to be understood and remembered by listeners. Furthermore, the rhetorical value of repetition is widely recognized. An oral argument or address that includes various forms of repetition and restatement invites greater listener participation—and is more likely to be persuasive and memorable—than one that does not. Preachers who desire to use the musical instinct of repetition skillfully in their preaching must first recognize the necessity of repetition for the participation, satisfaction, and ultimately even the persuasion of listeners. Repetition is a requirement of memory itself. Whether it be the acquisition of a physical skill or some form of cognitive knowledge, repetition is integral to the process of

---

[147] Arthurs, *Preaching as Reminding*, 18. As Arthurs states elsewhere, "Forgetting God is tantamount to forsaking him to worship idols, and we are prone to do just that." Arthurs, *Preaching as Reminding*, 40.

[148] Samuel Wells, *Improvisation: The Drama of Christian Ethics* (Grand Rapids, MI: Brazos Press, 2004), chap. 8.

[149] Arthurs, *Preaching as Reminding*, 6. See also chaps. 4-7 for an examination of various "tools for stirring memory." For more on what it means to promote the church's "inhabitation" of the biblical story through preaching, see Michael Pasquarello III, "Narrative Reading, Narrative Preaching: Inhabiting the Story," in Joel B. Green and Michael Pasquarello III, eds., *Narrative Reading, Narrative Preaching: Reuniting New Testament Interpretation and Proclamation* (Grand Rapids, MI: Baker Academic, 2003), 177-93.

learning. Moreover, repetition increases participation and satisfaction by enabling listeners to make successful predictions regarding what comes next.

Yet preachers must also remain cognizant of the larger spiritual significance of repetition. The goal of using repetition to enhance listener memory and participation must be understood not only with regard to the memorability and persuasive effect of individual sermons, but indeed as the very means by which long-term theological "listening schemas" are established in the lives of worshipers. In other words, repetition is an integral tool in discipleship. The ultimate goal is character formation. Both small-scale and large-scale repetition in preaching must be recognized, therefore, as a powerful tool whereby the church acquires the patient disposition of faithfully telling and re-telling, hearing and re-hearing, the story of God's covenant faithfulness. In that sense, "the Lord's remembrancers"[150] is a fitting way to characterize the vocation of preachers. Or as William Willimon puts it, citing Karl Barth, "We preachers must discipline ourselves to repeat ourselves."[151]

REPETITION IN PRACTICE

The following excerpt of a sermon by Lisa Weaver exemplifies the skillful use of repetition, in the form of two separate phrases that Weaver repeats at different points in the sermon.[152] This sermon was preached at the conclusion of a three-day worship conference that brought together pastors, worship leaders, scholars, and lay leaders from a variety of Christian traditions.

Weaver begins the sermon by setting it in the context of the other Scripture texts that had been preached at previous worship services throughout the conference, all of which had focused on Jesus' post-resurrection appearances. She notes the "summary" nature of Acts 1:1-11 and asks a provocative question: Why don't we have more stories from the 40 days between Jesus' resurrection and ascension? The answer, Weaver suggests, is found in a phrase from John 14:12, "greater works."

The focus of the ascension narrative, Weaver says, is rightly shifting from Jesus's work to the church's work. If we had more postresurrection

---

[150] Arthurs, *Preaching as Reminding*, 3-9 .

[151] Willimon, *Undone by Easter*, 65.

[152] Sermon text excerpt: Lisa Weaver, "Invited Again," Ascension sermon on Acts 1:1-11 (at the 2018 Calvin Symposium on Worship: https://worship.calvin.edu/resources/resource-library/closing -communion-worship-the-ascension, starting at 20:10). Used by permission.

stories, she jokes, the church may still be sitting around arguing about the division of labor—whether certain works are supposed to be Jesus's responsibility or ours. Weaver elaborates on this idea, using the repeated refrain "a greater work":

> Jesus said, "Greater works than these [shall he do]," so I imagine that John said, "No, this is not going to be a post-resurrection recitation on what Jesus does, but the world is now going to have to start to mark what the church does, because the church has to pick up the ministry of Jesus Christ."
>
> Curing cancer, diabetes, heart disease, and every other form of disease—a greater work. Dismantling racism, sexism, classism, and every form of ideological heresy contrary to the gospel of Jesus Christ in all its forms is a greater work. Eradicating human exploitation, trafficking, and oppression in all its forms—a greater work. Ending war—a greater work. Making sure every person on the planet has enough food to eat—a greater work. Making sure every person on the planet has access to clean water—a greater work. Making sure every person has the unhindered ability to pursue abundant life, complete liberty, and the pursuit of happiness on their own terms—a greater work. Creating the beloved community here on earth—a greater work.[153]
>
> We don't have Jesus's record because the work is no longer his; it belongs to the church. "Your kingdom come, your will be done on earth as it is in heaven"— a greater work.

Weaver then goes on to note that, just as Jesus invites the church to repeat and extend his pre-resurrection works after his resurrection and ascension, Jesus also invites his disciples to another "repeatable act"—the Lord's Supper, which strengthens us for the "greater works" to which we are called. Alongside this repeatable act, the church universal prompts us to continue confessing our faith together. The sermon continues:

> We have or will experience ministry burnout and faith fatigue. But when we confess our faith in the triune God, we are reminded that there is a creator of everything. We are reminded that there is a savior, consubstantial with the

---

[153]Weaver takes the risk of providing great specificity here, in order to prompt listeners to recognize the multiple mundane forms of "greater works" through which the church continues to carry on Jesus's mission. The focus here is decidedly "this-worldly," which could perhaps become an issue if it were not balanced out by the eschatological focus of the final section of the sermon. A significant part of the overall rhetorical power is the musicality of the vocal performance techniques Weaver uses in speaking these words.

creator, who for us and our salvation was made human, died, and rose again. When we confess our faith, we are reminded that there is a Holy Spirit, coequal with the creator and the savior, who speaks to us and leads us and guides us in all truth.[154]

When we confess our faith, we are reminded that we do not do these greater works alone. When we confess our faith, we are reminded that when we wrestle against powers and principalities and spiritual wickedness in high places, there is someone to go before us and with us. When we confess our faith in the universal church, we are reminded that, though we go through the fire, we shall not be consumed by it. When we confess our faith, we are reminded that there is a day when the wicked will cease from troublin' and Sunday will have no end. When we confess our faith in the church, we get a little help on the journey. So while we say what we believe, we get strength from the Meal[155] that will keep us strong enough to do the greater work to which we have been called.

When we confess our faith in the church, we get strength for the journey. And so, being invited, again, to this holy meal and to confess our faith in the triune God, when we leave this place, let's glance toward heaven and just remember the last line of our text today: "This Jesus who has been taken from you into heaven will come to you in the same way you saw him go." He will come again. And so, as we come again to the Table, we do so proclaim the Lord's death until he comes. And we are invited again to participate in our Savior's great feast for us. In the name of the Father, and [the] Son, and the Holy Spirit. Amen.[156]

With the sermon now concluded, worshipers are invited to rise and profess their faith together, using the words of the Nicene Creed, which then leads into a time of prayer and the celebration of the Lord's Supper.

---

[154]Here Weaver models multiple dimensions of repetition. There is, of course, the surface repetition found in the anaphora, "When we confess our faith . . ." But there is also the repetition of the church's story in the language she borrows from the Nicene Creed. The following sentences then set creedal language alongside scriptural language, further amplifying the repetition of the church's story.
[155]Here the preacher gestures toward the Lord's Table.
[156]The "repeatable acts" of confessing faith and receiving the sacrament now become the final layer of repetition—creating multiple overlapping waves in the metric hierarchy of the sermon, the worship service, and the dispersed community's life of faith.

4

THE END(S) OF THE SERMON

TELEOLOGY AND HOPE

MANY A DISORGANIZED SERMON (or a disorganized public speech of any kind) has provoked among listeners the exasperated question, "Where is this going?" In the case of preaching, however, the stakes are raised, as preaching aims for much higher ends than simply keeping listeners' attention, or making people laugh, or informing the audience about a topic, however lofty that topic may be. Ultimately, preaching witnesses to nothing less than God's coming kingdom and the new creation that is springing forth even now among those who, through faith in Jesus, by the power of the Holy Spirit, are being transformed from one degree of glory to the next (2 Cor 3:18). So the question, Where is this going? takes on an even larger significance (an eternal significance!) with regard to preaching.

Skilled musicians—including songwriters/composers and performers—have developed instincts for leveraging a sense of purposefulness or directionality (i.e., a strong teleological dynamic) in the music they create. Failure to cultivate listeners' desire to find out "where this is going" will eventually result in the loss of listeners' attention, or at the very least, an unsatisfying listening experience.

This chapter will examine the musical-homiletical characteristic of teleology, demonstrating the formative potential of connecting the musical instinct of teleology to the eschatological impulse embedded in the call to preach the gospel.

TELEOLOGY AND MUSIC

The third and final shared characteristic between the art of music and the art of preaching is *teleology*. As has been stated in a variety of ways throughout this project, most music in its very ontology involves the creation of a sense of movement through time within "acousmatic space," a quasi-spatial sonic realm generated through the *Gestalt* experience of musical tone.[1] Furthermore, in most pieces of music that adopt the Western system of tonality, the movement heard within this acousmatic space has a sense of directionality to it. "All tonal music," writes Roger Scruton, "moves to its conclusion through regions of tonal space."[2] Listeners need not be able to name exactly what is happening with absolute precision or through the use of official nomenclature in order to nonetheless hear, understand, and enjoy the "journeys of tension and resolution" generated on both large and small scales in the rhythmic and tonal patterns of a musical work.[3]

Although important critiques have been leveled against the implicit, if not overt, mythology of "conquest" commonly embedded in musical works within the Western classical genre (and their attendant performance rituals),[4] and although this "conquest" mythology is oftentimes found alongside culturally myopic claims regarding the superiority of the Western tonal system among the world's musical systems,[5] the creation of a sense of tension and resolution nonetheless remains vital to the experience of hearing musical sounds *as music*, at least in the Western tonal tradition. Whether referred to as "tension and release," "attraction and repulsion," "saturation and unsaturation," or "pain and soothing," a certain quasi-narrative teleological dynamic "lies in the nature of tonality."[6]

Although not a musical term per se, "teleology" remains perhaps the best descriptive term for the sense of directionality that is generated in and through the rhythmic, melodic, and harmonic patterns in a piece of music. As Begbie explains,

> Tonal music operates to a large degree according to teleological principles. Typically it possesses an integral relational order which in its large-scale and

---

[1] Roger Scruton, *The Aesthetics of Music* (Oxford: Oxford University Press, 1997), 75-77.
[2] Scruton, *Aesthetics of Music*, 401.
[3] Scruton, *Aesthetics of Music*, 401.
[4] Christopher Small, *Musicking: The Meanings of Performing and Listening* (Middletown, CT: Wesleyan University Press, 1998), chap. 11.
[5] See the discussion in Kathleen Marie Higgins, *The Music Between Us: Is Music a Universal Language?* (Chicago: The University of Chicago Press, 2012), 4-8.
[6] Scruton, *Aesthetics of Music*, 266.

small-scale organization is sensed as directional, driving towards rest and closure, often (but not always) leading to some kind of goal or "gathering together" of the whole temporal process. We sense "it is going somewhere." This teleological dynamic is generated primarily through the twin elements of tension and resolution. Configurations of tension and resolution work in many different ways and at many different levels, potentially engaging every parameter of music.[7]

The previous two chapters briefly examined the twin phenomena of meter and tonality, yet in relative isolation; teleology is the dynamic that emerges when these two phenomena are united in the practice of making music.

The teleological quality of music might thus be understood as the sense of directionality that emerges amid the multiple interpenetrations of metric and tonal patterns that constitute a piece of music—as rhythmic, melodic, and harmonic lines converge in a complex metrical matrix of tensions and resolutions.[8] There is a certain undeniable "magnetism" heard in musical sounds:

> Tones seem to incline towards each other, fall away from each other, as though they were incomplete entities which are magnetized by their neighbors and eager to cling to them. To a certain extent they resemble words in a language, which are restless and ambiguous until surrounded by a completing sentence. But words do not exhibit the peculiar tension that leads us, on hearing one tone, to want its resolution in another.[9]

The "magnetism" identified here—the restlessness and ambiguousness that longs for completion—is but one of many possible metaphors for the teleological quality of musical sounds.

It is crucial to note, however, that the creation of a sense of directionality in music—a teleological dynamic—presupposes the existence of certain listening habits within a musical culture, habits which can be relied on to create

---

[7]Jeremy Begbie, *Theology, Music and Time* (Cambridge: Cambridge University Press, 2000), 37-38. Begbie is careful to specify here that he is using the word tension "in a very wide sense" to describe a sense of incompleteness, which implies "a later closure." Thus musical tension need not be understood as necessarily implying a high degree of "conflict or antagonism."

[8]For a succinct explanation of the metric and tonal phenomena that underlie teleological processes in music, see Begbie, *Theology, Music and Time*, 39-51. Begbie defines rhythm as "motion in the dynamic field of meter" and melody as "motion in the dynamic field of key." The goal directedness that is heard in rhythmic and melodic motion, to name only two musical parameters, becomes integral to the teleological quality of the music as a whole.

[9]Scruton, *Aesthetics of Music*, 52.

listener expectations as to "what happens next." David Huron has closely analyzed the heuristic knowledge on which listeners draw as they actively, and even unconsciously, anticipate musical events. In this examination of musical teleology, Huron's study of the heuristic knowledge on which listeners draw—specifically as they listen to melodies—becomes especially relevant.

Interestingly, Huron has discovered that, in the case of melodic progressions, "experienced listeners of Western music rely on patterns that are serviceable, but not exactly right."[10] In other words, listeners had formed close approximations of the rules that govern melodies in actual practice, yet there are marked differences between the actual rules of melodic progression and the approximate rules that listeners had developed to govern their apprehension of the teleological trajectory of tones in a melody.[11] Yet, as Scruton emphasizes, listeners need not be able to name precisely what is happening in order to hear musical sounds as progressing from tension to release. What is most important is that listeners are engaged in discerning and anticipating the teleological trajectory of the music, whether or not their heuristic knowledge is completely accurate.

According to Huron, a large sample of art and folk melodies from not only Western music but also a number of other musical cultures[12] demonstrates several pervasive teleological tendencies with respect to melodic progressions, including pitch proximity, step declination, step inertia, melodic regression, and melodic arch.[13] Distilling these tendencies into statistical rules, Huron argues that "in an ideal world" listeners would form the following heuristic patterns as they listen to melodies and attempt to anticipate what happens next:

1. Pitch proximity: Listeners would expect an ensuing pitch to be near the current pitch.

2. Regression to the mean: As the melody moves farther away from the mean or median pitch, listeners would increasingly expect the next pitch to be closer to the mean.

---

[10]David Huron, *Sweet Anticipation: Music and the Psychology of Expectation* (Cambridge, MA: The MIT Press, 2006), 94.

[11]Huron, *Sweet Anticipation*, 91-94.

[12]Huron lists "Albanian, American, Bulgarian, Chinese, English, German, Hassidic, Iberian, Irish, Japanese, Macedonian, Norwegian, Ojibway, Pondo, Venda, Xhosa, and Zulu." Huron, *Sweet Anticipation*, 74.

[13]Huron, *Sweet Anticipation*, 74-88.

3. Downward steps: Listeners would expect most intervals to be descending steps.

4. Arch phrases: Listeners would expect phrases to begin with ascending pitch sequences and to end with descending pitch sequences.[14]

Instead of these actual statistical rules, however, Huron found that experienced listeners demonstrate the following expectational tendencies:

1. Pitch proximity: Listeners expect an ensuing pitch to be near the current pitch.

2. Post-skip reversal: Listeners expect a large interval to be followed by a change in pitch direction.

3. Step inertia: Listeners expect a small interval to be followed by a subsequent small interval in the same direction.

4. Late-phrase declination: Listeners expect pitches to descend in the latter half of phrases.[15]

These two sets of rules are noticeably similar, but not exactly the same; the actual statistical rules that govern melodies are inexactly approximated in the rules that experienced listeners use to govern their expectations of what happens next. The question is, however, do these differences matter?

From a biological standpoint, Huron contends, the answer is yes; these differences do matter because an incorrect prediction can potentially lead to danger. From an artistic standpoint, however, the answer is no; the inexact heuristic approximations listeners use do not diminish their enjoyment of music.[16] What is more important is simply to note that under the same musical conditions individual listeners will form broadly similar expectations.[17] In other words, creating a musical listening culture requires a group of listeners who can discern teleological dynamics in a roughly similar manner, whether

---

[14]Huron, *Sweet Anticipation*, 93.

[15]Huron, *Sweet Anticipation*, 94.

[16]Huron, *Sweet Anticipation*, 98. Despite the negligible artistic significance of listeners' inexact heuristic patterns, this finding should nonetheless serve as a reminder of the dangers of naive realism in music theory. As Huron explains, music theorists can no longer assume that "the structures we see are ones we experience, and that the structures we experience can be seen in the notation." Huron argues instead for more "careful statistical analysis" in the practice of music theory. Huron, *Sweet Anticipation*, 99.

[17]Huron, *Sweet Anticipation*, 98.

or not the rules they use to govern their expectations match precisely with the statistical patterns evident in the melodic progressions they are hearing.

Exploring the issue of heuristic knowledge from a slightly different angle, Huron also sought to categorize the distinctive sensations—or, in his terminology, the distinctive *qualia*—that adhere to various tones within a tonal system. In order to test the consistency of these *qualia* among listeners within a given listening culture, he gathered ten experienced Western-enculturated musicians and asked them to describe the different scale degrees for the major key, including all twelve tones within the octave (tonic, raised tonic, supertonic, etc.).[18] Surveying the responses, he reports a "remarkable level of agreement" in the various musicians' experience of the different scale tones. "For example, seven of the ten participants used the word 'unstable' in describing the leading-tone. Six of the ten participants used the word 'bright' in describing the median pitch. All of the participants associated the tonic with pleasure, satisfaction, and contentment."[19] The simple conclusion that might be drawn from this high level of agreement is that "scale degrees are wonderfully evocative" (or, in Scruton's terms, "magnetic").[20] Within a particular key, a simple pitched tone is capable of evoking a remarkable array of impressions or feelings that are not merely idiosyncratic to different listeners, but are rather surprisingly similar among Western-enculturated listeners.[21] In other words, within the listening culture of Western tonality, the teleological tendencies of various scale tones appear to be more or less "built in."

In order to further analyze and perhaps even to explain this remarkable level of agreement, Huron grouped the various *qualia* into seven broad categories: (1) certainty/uncertainty, (2) tendency, (3) completion, (4) mobility, (5) stability, (6) power, and (7) emotion.[22] Consistent with the overall aim of his research project, Huron hypothesized that "the statistical properties related to different scale degrees [might] account for their distinctive *qualia*."[23] Though not fully conclusive, Huron believes that there are likely statistical

---

[18]Huron, *Sweet Anticipation*, 144.

[19]Huron, *Sweet Anticipation*, 146. Of course, there were some discrepancies as well. But overall, "such discrepancies were the exception: the descriptions showed a relatively high level of agreement."

[20]Huron, *Sweet Anticipation*, 147. Scruton, *Aesthetics of Music*, 52.

[21]Huron, *Sweet Anticipation*, 147.

[22]Huron, *Sweet Anticipation*, 163.

[23]Huron, *Sweet Anticipation*, 163.

causes to be found for the various *qualia*. The following passage offers an example of the connections he identifies:

> The *tendency* category seems to correlate with the absence of statistical flexibility for pitch continuations. Scale tones described as "tending," "leading," or "pointing" included the raised dominant and the leading-tone—both tones that are statistically limited in their possible continuation tones. By contrast, the word "possibility" was applied to the most statistically flexible of pitches, the dominant.[24]

Huron attempts to explain all of the aesthetic categories that emerged from this study in this same way, though admittedly with less success in some cases than in others. What is most important, however, is not the irrefutable explanatory success of the statistical causes he submits, but rather the more general discovery of a broadly agreed-on set of sensations evoked by various tones within a tonal system, for it is these sensations—these *qualia*—that enable musicians to develop a teleological dynamic, a sense of directionality, in their performances. The various *qualia* of individual scale tones might therefore be understood as providing a kind of teleological vocabulary from which musicians may draw in the composition and performance of works of music.

Cadences. Many of the metric and tonal features of this teleological vocabulary—the rhythmic, harmonic, and melodic means by which music creates a sense of both predictability and surprise—have been explored in previous chapters, and Huron's seminal text includes an abundance of further examples that will remain unexplored in the present project.[25] Yet there remains one musical phenomenon that must be included in the present discussion, as the teleological dynamics of music are perhaps nowhere more clearly evident than in the approach to and arrival of moments of resolution or closure. Indeed, these moments of closure are the very telos toward which works of music, on both the small and the large scale, sound as if they are moving. Without these large and small resolutions, much tonal music would, in major regards, fail to satisfy.[26]

In musical terms, moments of resolution or closure are referred to as *cadences,* and on the harmonic level there are many stereotypical forms in

---

[24]Huron, *Sweet Anticipation*, 163.

[25]See especially Huron, *Sweet Anticipation*, chaps. 9-16.

[26]For further discussion, see Huron's analysis of the "contracadential music" of Richard Wagner in *Sweet Anticipation*, 334-39. See also Begbie's analysis of the nonteleological music of John Tavener in *Theology, Music and Time*, 128-44.

which cadences can occur.[27] The stereotypical harmonic pattern that creates the strongest sense of resolution is the authentic cadence (also sometimes called the final cadence or full cadence), which is "the progression from the dominant harmony to the tonic harmony, V-I."[28] This type of cadence, seen in figure 4.1, is "virtually obligatory as the final structural cadence of a tonal work."[29] A somewhat weaker sense of finality is conveyed by the plagal cadence (fig. 4.2), which is the progression from the subdominant harmony to the tonic harmony, IV-I.[30]

Figure 4.1. Authentic cadence in the key of C

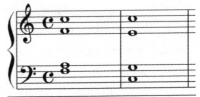
Figure 4.2. Plagal cadence in the key of C

Also common is the deceptive cadence (fig. 4.3), in which the V chord progresses to the VI chord instead of resolving to the tonic (the I chord), as expected. The deceptive cadence, as its name implies, creates an unanticipated prolongation of the harmonic progression. Finally, a half cadence (fig. 4.4, also called an imperfect cadence) occurs when a phrase or section ends on the dominant (V) rather than the tonic (I), and "is frequently encountered at the conclusion of the first part of shorter pieces in binary form."[31] The half

Figure 4.3. Deceptive cadence in the key of C

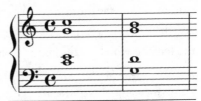
Figure 4.4. Half cadence in the key of C

---

[27] As briefly noted in the previous chapter, cadences are not only key in the creation of "a sense of repose or resolution," but are also "the principal means by which tonal music projects the sense of one pitch as a central or tonic pitch in a passage or work," since certain cadential patterns are among the statistically most prevalent features of music and are thus essential in creating a sense of "home." See Don Michael Randel, "Cadence," in *The New Harvard Dictionary of Music*, ed. Don Michael Randel (Cambridge, MA: Belknap Press, 1986), 120.

[28] Randel, "Cadence," 120.

[29] Randel, "Cadence," 120-21.

[30] Randel, "Cadence," 121.

[31] Randel, "Cadence," 121.

cadence creates a sense of provisional rest, a temporary stop along the way. These and other cadential patterns serve as a vital means by which harmonic tension is resolved and a teleological dynamic—a sense of moving toward, and arriving at, a goal—is created.

Huron notes that because cadences are among the most predictable elements in works of music, there are several compositional and performative techniques that have emerged in order to increase and prolong a sense of tension and thereby enhance the satisfaction that results from the eventual arrival of the resolution. On the harmonic level, two compositional techniques that have emerged are the anticipation and the suspension. The anticipation (fig. 4.5), which Huron calls "the quintessential expectation-related embellishment," introduces a hint of the resolution before the full resolution actually occurs, and thus heightens the listener's awareness of the ensuing cadence.[32] This technique enhances the pleasure of listening to a cadence through a combined increase and decrease of predictability. The anticipation reduces listeners' uncertainty about both the *what* and *when* of the ensuing resolution, which leads to a more positive (post-outcome) prediction response.[33] Before the advent of the resolution, however, the anticipation causes the sonority of the music to become more dissonant, which evokes a negative valence. Yet at the same time, the anticipation also dramatically increases the expectation of resolution. Thus, even though experienced listeners, on hearing an anticipation, will be fairly certain of what is coming next, this increased certainty also increases the yearning or craving for resolution, paradoxically increasing the tension while decreasing the uncertainty.[34] When combined with the positive response of increased certainty in prediction, the increase in tension serves to heighten the pleasure of the resolution. "All things being equal," then, "a cadence that includes an anticipation tone should be more pleasant than one without it."[35]

A similar dynamic occurs in the case of the suspension (fig. 4.6). When the suspended note occurs, the dissonance increases. At the same time, for Western-enculturated listeners, the predictability that the suspended note

---

[32]Huron, *Sweet Anticipation*, 308.
[33]Huron, *Sweet Anticipation*, 308.
[34]Huron, *Sweet Anticipation*, 308.
[35]Huron, *Sweet Anticipation*, 309.

Figure 4.5. Anticipation in the key of F

Figure 4.6. Suspension in the key of F

will resolve downward by a semitone approaches certainty. Even though the *when* of the resolution is still somewhat uncertain, the *what* of the resolution is highly predictable, and thus the overall certainty of the resolution remains relatively high. As a result, "there is a strong feeling of anticipation attending the suspended moment."[36] At one and the same time, then, when the suspension is resolved, "a formerly dissonant sonority" is "replaced by a chord with comparatively low sensory dissonance," and a high positive valence is achieved as a result of a correct prediction as to the manner in which the suspension is resolved.[37]

In addition to these compositional techniques for increasing the pleasure of harmonic tensions and resolutions, there are also several performative techniques that create this same dynamic. The most notable of these is *rubato*, the purposeful speeding up and slowing down of the tempo within a piece of music in order to enhance the expressive dynamic of phrases. More specifically, researchers have noted a consistent pattern of *ritardando/accelerando* at phrase boundaries.[38] "Performers typically slow down when approaching the ends of phrases and just before hypermetric downbeats," explains Huron. "They then accelerate as the new phrase, period, or section begins."[39] Moreover, the degree of tempo variation in performers' *rubato* seems to correlate with the importance of the phrase boundary within the overall metrical structure, with a modest ritard occurring at subphrase boundaries and a more dramatic slowing occurring at major transitions between large musical sections. The final ending will commonly provoke the greatest reduction in tempo among

[36]Huron, *Sweet Anticipation*, 309.

[37]Huron, *Sweet Anticipation*, 310.

[38]See, for example, David Epstein, *Shaping Time: Music, the Brain, and Performance* (New York: Schirmer Books, 1995), 373-74.

[39]Huron, *Sweet Anticipation*, 316.

performers. The biggest ritard is typically reserved for the points of greatest closure.[40] Thus music theorists commonly understand the ritard "as a gesture that clarifies the musical structure."[41]

According to Huron's musicological theory, however, there is a more plausible explanation for ritardandos at the ends of phrases than the simple clarification of structure. The final cadence involves high predictability in three elements simultaneously: melody, harmony, and meter. Such a high degree of predictability in three simultaneous musical parameters therefore "provides an opportunity to heighten the tension response and thereby to increase the pleasure evoked by contrastive valence."[42] Rather than simply delineating the music's structure, then, Huron suggests that performers are more likely drawn to this technique during moments of high predictability because it provides an opportunity to leverage tension. While it is true that the ritard surely becomes a learned association in cadential contexts, Huron believes that its origin is in the creation of contrastive valence. In support of this view, he cites the widespread tendency for performers to slow down at other instances of high predictability, even when those instances are not structural or related to closure.[43]

The combination of these compositional and performative techniques for heightening tension in cadential contexts affords musicians a highly effective means of leveraging the emotional impact of cadences. Beyond that, cadences themselves—and the compositional and performative techniques that often accompany them and heighten their effect—prove essential to the overall teleological dynamic of a piece of music. A great sense of satisfaction is generated through the "tension and release" of approaching and arriving at these moments of resolution or closure. Indeed, cadences, and especially final cadences, are, in aural terms, the ultimate "goals" toward which teleologically oriented music sounds as if it is moving.

Predictability and cliché. Before proceeding to an examination of the teleological dynamics of preaching, one final question that must be addressed with regard to musical teleology is the question of cliché. In the previous

---

[40]Huron, *Sweet Anticipation*, 316.
[41]Huron, *Sweet Anticipation*, 316.
[42]Huron, *Sweet Anticipation*, 316.
[43]Huron, *Sweet Anticipation*, 316.

chapter, the question arose as to how music is able to retain listeners' interest despite the high degree of repetition that is inherent to musical structure. In the present examination of the teleological nature of music, the question arises as to how music is able to avoid cliché despite the high degree of predictability that has been identified in the conventional patterns of tension and resolution that have emerged in tonal systems, especially in cadential contexts.

Of course, the issue of cliché—including, perhaps, its very definition—is inevitably bound up with complex questions of philosophical aesthetics that cannot be thoroughly explored in the present context. However, it is worth noting that, given Huron's commitment to the empirical study of the dynamics of aural pleasure, the absence of any thorough analysis of an aural "law of diminishing returns" in his writing is surprising.[44] Although Huron devotes much analytical attention to the enhancement and prolongation of tension, which leads to a greater sense of pleasure in moments of musical closure, he avoids the higher-level aesthetic question of whether or not a tonal system— or, at the very least, a certain pattern within a tonal system—might ever exhaust itself, and under what circumstances such exhaustion might occur.

In aesthetic terms, a cliché might be understood as a musical figure that has exhausted its possibility of producing a desired effect. Thus, a cliché is a figure, or perhaps even an entire system, that is "no longer available" to an artist who desires emotional authenticity.[45] With such a high degree of predictability in the approach to and arrival of cadences, the question arises as to how musicians are able to avoid the ring of inauthenticity that might result from the overuse of certain patterns of tension and release within a tonal system.

The twentieth-century music theorist Theodore Adorno famously claimed that the entire system of Western tonality had exhausted itself, having degenerated into banality and cliché by the end of the nineteenth century.[46]

---

[44]Huron does make brief mention of the changing effects of repeated listening as it relates to the induction of feelings of surprise, frisson, and awe, but these effects are analyzed and explained in purely evolutionary terms, i.e., within the "fight, flight, and freeze" responses that have become so common in scientific accounts of human behavior. See Huron, *Sweet Anticipation*, 292-94.

[45]Scruton, *Aesthetic of Music*, 490.

[46]Scruton, *Aesthetics of Music*, 468-74. Adorno was joined in this opinion by nearly every proponent of musical modernism (i.e., atonality), most notably Arnold Schoenberg, who believed that tonal music had become confined to "sentimental gestures." See Scruton, *Aesthetics of Music*, 479-85. For a rebuttal of the claim that "tonal music in the West suffered a major disintegration around the end of the nineteenth century," see Begbie, *Theology, Music and Time*, 37-38n27.

Although critical of Adorno's Marxist ideology and sweeping generalizations, Roger Scruton finds much in Adorno's attack of tonality that is worthy of careful consideration.[47] There are indeed certain musical patterns, Scruton acknowledges, that are no longer available to musicians who want to avoid conveying a certain emotional laziness.[48] "It is undeniable that there are musical clichés [in addition to linguistic clichés]—chord progressions that have been too often used and which no longer surprise us, melodic devices (the upbeat in Mahler, for example) which launch us too easily and unthinkingly into the movement of the tune; the rhythmic clichés of the waltz and the tango."[49]

Crucially, however, Scruton does not believe that musicians can never use such patterns again. Rather, musical clichés must be "rescued from the inattention of the listener, by throwing them into sudden and unexpected relief."[50] Offering several examples from such composers as Strauss, Berg, and Ravel, Scruton contends that musical clichés can be "rescued from inattention" through an approach similar to the rescue of verbal clichés that is found in a writer like Samuel Beckett.[51] Perhaps in addition to the compositional techniques identified by Scruton, the performative techniques for increasing tension identified by Huron, such as *rubato*, have arisen for precisely this purpose—to rescue the highly stereotypical patterns of cadences from the inattention of the listener.

Thus Scruton rejects the alternative atonality that is proposed by Adorno and his contemporaries, since "there is no guarantee that the faults that Adorno discerns in the tonal idiom will be avoided—or avoided for long—by adopting some rival musical 'syntax.'"[52] In fact, despite Adorno's contention that the atonal idiom would be immune to standardization, "the revolt against tonality [has] produced a wealth of atonal clichés."[53] This, Scruton argues, is because "cliché is an *aesthetic*, not a syntactical, defect—a misuse of language

---

[47]Roger Scruton, *Understanding Music: Philosophy and Interpretation* (New York: Bloomsbury, 2009), 212.
[48]Scruton, *Understanding Music*, 220.
[49]Scruton, *Understanding Music*, 221.
[50]Scruton, *Understanding Music*, 221.
[51]Scruton, *Understanding Music*, 221.
[52]Scruton, *Understanding Music*, 222.
[53]Scruton, *Understanding Music*, 222.

that belongs to the order of style rather than that of grammar."[54] The emergence of clichés, therefore, cannot be avoided through the invention of a new musical syntax, for a new syntax "will be no more proof against cliché than a new fashion in dress is proof against the aesthetic defects of the old. Everything will depend upon the creativity and taste with which the new idiom is used—and the same goes for the old idiom too."[55]

Clichés do not emerge simply from constant use, therefore, but rather from a certain kind of *overuse*, or perhaps even a kind of *misuse*. "A musical device becomes banal when it is *borrowed*, but not earned."[56] An analogy from the world of language helps to illuminate this distinction:

> The word "apple" has been used by me, you, and our companions countless times: but in its ordinary literal meaning, it could never be a cliché, because it *does not pretend to any effect*. It is doing its ordinary job of work, and makes no claim to expressive power. The phrase "apple of my eye" is, however, although used far more rarely, a cliché. For it is pretending to be expressive when it has lost the power of being so. It makes a promise of effect which it can no longer fulfill.[57]

Similarly, there are certain conventional musical devices that form the building blocks of tonality, but are not clichés in themselves; "rather, they form part of the grammar of musical utterance."[58]

The question of cliché, then, involves not simply quantitative analysis as to the number of times a certain musical device is used, but also qualitative judgments as to the manner and context in which a device is used, including its intended effect. Therefore, as Scruton helpfully points out, the question of cliché is inevitably bound to questions of *character formation* among both performer and audience.[59] Musical clichés abound in contexts that lack emotional depth; banality and sentimentality are thus closely linked. But, as Scruton contends, the word *sentimental*, "in its primary occurrence, applies

---

[54]Scruton, *Understanding Music*, 222.
[55]Scruton, *Understanding Music*, 222.
[56]Scruton, *Aesthetics of Music*, 482.
[57]Scruton, *Aesthetics of Music*, 480.
[58]Scruton, *Aesthetics of Music*, 480.
[59]On the question of music, emotion, and character formation, see also Jeremy Begbie, "Faithful Feelings: Music and Emotion in Worship," in *Resonant Witness: Conversations between Music and Theology*, ed. Jeremy S. Begbie and Steven R. Guthrie (Grand Rapids, MI: Eerdmans, 2011), 323-54.

to people," and thus cannot be described in purely musical terms.[60] The evaluation of a particular musical figure or work as a cliché or as sentimental, therefore, involves the identification of emotional manipulation and inauthenticity among performers and listeners. Thus, moral and aesthetic judgments are intricately bound together in the question of cliché.[61]

A cliché is not determined simply by the number of times a figure is used, but rather by the larger contextual ends toward which a figure is applied. Sentimentality in art is detected when the resolution of tension seems to come too easily, alerting listeners to an attempt on the part of the musicians to generate emotions "on the cheap."[62] A musical cliché thus becomes an invitation "to pretend at an emotion, without really feeling it," and even more importantly, without connecting that emotion to costly, relational action.[63] There is a real danger, therefore, of whole groups of people becoming complicit in the creation and perpetuation of clichés, seeming noble in their own eyes, without the cost of being truly so.[64] Nonetheless, the fault in such cases is not necessarily to be found in the conventional patterns that form the tonal syntax itself, but rather in the ends toward which such patterns are directed contextually—whether or not they are tied to true feelings in a context of costly interpersonal action.

While it is certainly true that a conventional musical pattern can result in banality through overuse, the latter is not strictly the cause of the former. Rather, both are symptoms of the true cause: emotional pretense. Therefore, in contrast to Adorno and his sympathizers, Scruton does not believe the tonal system to be totally beyond rescue and renewal, for such a blanket

---

[60]Scruton, *Aesthetics of Music*, 485.
[61]As Scruton powerfully summarizes,

> The sentimentalist is therefore a paradigm immoralist. His carefree existence is not a happy one: for it lacks the essential ingredients—love and friendship—on which happiness depends. The sentimental friend is not a friend: indeed he is a danger to others. His instinct is to facilitate tragedy, in order to bathe in easy sympathy; to stimulate love, in order to pretend to love in return, while always reserving his heart and mind, and calculating to his own advantage. He enters human relations by seduction, and leaves them by betrayal. (Scruton, *Aesthetics of Music*, 487)

[62]Scruton, *Aesthetics of Music*, 486.
[63]Scruton, *Aesthetics of Music*, 487. "The other person enters the orbit of the sentimentalist as an *excuse* for emotion, rather than an *object* of it," since true emotion would involve a person in a potentially costly interpersonal relationship, whereas sentimental emotion does not involve a costly relational response. Scruton, *Aesthetics of Music*, 486.
[64]Scruton, *Aesthetics of Music*, 488.

pronouncement would ironically "kill off the critical attitude that [Adorno] supposed himself to be encouraging."[65] Although in strictly musical terms, Scruton himself is quite critical of much popular music—and for that matter, much classical music[66]—he does not believe ordinary listeners to be incapable of aesthetic education. Rather, "by making discriminations *within* the realm of popular music," Scruton believes, "we can encourage young people to recognize the difference between genuine musical sentiment and kitsch."[67]

This does not entirely resolve all the issues identified by critics of the teleologically oriented, resolution-focused music of the Western tonal tradition. Yet it does suggest a helpful frame within which to evaluate the use of certain conventional musical patterns, especially those found in cadential contexts. It is not simply a matter of either "total condemnation" or "anything goes." Distinctions are possible with respect to contextual factors that impinge on the authenticity sensed in the use of conventional patterns of musical tension and resolution. A cliché cannot be identified simply by counting the number of times a certain stereotypical pattern is used; rather, an assessment of the larger contextual ends toward which such patterns are directed is also necessary. Clichés arise in the context of musical cadences when gestures feel borrowed and resolutions seem to come too easily, without appropriate relational cost to the artist and to the community.

TELEOLOGY IN PREACHING

Having explored some aspects of the teleological dynamics of music, especially with regard to the distinctive *qualia* of various scale tones and the stereotypical patterns of harmonic resolution in cadential contexts, the discussion will now turn toward the teleological dynamics of preaching. Two homileticians who have developed the theme of teleology through musical analogies are Clayton Schmit and Eugene Lowry. A brief overview of Schmit's work will lead into a more substantial analysis of Lowry's method of developing the teleological trajectory of preaching. Some summary observations on teleology and eschatology in preaching will follow, leading ultimately to an exploration of the theological theme of hope.

---

[65]Scruton, *Understanding Music*, 218.
[66]See Scruton, *Aesthetics of Music*, 493-508.
[67]Scruton, *Understanding Music*, 219.

According to Schmit, "'What comes next?' is a question all preachers need to contend with."[68] In every step of crafting a sermon, from exegesis to preparation to performance, preachers who are guided by this question learn "to develop habits for knowing what comes next and for determining what does not come next."[69] Artists, Schmit writes, are guided by this question as well. In particular, "musicians, as a matter of training and habit, acquire sometimes prodigious skill at knowing what comes next."[70] An inquiry into the habits of musicians "can refresh our perspectives on the theology and performance of preaching," especially as it relates to "the qualities of anticipation and inevitability in musical performance."[71]

Though Schmit does not use the word "teleology" explicitly, the analogy he develops between music and preaching is clearly related to the teleological dynamic of both art forms. In the case of music specifically, Schmit writes, "Through knowledge of music's conventions, a performer acquires a sense of musical inevitability and a corresponding sense of anticipation regarding where the music needs to go."[72] Offering several musical examples, including the resolution of a dominant chord into a tonic chord, Schmit reaffirms the inherent directionality of musical sounds, concluding, "All music is built on conventions that create a sense of inevitability which in turn advances a sense of anticipation in the performance."[73] This is true, he maintains, whether the music in question is a highly orchestrated classical work or a highly improvisatory jazz piece. Moreover, the sense of anticipation and inevitability is just as strong— or perhaps even more so—in the listener as in the performer of music.[74]

Similarly, Schmit writes, there is a sense of inevitability and anticipation— a teleological dynamic—that is created in the practice of preaching, except that there is a larger theological significance attached to the practice of preaching that "informs the way sermons are prepared and performed."[75] As Schmit explains:

---

[68]Clayton J. Schmit, "What Comes Next? Performing and Proclaiming the Word," in *Performance in Preaching*, ed. Jana Childers and Clayton J. Schmit (Grand Rapids, MI: Baker Academic, 2008), 169.
[69]Schmit, "What Comes Next?," 169.
[70]Schmit, "What Comes Next?," 170.
[71]Schmit, "What Comes Next?," 171.
[72]Schmit, "What Comes Next?," 181.
[73]Schmit, "What Comes Next?," 182.
[74]Schmit, "What Comes Next?," 183-84.
[75]Schmit, "What Comes Next?," 185.

Unless a sermon is to be perceived as "preachy," it will present a natural unfolding of the logic of salvation. The sermon will have the same shape as the structure of the scriptural record: fall and redemption. The fact of sin leads, in
Scripture, inevitably toward the necessity that God will provide a means by
which to reconcile humankind. The structure of salvation, whereby God gives
God's self to atone for human sin, creates a gravitational force of grace that
pulls those caught in the fall, or free fall of sin, toward itself. This is the great
"five-one impulse" of the law and the gospel. As a dominant seventh played as
the penultimate chord in a piece of music leans toward and wants to capitulate
to the tonic, so the declaration of the law leans toward the inevitability of grace
and wants to capitulate to its resolving power.[76]

Like the musical conventions that increase predictability in cadential contexts
and generate the distinctive *qualia* of individual scale tones, "the proper bal-
ancing of the judgment and gospel tones in preaching is a theological convention. The naming of sin must be followed by the pronouncement of grace."[77]
For Schmit, this "divine dialectic" is essential in the practice of preaching.

Of course, this theological convention can be expected to sound different
in different contexts, yet the underlying pattern must be present if it is to be
heard within the "tonal system" of Christian preaching. As Schmit explains,

> This does not mean that sermons are prohibited from improvising on these
> themes. They can be stated in as many ways as there are preachers, multiplied
> by the number of occasions on which they preach. *Every* sermon needs to be
> a fresh structuring of this motif. But each sermon will express a version of this
> dialectic or it will not be *actio divina*, the kerygmatic Word that God self-
> performs through the speech of the preacher.[78]

If this theological convention of *law resolving into gospel* is not present in
some way, a sermon "becomes something other than proclamation."[79]

In support of this rather bold claim, Schmit cites the work of Richard
Lischer, who draws a clear distinction between gospel-centered preaching
and moralism. The former, Lischer explains, "takes on an eschatological

---

[76]Schmit, "What Comes Next?," 185.
[77]Schmit, "What Comes Next?," 185.
[78]Schmit, "What Comes Next?," 186. Here Schmit draws heavily upon the understanding of preaching advanced in Charles Bartow, *God's Human Speech: A Practical Theology of Proclamation* (Grand
Rapids, MI: Eerdmans, 1997).
[79]Schmit, "What Comes Next?," 186.

importance," while the latter is content to "hold up the virtues, be they yester-day's piety, courtesy, and cleanliness, or today's openness, frankness, and freedom," and to exhort one's listeners toward the realization of these virtues without offering them the grace that is necessary to achieve them.[80] Moralism is, according to Lischer, "a deadly transposition" of the conventional theo-logical pattern of proclamation: "Instead of offering its list of virtues as pos-sible goals or consequences of the gospel, moralism subtly *prescribes* them as the *means* by which the grace of God is apprehended."[81] Assessing the state of contemporary preaching through this "tonal system" of law resolving into gospel, Lischer soberly concludes that at least half of the sermons he hears are moralistic. Such sermons, he explains, "usually preach Jesus-our-example and think that by mentioning his good behavior they have preached the gospel."[82]

In light of this stark assessment, Schmit is amply justified in his identifica-tion of the law/gospel dialectic as the essential pattern of tension and resolu-tion within the "tonal system" of Christian proclamation. Absent this teleological orientation of law resolving into gospel, a sermon becomes "some-thing other than proclamation." "The task of the preacher in training," then, "is to acquire the theological habit of knowing the inevitable shape of grace."[83] The gospel is the tonic chord into which the tension of the world's trouble must resolve.[84] "Like music that ends on the tonic, or home tone, preachers need to learn that sermons must find their end in the home tone of God's love." They must learn, Schmit writes, to feel "the gravitational pull of the good news."[85]

A similar teleological understanding is developed in much greater detail in the homiletical theory of Eugene Lowry. In his most recent work, *The Homi-letical Beat*, Lowry explicitly sets his own narrative homiletical project within the context of Begbie's musical-theological project, drawing specifically on Begbie's understanding of the metrical matrix—the ascending hierarchy of

---

[80]Richard Lischer, *A Theology of Preaching: The Dynamics of the Gospel* (Eugene, OR: Wipf and Stock, 1992), 44.

[81]Lischer, *Theology of Preaching*, 44. As Lischer further explains, "Even faith is not immune to this subtle confusion of law and gospel. Moralism confuses exhortations to faith ('We all need to return to the bedrock of belief!') with faith itself; with the result that faith, as the open hand that grasps the gift, is preached as a *work* and is added to moralism's checklist of virtues."

[82]Lischer, *Theology of Preaching*, 45.

[83]Schmit, "What Comes Next?," 187.

[84]Paul Scott Wilson, *The Four Pages of the Sermon: A Guide to Biblical Preaching* (Nashville: Abing-don Press, 1999), 155-59.

[85]Schmit, "What Comes Next?," 187.

metrical waves of tension and resolution generated in a piece of music.[86] Narrative homiletics, Lowry insists, resembles the teleological dynamic of music in that one possible meaning of the term narrative refers to the strategic aim that is embodied in the form of the sermon.[87] In Lowry's homiletical theory, tension is leveraged through the strategic delay of resolution in order to maximize the impact of the resolution when it occurs.[88] The gospel is unquestionably the resolution Lowry assumes throughout his writing, yet he also insists that, since the art of preaching inevitably involves a movement through time, "*the timing of the announcement [of the gospel] is everything.*"[89] The shaping of time in preaching through careful attention to this teleological dynamic thus becomes the distinguishing feature of Lowry's homiletical theory.

The most powerful preaching, according to Lowry, is that which best leverages the tension of the sermon in order to increase the impact of the resolution when it occurs; thus, a step-by-step approach for leveraging tension is proposed, with four or five separate stages in the homiletical plot. In its original iteration the five stages of Lowry's homiletical plot are (1) upsetting the equilibrium, (2) analyzing the discrepancy, (3) disclosing the key to resolution, (4) experiencing the gospel, and (5) anticipating the consequences.[90] More recently, Lowry has loosened the order of these elements and applied different terms, allowing for various scenarios in which, for instance, the fourth stage— the experience of the gospel—can occur "just before, just after, or precisely at the sudden turn of the sermon."[91] As Lowry notes regarding the latest version of his narrative homiletical plot, represented visually in figure 4.7, "the crucial visual clues here involve noticing that the thought grows deeper into greater perplexity for more than half of the sermon."[92] The sudden shift, the reversal, the move toward resolution—whatever term is used—occurs well beyond the temporal midpoint of the sermon.[93] Again, this strategic delay allows the

---

[86]Eugene L. Lowry, *The Homiletical Beat: Why All Sermons Are Narrative* (Nashville: Abingdon Press, 2012), 19-20.

[87]Lowry, *Homiletical Beat*, 18-25.

[88]Lowry, *Homiletical Beat*, 12-13, 38-39.

[89]Lowry, *Homiletical Beat*, 59 (emphasis original).

[90]Lowry, *Homiletical Beat*, 28-87.

[91]Lowry, *Homiletical Beat*, 33.

[92]Lowry, *Homiletical Beat*, 34. In the afterword to the expanded edition of *The Homiletical Plot: The Sermon as Narrative Art Form*, expanded ed. (Louisville, KY: Westminster John Knox, 2001), Lowry provides the following alternative names for the stages represented in fig. 4.7: oops= conflict, ugh=complication, aha=sudden shift, whee=good news, and yeah=unfolding.

[93]Lowry, *Homiletical Beat*, 34.

concluding stage—the anticipation of the future "made new by the good news of the gospel"—to acquire a more powerful force, as the tension leading up to the resolution of the sermon has been prolonged and deepened.[94]

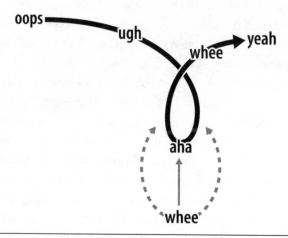

Figure 4.7. Eugene Lowry's revised homiletical plot, based on Eugene Lowry, *The Homiletical Beat: Why All Sermons Are Narrative* (Nashville: Abingdon Press, 2012), 33.

This transposition of the law/gospel dialectic into a specific homiletical form involving the strategic prolongation of tension has the advantage of providing preachers with a readily accessible, step-by-step process for enhancing the teleological dynamics of their sermons.[95] Yet it has not been without its critics. In *Preaching Jesus*, Charles Campbell expresses concern that an increased focus on narrative form, oftentimes tied to an analysis of certain supposedly generic features of all narratives, will result in a diminished focus on the specific character whose identity is rendered in the biblical narrative, Jesus Christ.[96] Drawing on the postliberal theology of Hans Frei, Campbell warns of a homiletical method that loses its ability to discern the extent to which sermons with an excellent *plot* fail to bear faithful witness to the *character* of Jesus Christ:

---

[94]Lowry, *Homiletical Beat*, 34. Of course, the implication that this strategy of regularly and deliberately delaying the announcement of the good news will retain its effect in the weekly worship life of a congregation deserves critical examination.

[95]See Paul Scott Wilson, *Preaching and Homiletical Theory* (St. Louis: Chalice Press, 2004), 87-89.

[96]Charles L. Campbell, *Preaching Jesus: New Directions for Homiletics in Hans Frei's Postliberal Theology* (Eugene, OR: Wipf and Stock, 1997), 167-88.

The gospel narratives—and the biblical narrative as a whole, which renders the identity of God in Jesus Christ—point us beyond formal considerations of sermon structure to the crucial matter of Christology. It is the central character rendered by the gospel narratives, not narrative plot in general, that is at the heart of preaching shaped by the biblical story. An older, discursive sermon that focuses on the identity of Jesus Christ within the framework of the gospel narratives can be more faithful to those narratives than a "narrative sermon" that fails to render the identity of God in Jesus Christ in any concrete way.[97]

For Campbell, the danger of transposing the teleological dynamic of the gospel into a more generalized sermon form, as in Lowry's homiletical theory, is that Jesus himself might be inadvertently removed from the central place in the gospel proclamation. As Campbell observes, "In narrative preaching it has generally been the case that narrative equals parable. And in the parables, of course, Jesus is not a character, except as the narrator."[98] As a result, the mindset seems to be, "If you've got a good parable, you don't need Jesus."[99] Despite its many strengths, therefore, Campbell believes that a major weakness of Lowry's homiletical theory is its overreliance on form—which for Lowry almost inevitably assumes the form of a parable—as a means of proclaiming the gospel.[100]

---

[97]Campbell, *Preaching Jesus*, 173. For an example of a homiletical theory based on generic features of narrative, see Lowry's appropriation of Aristotle in *Homiletical Beat*, 49-73.

[98]Campbell, *Preaching Jesus*, 174.

[99]Campbell, *Preaching Jesus*, 174. Campbell notes that this phrase is a riff on a statement made by the character Hazel Motes in Flannery O'Connor's novel *Wise Blood* and is obviously presented somewhat tongue-in-cheek.

[100]Campbell, *Preaching Jesus*, 174. As Campbell notes, "Every sermon, for Lowry, should be 'parabolic'; it should have a plot leading from disequilibrium through reversal to a new equilibrium." Campbell, *Preaching Jesus*, 174, citing Eugene L. Lowry, *How to Preach a Parable: Designs for Narrative Sermons* (Nashville: Abingdon Press, 1989), 21-23. In a revealing confirmation of the overreliance on parabolic form, Campbell finds that only one of the sermons examined in Lowry's book, *How to Preach a Parable*, "is actually based on a New Testament parable." Campbell, *Preaching Jesus*, 174. Thomas Long defends the impetus for Lowry's narrative homiletic against this criticism, writing,

Lowry develops his plotted scheme of preaching not simply because this sequence of movements will be more engaging and interesting to listeners. No, Lowry settles on narrative structure because of his conviction, widely held by others, that listeners are intrinsically makers of narrative and dwellers in narrative. Lowry's narrative structure is designed to match a narrative-shaped, ambiguity-resolving, meaning-constructing capacity in human consciousness. (Thomas G. Long, "Out of the Loop," in Mike Graves and David L. Schlafer, eds., *What's the Shape of Narrative Preaching?* [St. Louis: Chalice Press, 2008], 120)

Yet this very defense seems only to confirm Campbell's concern that, in Lowry's work, attention to the more general category of narrative has been allowed to overwhelm the more specific character of Jesus Christ within the biblical narrative.

Although Campbell is undoubtedly justified in his concern that sermons crafted according to Lowry's narrative homiletical form might focus so much on teleological strategy that they unintentionally dilute the character of Jesus, the force of the critique is weakened when one recalls Lowry's central goal: to craft a homiletical theory that follows the teleological dynamic of the gospel in the very form of the sermon, in order that the good news of Jesus might be preached not just in *what* is said but also *how* it is said. Whether successful or not, Lowry's simple desire is for form to match content as closely as possible in the practice of preaching. Nonetheless, Campbell's observation of the possible eclipse of the character of Jesus through homiletical form is insightful and may in fact have even wider-ranging implications than Campbell himself allows. It may be, in fact, that when preachers come to rely too heavily on homiletical form to create an experience of the gospel, not only may the character of Jesus rendered in and through the scriptural narrative be eclipsed, as Campbell proposes. It may be, even further, that form-focused preachers can lose sight of the very presence of Jesus himself, the living Word, who promises to speak through the Holy Spirit in the proclamation of the gospel.

The teleological dynamic of the gospel, in other words, must not be reduced to a particular understanding of homiletical form, or even to a particular understanding of narrative rendering of character, but must rather be rooted in the spiritual realities to which the human speech of gospel proclamation gives witness. As Trygve Johnson writes, "The gospel is not an idea, but is grounded in the continual work of the risen Christ who through the Spirit has now laid out a new creation and put this new action of creation in us."[101] This confession of faith—that Christ is present in and through the human words of preachers—is the basis of all gospel proclamation: "The Christian preacher is always working in and with the reality of Jesus' work."[102] As Charles Bartow puts it, "In the reading of the Scriptures and in preaching we seek to be faithful to the One who has borne—and who continues to bear—faithful witness to himself with the words of prophets and apostles."[103]

---

[101]Trygve David Johnson, *The Preacher as Liturgical Artist: Metaphor, Identity, and the Vicarious Humanity of Christ* (Eugene, OR: Cascade, 2014), 162.

[102]Johnson, *Preacher as Liturgical Artist*, 162.

[103]Bartow, *God's Human Speech*, 45.

Among the many consequences of this trust in Christ's presence in and through the human words of preachers is the reframing of the very concept of teleology in the practice of preaching. The telos toward which preaching rightly aims must be greater than the simple resolution of a homiletical plot, even if that homiletical plot is patterned after the shape of the gospel. The true telos of preaching, Johnson reminds us, is nothing less than the risen Christ himself bringing about the fulfillment—the telos—of creation:

> The one who created all things with his Father in the Spirit is now alive beyond death and creating a new world as he speaks as the resurrected Lord. In Jesus' proclamation of the kingdom of God, his words create a world for others to step into and be healed, and consequently is understood to move us towards the fulfillment, or *telos*, of creation. When the Word speaks to people something creative happens. . . . In short, the Word creates reality.[104]

A robust, gospel-centered understanding of teleology in preaching must therefore always keep this larger teleological vision in view: the new creation that Christ is bringing about through the Spirit.

Of course, Lowry's point still holds that form and content can and should work in concert, as much as possible, to witness to the dynamics of the gospel. Yet there is a further danger in adopting certain teleological strategies that Lowry and other advocates of narrative preaching leave surprisingly under-developed—the danger of cliché. Just as it is possible to identify a musical cliché through certain tonal patterns that signal a cadential resolution that is, in Scruton's words, "borrowed but not earned," surely it is also possible to identify a homiletical cliché through certain speech patterns that signal a homiletical resolution that has come "on the cheap." It is surprising, therefore, that for all of the supposed teleological deficiencies Lowry and other "pillars of the New Homiletic" identify in the "old style" traditional preaching, they pay so little attention to the potential that their own, newer homiletic models—narrative, inductive, etc.—might also become cliché in the various contexts in which they are used and with respect to the larger ends toward which they are directed.

---

[104]Johnson, *Preacher as Liturgical Artist*, 162.

If the law/gospel dialectic is to be understood as the essential theological pattern of tension and resolution in Christian preaching, whether this dialectic is found solely in a sermon's content or in its form as well, it is essential that the full spiritual import of the gospel be kept central. Preachers' understanding of the narrative tension that builds in the sermon and ultimately resolves in the announcement of the gospel must never become a "pretended effect." It must always remain connected to life-and-death, earthly realities. Luke Powery poignantly captures this necessity:

> The world is brewing with ongoing trouble—war, famine, genocide, governmental corruption, economic instability, to name a few. To ignore these expressions of death is to be homiletically blind and irrelevant. In African American communities alone, the existential devastation is vast. There are megachurches that preach a mini-gospel at times, one that promotes a feel-good religion. Yet the people in the pews and in the surrounding communities are not always feeling good because that is not the earthly reality.[105]

In light of this earthly reality, Powery considers it "preposterous that some preachers can separate the gospel from the presence of death in the world as a way of avoiding it in the pulpit."[106]

Inasmuch as the supposed "resolution" of the gospel remains distanced from the depth of the earthly reality of listeners' lives and the costly relational response that results from an acknowledgment of this reality, it becomes cliché. On the other hand, inasmuch as the supposed "resolution" of the gospel remains focused solely on human action—human responses aimed at producing purely immanent solutions and "this-worldly" hopes—it also becomes cliché. No matter how skillfully the narrative tension of a sermon might be maintained, no matter how well a sermon's resolution might be strategically delayed, no resolution can be considered truly hopeful if it remains disconnected from the full eschatological import of preaching: the ultimate triumph of Christ's resurrection over the powers of sin and death.[107]

The vision in Ezekiel 37 of the valley of the dry bones thus remains a crucial homiletical metaphor in contemporary times because this vision, writes

---

[105]Luke A. Powery, *Dem Dry Bones: Preaching, Death, and Hope* (Minneapolis: Fortress, 2012), 8.
[106]Powery, *Dem Dry Bones*, 9.
[107]Powery, *Dem Dry Bones*, 79-85.

Powery, "uses death to awaken us from our homiletical sleep in order to realize what is at stake when we preach in the valley of the dry bones and to reclaim the importance of preaching today because when we preach in the Spirit, the possibility of hope is always present."[108]

The teleological dynamic of the gospel in preaching becomes recognizable by the presence of true, deep, and abiding hope even in the face of suffering. When the conventional theological pattern of the law/gospel dialectic is used in such a way that the aural satisfaction of proclaiming "good news" seems to come much too easily—that is, in the absence of costly relational action and costly public witness to the lordship of Jesus—then the gospel is at serious risk of becoming a cliché.

Clichés in preaching, therefore, are ultimately a spiritual matter—and a grave one at that—and can only properly be addressed on the spiritual level in the heart of the preacher, not simply through the adoption of a different form or technique, no matter what the purported benefits are of that particular form or technique for effective gospel proclamation.[109] As Willimon writes,

> My homiletical attempts to substantiate God in a way that grips my audience are also another attempt at utilizing Jesus Christ in a vain effort at "self-substantiation." My preacherly self (or the selves within my congregation) becomes more important in the process of gospel communication than Christ, the Agent of proclamation.[110]

It is essential, therefore, to remain grounded in "the Easter basis of preaching," the preacher's trust in the risen Christ who is the active agent in our humble speech. "We preachers can be so bold" as to repeat the gospel—the ultimate eschatological resolution to the world's troubles—again and again because of our faith "that there is only one preacher, Christ. And he will preach."[111]

---

[108] Powery, *Dem Dry Bones*, 81.

[109] A caution should be noted here regarding the ability of someone who lacks sufficient understanding of a given context to judge the presence of a cliché. See, for instance, Cleophus LaRue's positive appropriation and cataloging of oral formulas in Black culture, which are "made up of clichés, colloquial expressions, adages, aphorisms, maxims, and mottos." The use of these formulas in Black culture is not a sign of sentimentality, however, but is simply "a part of the black way of being in the world." Cleophus J. LaRue, *I Believe I'll Testify: The Art of African American Preaching* (Louisville, KY: Westminster John Knox, 2011), 135-38.

[110] William H. Willimon, *Undone by Easter: Keeping Preaching Fresh* (Nashville: Abington, 2009), 65.

[111] Willimon, *Undone by Easter*, 67.

SUMMARY: TELEOLOGY IN MUSIC AND PREACHING

In light of the preceding analysis of teleology in music and preaching, some summary observations are now appropriate. As demonstrated above, a sense of directionality—a teleological dynamic—in both music and preaching is created largely through the use of conventional patterns of tension and resolution. In order to maintain the interest of one's listeners, a certain "magnetism" is created in the unfolding of a musical or homiletical theme. In the case of music specifically, listeners are given a sense that this tone or this melody or this rhythm is going somewhere—a sense of developing tension that demands resolution, even if that resolution is different from what listeners are expecting. With musical sounds, a process of statistical learning through enculturation into a system of tonality enables listeners to develop heuristic knowledge that can be used to anticipate future sound events. This heuristic knowledge is what enables, for example, particular scale tones to produce particular *qualia* (distinctive sensations) in the ears of listeners, whether it be a sense of instability created by the leading-tone or a sense of restfulness created by the tonic.[112]

In preaching, one major theological pattern of tension and resolution was found to be essential in creating a teleological dynamic: the law/gospel dialectic. Preachers, according to Schmit, Lischer, Wilson, and others, must learn to sense the inevitable pull of grace, which resolves the tension of sin/law/trouble that has been building throughout the sermon. In the work of Eugene Lowry, preachers are even given a step-by-step method by which to create this tension and resolution. Stewardship of the teleological trajectory of the sermon creates the conditions whereby the gospel can be experienced as a pleasing homiletical resolution to the tension created by the "trouble" in the text and in the world. Yet in both music and preaching, a special concern emerges with respect to cadences (or resolutions), in that special care must be taken to avoid cliché, since the ends of phrases are the most predictable elements in both of these arts. The very same mechanism—a sense of inevitability—that enables a teleological dynamic to be created in the first place also necessitates a steadfast refusal to allow the resolution of the musical or homiletical moment of tension to come too easily. In the case of

---

[112]Huron, *Sweet Anticipation*, 144-47.

preaching more specifically, this involves a steadfast refusal to provide simple answers to complex questions of human sin, systemic evil, and all manner of earthly troubles.

It must further be acknowledged, however, that in contrast to the creation of teleological dynamics in music, there is also an inescapable eschatological dimension to the creation of a hopeful teleological trajectory in preaching, since the linguistic nature of preaching affords it the ability to point beyond itself to unseen realities known only by faith. Teleology in preaching is not merely about the creation of narrative tension and resolution within the sermon itself, therefore, without reference to the greater spiritual realities to which preaching witnesses and in which the ultimate tension and resolution of the gospel is rooted. Teleology in preaching inevitably retains an eschatological dimension, by which preachers use tension and resolution not merely for interest's sake, but rather for truth's sake. The telos toward which preaching ultimately aims is nothing less than the new creation that God is bringing about in Christ through the power of the Holy Spirit.

Yet, as Thomas Long notes, this presents a problem for many contemporary preachers, as "today's mainstream pulpit" has grown largely silent about matters of eschatology: "Among educated clergy in the churches we have come to call 'mainline,' the language of heaven, hell, Christ's coming reign, and the final judgment were recurring and important topics of sermons in the nineteenth century, but by the close of the twentieth century a veil of embarrassment had been thrown over the whole matter."[113] Long himself attributes this contemporary eschatological embarrassment to the collapse of postmillennial eschatological thought in the early twentieth century, a loss from which mainline preaching has yet to recover.[114] Having now morphed into any number of secular varieties of the doctrine of progress, the transcendent hope of the gospel has been transformed into purely immanent hopes. "In our own day," Long writes, "both on the left and on the right, there continues the sucking up of eschatological hope into the energies of present-tense optimism and progress."[115] When eschatology is replaced by the doctrine of

---

[113]Thomas G. Long, *Preaching from Memory to Hope* (Louisville, KY: Westminster John Knox, 2009), 112.
[114]Long, *Preaching from Memory to Hope*, 113-17.
[115]Long, *Preaching from Memory to Hope*, 118.

progress, preachers unwittingly become pragmatic atheists: "God is dead. Ad lib the ending."[116] But this large-scale eclipse of eschatological hope by purely immanent visions of progress is ultimately detrimental to the proclamation of the gospel: "When the church and its preachers become apostles of progress, in its various forms, we unwittingly become enemies of the faith."[117]

Thus, contemporary preachers find themselves in a precarious position with regard to matters of teleology and eschatology. For instance, Samuel Wells recounts his own purposeful resistance to the purely immanent focus of the modern research university and his subsequent determination to pursue an explicitly "teleological agenda" when he assumed the office of Dean of the Chapel at Duke University.[118] In the present-day academic environment of such an elite university, however, any talk of teleology is met with deep suspicion:

> It is widely supposed today that the only goods one can discuss publicly are instrumental goods (that is, qualifications that will take you to the next good place), not final goods (that is, ultimate goals). . . . This makes speaking on significant public occasions very difficult. There is little to hope for but peace and security, a safe world in which to . . . nobody says quite what.[119]

Wells was acutely aware of the provocative nature of bringing teleological questions to the fore in his preaching and public speaking at the university. Yet despite deep suspicions that any attempt to speak about final goals in a university setting is a veiled attempt at coercion, he remained convinced that preachers in pluralistic settings "should have the courage to name and display the goal to which [they] assume the audience is or should be striving."[120]

---

[116]Long, *Preaching from Memory to Hope*, 118. For further discussion of eschatology in relation to the secular doctrine of progress, see Richard Bauckham and Trevor Hart, *Hope Against Hope: Christian Eschatology at the Turn of the Millennium* (Grand Rapids, MI: Eerdmans, 1999).

[117]Long, *Preaching from Memory to Hope*, 118. For a comprehensive historical account of the emergence of the "immanent frame" as the dominant—or indeed the only—frame of legitimate discourse in our present "secular" age, see Charles Taylor, *A Secular Age* (Cambridge, MA: Belknap Press, 2007), esp. chap. 15. See also David Zahl's more recent analysis of contemporary culture's search for salvation in purely secular terms in *Seculosity: How Career, Parenting, Technology, Food, Politics, and Romance Became Our New Religion and What to Do about It* (Minneapolis: Fortress Press, 2019).

[118]Samuel Wells, *Speaking the Truth: Preaching in a Pluralistic Culture* (Nashville: Abingdon Press, 2008), 30.

[119]Wells, *Speaking the Truth*, 28 (first ellipsis added, second original).

[120]Wells, *Speaking the Truth*, 30.

Similarly, Thomas Long contends, "Vibrant Christian preaching depends upon the recovery of its eschatological voice."[121] Preachers ignore the ultimate teleological trajectory of their preaching at their own peril, for, as Long asserts, "life under the providence of God has a shape, and . . . this shape is end-stressed; what happens in the middle is finally defined by the end."[122] This is the teleological dynamic of hope that must form the movement from tension to resolution in Christian preaching. As Long concludes: "If Jesus is Lord, if Jesus is raised from the dead, then this puts eschatological pressure on the present. All that damages human life is obsolete, passing away, and the preacher can stand up there boldly speaking in the future-present tense."[123] To embrace the eschatological dimension of preaching is, as Luke Powery summarizes it, to "[situate] preaching in its proper place as a ministry of hope in the Spirit of hope while in the midst of groaning realities of death."[124]

Clearly, then, faithful stewardship of the teleological trajectory of the sermon requires preachers to develop an instinct for situating themselves within God's work of new creation, delighting themselves to witness in all times and places to the in-breaking of the age to come within the present age. Every resolution or conclusion in every sermon, whether it be an intermediate resolution or final conclusion, must ultimately situate itself in relation to this ultimate telos. As Michael Pasquarello III affirms, "The heart of the New Testament proclamation is that through the Son, the Father is leading the whole created universe—cosmos and history—to the ultimate fulfillment of the kingdom (Eph. 1:9-10)."[125] Preaching retains an advantage over music in that it is able to point beyond itself to this final end: "Through its weekly performance of the gospel story, the church gives voice to the apostolic witness that points to the age to come."[126] Thus throughout the process of development, rehearsal, and performance, preachers can learn instincts for leveraging the teleological trajectory of the sermon not primarily as a matter of skill, but rather as a matter of bearing witness, in word and deed, to God's promise of new creation.

---

[121]Long, Preaching from Memory to Hope, 123.

[122]Long, Preaching from Memory to Hope, 126.

[123]Long, Preaching from Memory to Hope, 131.

[124]Powery, Dem Dry Bones, 83.

[125]Michael Pasquarello III, Christian Preaching: A Trinitarian Theology of Proclamation (Grand Rapids, MI: Baker Academic, 2006), 183.

[126]Pasquarello, Christian Preaching, 185.

Just as musicians develop instincts for leveraging the teleological trajectory of a piece of music, shaping their performance at any given moment by means of a broader orientation regarding where they have been, where they are, and where they are going, so also might preachers develop eschatological instincts within which to root their own homiletical performance as a witness to the hope of the gospel. As Luke Powery so eloquently describes this eschatological homiletical instinct,

> To embrace the end, the eschaton, is to embrace the one who is our beginning and end in faith, love, and hope. The eschatological as a homiletical lens may help put congregational problems into perspective because eschatology implies that God is not finished with us yet. The journey of life continues and we have not reached our home, what we shall be. The struggles and pains of life, the little deaths, are not the totality of human existence, though they may appear to be at times. . . . The eschatological tells us that life is eternal and death will eventually die. In the Spirit, one can know this with hope as one yearns for and works toward God's future in the present.[127]

There is great power to be found in a homiletical commitment to embodying this hope-filled teleological instinct, not as a sentimental strategy for resolving tension "on the cheap," but rather as a joyful anticipation of God's future within the present moment in every sermon.

TELEOLOGY AND HOPE

The theological theme that ultimately emerges from this examination of teleology in music and preaching, then, is the theme of hope. Attention to the teleological trajectory of the sermon—the third major instinct in this musical homiletic—is thus envisioned as a means of forming hope among one's hearers. Although this theme relates closely to the theme of patience examined in the previous chapter, this final musical-homiletical task, focusing more on teleology than repetition, points beyond patience toward hope. Although patience is indeed a mark of hope ("But if we hope for what we do not see, we wait for it with patience" [Rom 8:25]), the end ultimately defines the middle. The Christian virtue of patience is therefore impossible without the cultivation of hope, and the formative potential of teleology in preaching is the cultivation of precisely this virtue.

---

[127]Power, *Dem Dry Bones*, 83.

Perhaps not surprisingly, one of the strongest themes throughout Jeremy Begbie's theology through music project is the theme of hope. As has been amply demonstrated, one of Begbie's key observations regarding music and the theology of time stems from his analysis of the interpenetrating temporalities that comprise the metrical matrix in a piece of music. Scrutiny of the metrical hierarchy, for Begbie, becomes an occasion for the reconfiguration of traditional conceptions regarding time and eternity, promise and fulfillment. In Begbie's view, the experience of performing and listening to music, especially with reference to its inherent teleological dynamic, has great potential to enhance our understanding of eschatology and hope.

Tension and resolution in music, Begbie explains, is a complex, multileveled phenomenon: "Within each bar, a pattern of beats is created which takes the form of a wave of intensification and resolution. This is played out in a hierarchy of levels. Resolution at one level increases tension on higher levels."[128] With regard to the theme of hope, therefore, Begbie notes that "there will always be levels in relation to which closure generates an increase in tension, giving rise to a stronger reaching out for resolution."[129] A similar pattern can be found in the biblical narrative of God's promises, Begbie argues. With each divine promise that is fulfilled, there is an intensification of hope for the future. On one level, there is closure, resolution; yet on a higher level, there is further intensification. "In this way, hope is intensified, re-charged, a more potent 'reaching out' engendered."[130]

This is consistent, Begbie argues, with the understanding of hope that is found in the scriptural narrative:

> In the history narrated in Scripture, this extra reaching for fulfillment arises in part because fulfillments are experienced as in some way inadequate to expectation. Every fulfillment is partial and provisional, and therefore a partial *non*-fulfillment. And yet, far from diminishing hope, we find that successive fulfillments increase the hope both in power and content. Deeply ingrained in the biblical testimony is a sense, sometimes acute, of the absence of an adequate

---

[128]Jeremy Begbie, *Theology, Music and Time*, 106.
[129]Begbie, *Theology, Music and Time*, 107. "Each fulfillment constitutes an increase in the demand for fulfillment at a higher level. Every return closes *and* opens, completes *and* extends, resolves *and* intensifies."
[130]Begbie, *Theology, Music and Time*, 108.

fulfillment of what has been promised, a lack or deficiency which impels the people of God to reach forward and strain more fervently for what is to come. ... Each downbeat brings an expectation and hope for *more*, so expanding the content and range of the original promise.[131]

Ultimately, hope is intensified by the expectation that each partial fulfillment hints at a resolution that will eventually occur in complete fullness.

This teleological dynamic of promise and fulfillment, of partial resolutions that serve to intensify the experience of hope, acquires an even greater significance with reference to the coming of Jesus, which is indeed the most important promise-fulfillment pattern in Scripture: "In the New Testament the coming of Jesus is presented as the completion of multiple implications inherent in the promissory story of Israel."[132] Yet although this fulfillment is "climactic and decisive," in some sense it only serves to intensify the longing for a full and final resolution:

> The first Christians are impelled towards a yet more fervent longing for a yet more glorious future. Again, this arises both because of a sense of the fulfillment's provisionality—the world has not yet reached its intended end—and a sense that *in him* the end has already arrived—Jesus Christ is raised as the first fruits of those who have died (1 Cor 15:20). Moreover, through the Spirit there can be many provisional fulfillments of the new promise set in motion by Christ (on the lowest level, as it were), without effacing belief in a terminating fulfillment at the eschaton, and without effacing the decisiveness of the fulfillment in Christ. To know Christ by means of the Spirit outpoured is to know the "first fruits" of the life to come (Rom 8:23).[133]

Thus, Begbie argues, music has the potential to free eschatology from "single-leveled, single-line models of temporality," which obscure the biblical understanding of the dynamics of promise and fulfillment.[134] "The hopeful dynamic

---

[131]Begbie, *Theology, Music and Time*, 108.
[132]Begbie, *Theology, Music and Time*, 109. Begbie clarifies, however, that this does not assume that there have been no prior fulfillments before the coming of Jesus.
[133]Begbie, *Theology, Music and Time*, 109.
[134]Begbie, *Theology, Music and Time*, 110. This observation seems particularly relevant in light of Thomas Long's speculation that the collapse of postmillennialist eschatology is responsible for the eschatological silence found in contemporary mainline preaching. For further discussion of eschatology, teleology, and temporal processes in music, see Borthwick, Hart, and Monti, "Musical Time and Eschatology," in *Resonant Witness: Conversations between Music and Theology*, ed. Jeremy S. Begbie and Steven R. Guthrie (Grand Rapids, MI: Eerdmans, 2011), 271-94.

of Christian faith," Begbie writes, "is carried forward not simply by what we do *not* possess but by what we *are* given now of the future."[135]

With regard to teleology, eschatology, and the cultivation of hope, the art of preaching might thus be understood to have certain advantages and disadvantages compared to the art of music. As demonstrated above, perhaps the biggest advantage preaching might have over music is the ability to specify one's goals, whereas music is able only to present a more general "dynamic of hopefulness" without specifying ultimate ends. Biblical hope, Begbie concedes, "though exhibiting this dynamic of hopefulness, is also normally quite explicitly directing attention to happenings of varying degrees of specificity."[136] Recalling Wells's insistence that preachers in a pluralistic culture must have the courage to specify their teleological commitments, lexical specificity gives the art of preaching an advantage over purely instrumental music in the delineation of an eschatological vision. On the other hand, because certain eschatological concepts inevitably involve models regarding the relationship of time and eternity, and because these models oftentimes defy the ability of language to adequately express,[137] perhaps the multileveled teleological dynamic of musical sounds might also have certain advantages over preaching in the ability to represent complex temporal models nonlinguistically.[138]

Clearly, then, in order for preaching to faithfully and reliably engender the hope of the gospel, a rich, multifaceted understanding of the teleological trajectory of the sermon must be developed. This homiletical understanding must encompass conceptual and aesthetic considerations on multiple levels, including the linguistic, the formal, and the performative. Since preaching differs from music in its ability to name unseen realities known only by faith, it is necessary to conclude this chapter with two final considerations regarding the creation of an integrated, hope-filled teleological dynamic in preaching.

---

[135]Begbie, *Theology, Music and Time*, 111.

[136]Begbie, *Theology, Music and Time*, 111. For a related account of the "ontological indeterminacy" that has developed in modern art, see Charles Taylor, *A Secular Age*, 352-61.

[137]For a helpful overview of the relationship between time and eternity, see Antje Jackelén, *Time and Eternity: The Question of Time in Church, Science, and Theology*, trans. Barbara Harshaw (West Conshohocken, PA: Templeton Foundation Press, 2005).

[138]For an extended discussion of biblical and musical models for the relationship between time and eternity, with special reference to two critical studies of the music of J. S. Bach, see Jeremy Begbie, "Bach, Modernity, and God," in Jeremy Begbie, *Music, Modernity, and God* (New York: Oxford University Press, 2013), 41-72, esp. 59-62.

The first consideration recalls the liturgical setting of preaching. In his book *Sent and Gathered: A Worship Manual for the Missional Church*,[139] Clayton Schmit proposes a model for conceiving of the teleological trajectory of individual worship services—and, by extension, of individual sermons within them—through the musical metaphor. Just as Begbie uses the musical metaphor of the multileveled metrical matrix to picture Christian hope as the cultivation of a "yet more fervent longing for a yet more glorious future" amid the provisional fulfillment of God's promises,[140] so also Schmit pictures the classic fourfold pattern of worship as being like the four beats of a bar of music, propelling the church forward into hopeful embodiment of God's mission in the world as a wider sense of God's story emerges through the ascending hierarchy of metrical waves that are generated by each individual worship service.[141] The embodiment of a hopeful, gospel-centered teleological trajectory in individual sermons might therefore involve the preacher's own reframing of the sermon event itself, with the individual sermon understood sometimes as a complete piece of music in itself with its own metrical hierarchy, and at other times as merely one bar within a multileveled metrical matrix of ever larger hyperbars that are generated by the worship service as a whole, and even further, by sermon after sermon and worship service after worship service throughout a preacher's lifetime.[142]

The second consideration related to teleology and hope in preaching involves an examination—even a potential cataloging—of various *qualia* that are seemingly built in to certain homiletical practices within a given listening culture, affording special attention to the shaping of homiletical cadences or conclusions. An example of this is found in Frank Thomas's scholarship on the Black preaching tradition. As examined in the first chapter, William Turner characterizes a common performative technique in traditional African American preaching as "start low, go slow, climb higher,

---

[139]Clayton J. Schmit, *Sent and Gathered: A Worship Manual for the Missional Church* (Grand Rapids, MI: Baker Academic, 2009).

[140]Begbie, *Theology, Music and Time*, 109.

[141]See especially Schmit, *Sent and Gathered*, 47-53.

[142]The metaphor could be extended even further, with the life of each individual preacher forming one bar within the ascending hierarchy of metrical waves of the single song of the church's witness throughout history.

strike fire, then sit down in the storm."[143] Similarly, building on Henry Mitchell's work on Black preaching, Frank A. Thomas has developed a comprehensive theology of preaching from the performative tradition of *celebration*, especially as found in the concluding emotional register of sermons in the African American tradition.[144]

The unabashed use of a strong emotional appeal to create a celebrative trajectory serves a pedagogical function in itself, Thomas asserts, inasmuch as "celebration is the natural response when one has received and appropriated the assurance of grace in the gospel."[145] Celebration in African American sermon design, according to Thomas, "help[s] people *experience the assurance of grace* that is the gospel."[146] Regardless of the precise words spoken, Thomas holds, the celebrative impulse itself communicates the nature of the gospel in a similar way to the manner in which gospel impulses are purportedly embedded in the "Lowry Loop" narrative form.

Thomas's proposal regarding the hope-filled teleological trajectory that is "built in" to celebrative conclusions in African American preaching has invited further refining by other scholars, most notably Cleophus LaRue. While seeking to affirm the general impulse toward celebration as an effective (affective) tool for generating an experience of the gospel in preaching, LaRue proposes a broadening of Mitchell's and Thomas's concept of celebration to include not just climactic utterance of any sort at the close of a sermon, but rather a fulsome appreciation of what it means for worshipful praise of God to occur. This necessarily involves the integration of rhetoric with content.[147] As LaRue writes, "A functional celebration, erroneously claiming to build up the church—that is, [Thomas's assertion that] people remember and do what they celebrate—causes us to end up with a feel-good religion but not a very

---

[143]William C. Turner, "The Musicality of Black Preaching: Performing the Word," in *Performance in Preaching: Bringing the Sermon to Life*, ed. Jana Childers and Clayton J. Schmit (Grand Rapids, MI: Baker Academic, 2008), 191.

[144]Frank A. Thomas, *They Like to Never Quit Praisin' God: The Role of Celebration in Preaching*, rev. ed. (Cleveland: Pilgrim Press, 2013).

[145]Thomas, *They Like to Never Quit*, 18.

[146]Thomas, *They Like to Never Quit*, 18.

[147]Cleophus J. LaRue, *Rethinking Celebration: From Rhetoric to Praise in African American Preaching* (Louisville, KY: Westminster John Knox, 2016), 24-29.

deep faith. What we desperately need is a clear understanding of celebration, first and foremost, as worshipful praise."[148]

Even a doxology that is "detached from any notion of emotion" can still faithfully steward the teleological trajectory of the sermon, LaRue believes, "if it is indeed a declaration of praise for God."[149] Therefore, in place of a more limited, rhetorically focused model of celebratory conclusions, which he believes sets preachers up to feel failures if the effect is somehow not achieved,[150] LaRue proposes four types of doxological endings that model a more robust "theology of praise in its multiple expressions."[151] Seen in broader perspective, LaRue's critique and expansion of the work of Mitchell and Thomas can be understood as a refinement and expansion of a "cataloging" of various homiletical *qualia* that help to enhance the teleological trajectory of a sermon, and thus lend themselves toward a more powerful proclamation of gospel hope.

Teleology in preaching is not simply a matter of holding listeners' attention and creating interest, but rather a matter of developing a listening culture that is formed by the hope of the gospel. Through the cultivation and leveraging of teleological impulses, hope is formed in the practice of preaching as listeners are sent away with the promise of grace ringing in their ears, sounding a triumphant note of reversal over the forces of sin and death that seek to define listeners' earthly reality. This necessarily involves the integration of linguistic, formal, and performative dimension to engender a deep, multifaceted dynamic of gospel hope. Moreover, as Powery, Long, Pasquarello, and Begbie all emphasize, Christian hope inevitably involves a robust understanding of eschatological time, leading preachers to proclaim not simply "what we do *not* possess" at the present moment but also "what we *are* given now of the future."[152] A truly hopeful teleological trajectory in the art of preaching therefore necessitates a robust eschatological vision, an ability to speak with boldness in the "future-present" tense.[153]

---

[148]LaRue, *Rethinking Celebration*, 29.

[149]LaRue, *Rethinking Celebration*, 56.

[150]LaRue, *Rethinking Celebration*, 21.

[151]These four types are (1) *Christological endings*, (2) *ethical-moral endings*, (3) *endings that use God's name*, and (4) *"best is last" endings*. See LaRue, *Rethinking Celebration*, 57-64.

[152]Begbie, *Theology, Music and Time*, 111.

[153]Powery, *Dem Dry Bones*, 91-103; Long, *Preaching from Memory to Hope*, 131.

CONCLUSION: ATTENDING TO TELEOLOGY IN PREACHING

Preachers who desire to use the musical instinct of teleology in their preaching can begin by specifying the particular listening habits they would like to develop among their listeners. More specifically, preachers should consider how they might best preach in a way that listeners learn to long for, and expect to hear, the cadence of the gospel—the pleasing homiletical resolution of God's grace to the tension of the world's trouble that has been building in the sermon. Of course, special caution must be taken to ensure that these gospel resolutions do not come "on the cheap" and thus become theological clichés, leading to a sentimentalized faith. Nonetheless, the triumph of God's grace over the powers of sin and death must not be muffled or unclear. In order for sermons to truly be rooted in gospel hope, rather than a secularized message of moralism or progress, the eschatological perspective of God's action to bring about the new creation in Christ through the Spirit must take precedence. Preachers would do well to regularly assess, through various formal or informal means, the extent to which this gospel cadence is taking root in the listening habits of one's listeners.

Ultimately, teleology is an important dynamic for preachers to attend to not simply for the goal of producing a secularized, human-centered inspirational speech, but rather so that the church may be formed in the hope that there is a new world coming.[154] This new world, moreover, is not something that we bring about ourselves, but is something that we receive and enter into as God's gift. Our hope is based on God's promise. The responsibility of preachers is to develop deep instincts—through patterns of study, preparation, action, and reflection—for always pointing toward that ultimate eschatological telos. In the sermon itself, preachers can draw on various homiletical tools such as language, form, and performance, for the cultivation of the teleological trajectory. The good news for every preacher, however, is that our words are powerful not because of our own ingenuity or skill, but because of our confidence "that there is only one preacher, Christ. And he will preach."[155] It is Jesus himself, the living Word, who gives us the ability to speak words of hope and

---

[154]William H. Willimon, "Formed by the Saints," in *Preaching Master Class: Lessons from Will Willimon's Five-Minute Preaching Workshop*, ed. Noel A. Snyder (Eugene, OR: Cascade, 2010), 89.
[155]Willimon, *Undone by Easter*, 67.

promise in the midst of suffering and difficulty—who indeed speaks through us. Our first and last instinct as preachers must be to rest in that good news.

TELEOLOGY IN PRACTICE

The following sermon excerpt from Mary Hulst exemplifies a robust teleological orientation leading to a hopeful conclusion.[156] However, the tension that is developed in this sermon is not resolved "cheaply" or prematurely. The weariness of the psalmist and in the lives of the present listeners receives honest, empathic attention. Yet, at the same time, Hulst calls attention to the time markers that help believers orient themselves within the larger story of God's faithfulness—remembering the past and hoping in the future.

Hulst begins by highlighting the spiritual weariness that is evident in the psalmist's words, especially in Psalm 42:3, "My tears have been my food day and night." Hulst acknowledges the myriad ways these words may resonate with her listeners. Yet she also highlights the "spiritual sloth" that is evident in the psalmist's words in verse 4, "I used to go to the house of God." Hulst identifies spiritual sloth as a particular temptation for those who are "professionally religious," like her audience of seminary students is presumably preparing to be. One of the most difficult experiences to deal with, however, is God's silence, evident in verse 9, "I say to God, my Rock, 'Why have you forgotten me?'" Yet in the midst of the silence and mourning and weariness, Hulst says, we are nonetheless invited by Psalm 42 into two specific practices: to remember and to hope. She continues:

> Now, [to remember and to hope is] good counsel from the psalmist. But the truth is, it doesn't really matter so much what we do. It matters what God does. It matters what God is up to. And nestled into this psalm, we have this verse that seems like it doesn't fit. Verse 8: "By day, the Lord directs his love, at night his song is with me, a prayer to the God of my life." So here the psalmist is naming the Lord's direct love in his life, he's naming his song, and he says, "This is the God of my life, my whole life—my past, my future, and my now. This is the God of my whole life, and even though my now is kind of miserable, this is my God; this is who he is."

---

[156]Sermon text excerpt: Mary Hulst, "For Weary Souls," on Psalm 42, at Gordon-Conwell Theological Seminary, April 9, 2019, www.youtube.com/watch?v=VZge_YfozDQ. Used by permission.

It's so important for us to remember that God is doing exactly what God wants to do in each of our lives right now. He's not worried about your life. He's not worried about you getting a job. He's not worried about your future. He's good! This is the God we serve. He's doing exactly what he wants to do in your life to make you—to make me—look more and more like Jesus Christ. That's what God is up to in our lives. And sometimes it comes through suffering, and sometimes it comes through sorrow, and sometimes it comes through a confession of sin, and sometimes it comes through these deep, dark places.[157]

By the way, never say that to somebody pastorally. That's for the person to figure out for themselves. That's their testimony to give; that's not your testimony to declare.

But the psalmist is very clear that God is up to something. Because he knows God to be a good God. Maybe you know that call and refrain, "God is good, all the time. All the time, God is good." And it can be really tempting to kind of edit that and to be like, "My experience of God is mostly good, some of the time."[158] But that's not what it's about. It's like saying, "Mary has green eyes all the time. All the time, Mary has green eyes." Green eyes are just a part of who I am. You may experience them as blue, but they are not; they are green. And God's goodness is part of who God is. We may not always experience that goodness, but it's part of who he is. Which is why the psalmist can make this declaration that God is up to something, he's directing this, he's in charge of this, it's all going to be okay, I just need to hang in there.[159]

"By day, the Lord directs his love, at night his song is with me, a prayer to the God of my life." The God whom he knows is with him.

Hulst goes on to tell a story about a time when she was in parish ministry and there was a boy in the youth group at her church who had a heart for people who are experiencing homelessness. One night, the boy convinced his parents to allow him to spend the night under a bridge downtown where people who are experiencing homelessness would often sleep.

---

[157]This bold statement of God's providential care and sanctifying presence in individual lives is spoken in a winsome manner, which aids the reception of the message. Also important is the pastoral aside that follows.

[158]Here again, the use of empathetic humor helps to draw listeners in and aid the reception of a somewhat difficult message about belief in God's unwavering goodness, even during times of great suffering.

[159]Hulst presents a clear teleological statement here, using the language of Psalm 42:8 to declare God's sovereignty as a cause for hope and a motivation for perseverance.

Unbeknownst to the 16-year-old boy, however, his father followed him down there that night and stayed near him, just out of sight, the entire night. Hulst continues:

> [The boy] had no idea that his father was there, but he was. We can have seasons of spiritual weariness when we have no idea that God is there, but he is. And as we move into Holy Week,[160] we remember that we have a God who doesn't just observe our suffering, but a God who moves into our suffering, a God who takes on our suffering, a God who says, "Your suffering is my suffering. I am with you in your suffering in ways that you cannot even imagine." And that helps us in our suffering. We remember what Christ has done, and we hope for what is yet to come, for we know that someday our Jesus will return! And there will be no more mourning or crying or sadness or pain, for all those things will have passed away, and God himself will wipe every tear from our eyes. That is our God. He is with us. He is with us. He is with us. Amen.

---

[160]Notice the connection Hulst draws between the time markers of the church's liturgical seasons (a cyclical mode of marking time) and the linear modes by which we make sense of our own story in light of God's actions in the past, present, and promised future.

5

A MUSICAL HOMILETIC
IN PRACTICE

DRAWING ON MUSICAL INSTINCTS in the practice of preaching will always be more a matter of cultivating practical know-how than articulating a sophisticated musical-homiletical theory. As Michael Polanyi has famously stated with regard to tacit knowledge, "we can know more than what we can tell."[1] The cultivation of practical wisdom, rather than the proliferation of academic theory, is the ultimate goal of this project. Yet even the best musical performers have found that knowledge of music theory is one of the many aids to their excellence in performance. I recall a time in college when my piano instructor patiently helped me to see how a harmonic analysis of the piece I was learning would help me to remember and perform it more fluently. In the same way, for those preachers who desire to develop their preaching instincts to become more fluent in the theological dynamics of how God works to form God's people in the preaching of the Word, there can be great value in careful reflection on the formative potential of a musical homiletic.

This chapter briefly reflects on, and then seeks to demonstrate, what it might look like to "put it all together." What does it look like in practice to apply a musician's sensibilities to the task of preaching?

PUTTING IT ALL TOGETHER

Synchrony, repetition, and teleology: these are not the only three characteristics that the art of music and the art of preaching share, but they are three

---

[1]Michael Polanyi, *The Tacit Dimension* (London: Routledge & Kegan Paul Ltd., 1966), 4. See also Michael Polanyi, *Personal Knowledge: Towards a Post-Critical Philosophy* (Chicago: University of Chicago Press, 1962), especially chaps. 4 and 5.

of the major ones. Other characteristics, such as tonality, receive less direct attention here, even though they play a major role in both arts as well. Nevertheless, the three shared characteristics that have formed the basis of this musical-homiletical conversation have themselves generated numerous valuable insights for the theory and practice of preaching. This final chapter seeks to demonstrate how preachers might go about practicing this musical homiletic more intentionally.

Some readers of this book may be preachers who, like myself, are musically trained and who have a vague sense of the musicality of their own preaching, but lack specificity as to how the two arts relate. This book has attempted to provide these sorts of preachers an opportunity to gain critical understanding about the relationship between the disciplines of music and homiletics. Other readers may be preachers who are not musically trained, but who are eager to gain insight from a range of artistic disciplines in order to refresh their own homiletical theory and practice. This book has attempted to provide these preachers as well a fruitful and stimulating proposal for understanding music and for incorporating musical instincts into their homiletical practice. Finally, with Jana Childers serving as a methodological exemplar and Jeremy Begbie serving as a theological guide, this book has attempted to speak into the conversation of what it might look like for theology to incorporate a "performative mode" into its methodology.

Yet the goal of this conversation is not simply to contribute to the discipline of theology—or even the discipline of practical theology—but to strengthen the church's witness. The summary observations and concluding thoughts found at the end of each chapter have already begun to address the homiletical implications of each characteristic individually; what remains is to demonstrate how the musical homiletic developed in this project might be put into practice in a more integrated way.

Perhaps the simplest way for preachers to think about putting it all together is to relate each of the three characteristics to a specific moment or movement in individual sermons. In other words, preachers could focus on the cultivation of synchrony at the beginning of the sermon, the use of repetition in the middle of the sermon, and the teleological trajectory at the end. This could extend further to the spiritual value to which each characteristic has been connected, with preachers focusing on cultivating congregational unity at the beginning of the sermon, patience in the middle, and hope at the end. Although it is ultimately artificial to separate these three characteristics into three separate movements, it may be helpful, especially as preachers are trying to consciously attend to the performative dimensions of their preaching, to focus on each of these three phenomena—and each of their related goals—individually and successively. A first step in developing a greater sense of homiletical musicality might be to practice one skill at a time.[2]

Eventually, though, it would be expected that all three characteristics—and countless more—would be practiced fluidly and concurrently in an integrated musical approach to preaching. After all, in both music and preaching, none of these three phenomena is possible without the presence of the others. Yet no matter how this musical homiletic is appropriated—whether these three shared characteristics are practiced simultaneously or separately, partially or fully—the musical homiletic proposed here is ultimately reliant on God's gracious promise to transform human speech and to use the act of preaching as "a conduit of the Spirit's transformative power"[3] in the life of the church.

The preceding chapters have attempted to demonstrate the power and effect of each of these musical characteristics in both music and preaching, providing sample sermon texts to further demonstrate their occurrence in practice. It is now appropriate in this final chapter to utilize the musical homiletic developed here as a tool for the analysis of an original sermon, in order to demonstrate the practical and theoretical import of the present musical-homiletical conversation for the development of an integrated musical approach to preaching.

The following is a sermon that I preached on April 13, 2014, in a small-town Presbyterian church in the Midwest. It was Palm Sunday, and I was serving as the guest preacher. However, I was not an unknown voice to most of the worshipers, as I had preached in this congregation on several previous occasions, and my family had worshiped regularly with this congregation for nearly a year. The congregation was mostly composed of people who were

---

[2]In the initial stages of learning, it might even be helpful for preachers to more deliberately develop each skill by focusing on *one skill per sermon*, rather than all three individually within the same sermon.
[3]James K. A. Smith, *Imagining the Kingdom: How Worship Works* (Grand Rapids, MI: Baker Academic, 2013), 15.

"born and raised" in this rural agricultural town, and who, for the most part, were not very fluent in theological language or concepts. From the combination of this (admittedly limited) contextual assessment and my own observations regarding a familiar but seemingly incongruous feature of the Palm Sunday liturgy, the major focus of the sermon emerged: a theological-liturgical reflection on the triumphant cry, "Hosanna!"

Similar to the technique of sermon analysis utilized by Mike Graves in *The Sermon as Symphony*, the text of the following sermon will be supplemented with annotated comments.[4] Just as Graves highlights portions of each sermon that demonstrate the form-sensitive theory he is advocating, the analytical comments here will attempt to demonstrate some of the features of the musical homiletic that has been developed in previous chapters. However, because the bracketed, italicized analysis that Graves intersperses in his text is quite disruptive to the flow of reading the sermon itself, the analytical comments will be placed in the footnotes, which will allow readers the opportunity to read the sermon text without interruption, if so desired, before attending to the analysis.

"SAVE US" BY NOEL A. SNYDER, ON MATTHEW 21:1-11

I'm not gonna lie; I love me some Palm Sunday hymns.[5] "Hosanna, Loud Hosanna." "All Glory, Laud, and Honor." Pretty much any other hymn or praise song that has the word *hosanna* in it. These are some great songs. Triumphant, exultant, soaring, bright, ecstatic. These are great songs for a palm processional. They're great songs for kids to tromp around to. These are great songs.[6] There's only one problem—I'm not sure that they're scored right. I'm not sure if the music quite matches up to the emotional tenor that I see in this story when it is read in its context.[7]

I wonder what would happen if we were to take these Palm Sunday hymns to a film score composer, and if we were also to give the composer a copy of the

---

[4]See, e.g., Mike Graves, *The Sermon as Symphony: Preaching the Literary Forms of the New Testament* (Valley Forge, PA: Judson Press, 1997), 53-60.

[5]The use of colloquial language aims to connect with listeners and hold their attention. As noted in chapter 2, in White mainline congregations, synchrony is more likely to be developed by creating movement in the content itself, rather than in creating audible "talk-back" participation.

[6]The mention of processing with psalms, with children leading the way, recalls an earlier part of that morning's service and focuses the congregation on a shared liturgical experience.

[7]In Eugene Lowry's terminology, this observation "disrupts the equilibrium" of the common Palm Sunday celebrations.

script that we just read—the story of Jesus riding into Jerusalem, what we now call the triumphal entry. I wonder what would happen if we were to say to the composer, "Here's the script, and here's the music that traditionally accompanies the script in our worship services." I wonder what a composer might have to say about the way these two things line up.[8] And then I wonder, what if we were to say to the composer, "Would you be so kind as to compose some music to accompany this scene, based on your own reading of it?" I wonder what it would sound like. Would it sound like [humming the hymn tune "Ellacombe"]?[9] I'm not so sure.

I'm having a hard time with this way of scoring Palm Sunday, because what I find in this story, which none of these bright *hosanna* hymns seems to capture, is a deep sense of foreboding. Which is to say that, for every word or action in the story, there is a second meaning, a double meaning. There's a sense of exultation mixed with a sense of imminent danger.[10] So we have all this royal imagery, with palm branches and coats being laid out before Jesus, but we're also on edge, because we know that Jesus is headed for a showdown with the temple authorities, which will ultimately end with these same royal images being used to mock Jesus as he's tortured and left to die.

So on the one hand, we have Jesus being hailed as the son of David, the one whom the people expect to fulfill the prophecies by overthrowing the current government and reinstating the Davidic kingship and sitting on the throne as David's rightful heir. And in that sense, it's perfectly appropriate to sing a song of triumph to the son of David, the anointed one who will save us from exile and restore the kingdom once and for all. But on the other hand, we remember all of the profound ways that these concepts are redefined by Jesus, because we know that this king's campaign does not result in the type of victory the people expected it to result in.

So here's what I'm imagining as a more appropriate way to score our Palm Sunday hymns. We can still have [humming "Ellacombe"]. But then over top of that, I think what we should add is some minor tones, some long drawn out string sounds, to create a sense of foreboding, to strike a note of imminent

---

[8]This imagined scenario seeks to capture the attention of listeners by inviting them to imaginatively step outside of their normal liturgical experience and reconsider the Scripture text for themselves.

[9]"Ellacombe" is the triumphant-sounding hymn tune to which the text "Hosanna, Loud Hosanna" is traditionally sung.

[10]Calling attention to this mix of exaltation and danger helps to transition from the musical-liturgical observation with which the sermon began to a more explicit theological-hermeneutical analysis.

danger.[11] I know you know what I'm talking about. I know you've seen movies where there's this kind of double meaning, where there's a scene of triumph or joy mixed with a sense of foreboding, as the characters enter into some unforeseen danger. And quite often, one of the things that tips us off to the danger is the soundtrack.[12]

When my sister and I were teenagers, I recall that my sister would often dream of what music she wanted to be played on her wedding day. And I can remember sitting with her in the living room on several occasions, and I would play songs on the piano as she pretended to march down the aisle. Of course, one of the songs that she was most fond of, like many brides, was Pachelbel's Canon in D. And I remember how fun it was to get her all riled up by hitting a bunch of wrong notes right at the climax of the piece. Right as the tune soars up high and she was pretending to make her grand entrance, I would suddenly make it sound like a bad dream, like a funhouse nightmare or something. I was a mean brother. But it was just so easy to get her with that trick! Many years later, I did end up playing the piano at her wedding, but I was under strict orders not to make it sound like a funhouse nightmare as she came walking down the aisle.

I think Palm Sunday is kind of like that.[13] It's a perfect reminder of this double sense that we learn to live with as followers of Jesus. All of our most cherished projects, all of our most dearly held beliefs, all of our grandest dreams and visions—all of them are subject to God's intrusion. Not that God is out to get us or that God takes pleasure in ruining all of the things we most enjoy. Not that we spend our entire lives waiting for the other shoe to drop, with this constant sense of fear that our lives are going so well right now—we're so happy at the present moment—that we can be sure that something bad is about to happen. That's not what I'm saying. But I am saying that as followers of Jesus, we learn to become living sacrifices. We learn to follow Jesus, not just to the Mount of Olives, not just to Jerusalem, but all the way to the cross. We learn that our entire lives

---

[11]After the service, one worshiper commented that it would have been interesting were I to have played an example on the keyboard to help the listeners hear, rather than simply imagine, what I was talking about. I found this to be a helpful suggestion.

[12]The hope of this extended focus on exegetical issues through the lens of musical scoring is that listeners will, by this time, be united in their experience of this juxtaposition of triumph and danger in not only their liturgical rhythms but also their individual lives of discipleship.

[13]The analogous connection between this personal illustration and the emotional tenor of Palm Sunday is somewhat risky, since in my illustration I play the part of the "mean brother," purposely teasing my sister. The danger is that God turns into the mean God, taking pleasure in purposely disrupting our feelings of joy. For that reason, I will clarify this analogy below.

are subject to redefinition, to revision, to crucifixion even, so that God may
bring about something much bigger than we could imagine.[14]

> A very large crowd spread their cloaks on the road, and others cut
> branches from the trees and spread them on the road. The crowds that
> went ahead of him and that followed were shouting, "Hosanna to the
> Son of David! Blessed is the one who comes in the name of the Lord!
> Hosanna in the highest heaven!" (Matthew 21:8-9)

As followers of Jesus, we learn to become living sacrifices. We learn that our
entire lives are subject to redefinition, to revision, to crucifixion even, so that
God may bring about something much bigger than we could ever imagine. And
there is no word in the whole Palm Sunday narrative that is more open to redefinition than this word, hosanna. What does the word hosanna mean? Does
anybody know?[15] It means, "Save us."

One of the reasons I'm concerned about the scoring of our Palm Sunday
hymns in such triumphant and exultant tones is that this word, *hosanna*, potentially becomes something like a synonym for the word *hallelujah*. The word *hallelujah* is in fact a proper exclamation of praise. The word *hallelujah* means,
"Praise the Lord." We're so used to this word *hosanna* that it becomes easy for us
to think of it as something akin to the word *hallelujah*, when in actuality it is a
deep cry of longing: "Save us! Please, somebody, save us!" It is a deep cry of
longing and of the hope that finally, at last, this is it! This is our guy! Somebody
has come to save us!

Hosanna! It's not so much an exclamation that you shout in celebration when
something good happens to you. Rather, it's more of a rally cry. It's more the
type of exclamation that you shout when you're watching the star of your favor-
ite soccer team driving toward the goal in the championship game: "Go! Go! Go!"
"Save us! Save us! Save us!" Finally! At last! Somebody has come to save us! This is
it! Blessed is the one who comes in the name of the Lord! But then in the Gospel
narrative, it's as if, as we're all watching the player drive toward the goal in the
championship game, the other team trips him, but there's no call. And every-
body's shouting, "He was tripped!" But the refs ignore it. And time runs out. And
our team loses. And now what has become of our *hosanna*?[16]

---

[14] I create here a phrase that will repeat itself many times throughout the sermon. This, then, will
serve as the theological "tonic," the "home base" to which we will repeatedly return.
[15] Whether or not anyone did actually know the meaning of the word *hosanna*, there was no visual
or verbal response of recognition, and it seemed that most did not know the meaning.
[16] Whether or not it was successful, the use of a modern sports analogy seeks to capture again the

As followers of Jesus, we learn to become living sacrifices. We learn that our entire lives are subject to redefinition, to revision, to crucifixion even, so that God may bring about something much bigger than we could ever imagine.[17] And there is no word in this whole narrative that is more open to redefinition than this word, *hosanna*. The scandal of the Holy Week drama that begins with the Palm Sunday narrative is that, just as we're hanging our heads and walking out to the parking lot in defeat, just as we're saying to ourselves, "We thought this was it. We thought this was our time. We were crying, 'Save us,' but now it's all over"—just as we're walking away in defeat, suddenly a voice pierces through our despair with an outrageous announcement: *That was it. I have saved you. I know it didn't look like you expected it to, but that's because I had my sights set on something bigger. I have conquered. I have disarmed the powers and principalities. It is finished.*[18]

There is no word in the Palm Sunday narrative that is more open to redefinition than this word, *hosanna*. Save us! And I might even go so far as to say that there is also no other word that better encapsulates our common human experience than this very same word, *hosanna*. Save us. We may not always articulate it quite like that, but the longing is still there. It shows up in all sorts of ways. In our culture, we see a mass numbing through the abuse of drugs and alcohol. Maybe also the abuse of power; the longing to either escape our condition or exercise total control over our condition. Both are manifestations of the longing to be saved. We want somebody to throw us a line, to fix our problems, to give us wings to fly away. Or simply to never disappoint us again. Hosanna! Save us! Either that or we try to save ourselves by finding the perfect ending to that wonderful phrase, "If only." If only I had [fill in the blank]. A better car, a better job, a better spouse, more freedom, more options. If only, then my life would be better. Then I would be happy. If only _____. Hosanna! Save us![19]

The quickest way to find out what it is that might need to be redefined, revised, or crucified in our lives is to fill in that blank, "If only _____." The people who surrounded Jesus that day in the grand drama of the triumphal entry, the

---

sense of exultation followed by defeat that is characteristic of Holy Week liturgical celebrations, patterned off of the shape of the Gospel narratives themselves.

[17]This is the third occurrence of this exact phrase, strengthening the sense of a theological "tonic" in the ears of listeners.

[18]The dramatic irony of the victory of the cross is now identified as God's surprising answer to humanity's cry, "Save us!"

[19]The repetition of the phrase, "Hosanna! Save us!" creates a "dominant" chord that leads into the "tonic" of God's surprising answer to our cry. Additionally, the attempt here is to identify the cry, *hosanna*, in the lives of contemporary listeners.

people who laid down their coats and their palms and cried, "Hosanna to the Son of David! Blessed is the one who comes in the name of the Lord! Hosanna in the highest heaven!"—those people had their own "if onlys." If only we could overthrow our Roman oppressors, if only we could restore the fortunes of Israel, if only the Messiah would come and take us back to the promised land, take us back to the way things used to be. If only.

And Jesus participates in this grand drama, which Matthew tells us is a fulfillment of the prophecy from Zechariah, but almost as soon as the procession reaches Jerusalem, the expectations of the people for the way that this prophecy would be fulfilled are redefined, revised, and crucified. Save us! Save us! Hosanna in the highest! So Jesus heads toward his showdown with the Jerusalem authorities, and in doing so he ultimately shows the people that their vision is too small. They want Jesus to restore the kingdom of Israel. Jesus comes to inaugurate the kingdom of God. They want Jesus to overthrow the oppressor *out there*. Jesus comes to disarm the forces of evil themselves, including both the corrupted powers *out there* and the very source of that corruption—the sinful heart *in here*.[20]

Jesus disarms the forces of evil themselves—not destroys just yet, but disarms nonetheless, so that they can no longer exercise their dominion over us. And in the process, Jesus disarms all of our if onlys, so that we can no longer pretend that all we need to be saved from is out there. Now we're forced to admit that it's in here as well. In order to truly save us, Jesus sets his sights higher than we ever had them set, because evil isn't just out there. It's in here. In order to truly save us, Jesus needs to save us not only from "them," but also from ourselves. That's what Jesus goes to the cross to do. Hosanna. Save us. And Jesus goes to the cross to do exactly that. And as the people walk away in disappointment and defeat, a whisper comes, "I have saved you." The strife is over, the battle won.[21]

What are we to say, then, about our joyful Palm Sunday hymns?[22] Is it right to sing *hosanna* in exultant tones? Looking back through the eyes of faith, I think there just may be a place for such a thing. We live in faith that Jesus reigns now

---

[20]By helping listeners to imagine the original context in which onlookers cried *hosanna* and subsequently had their hopes redefined, a certain "distance" is created in which listeners may also imagine the ways God might be redefining their own "if onlys."

[21]The use of a phrase from a traditional Easter anthem calls attention to the theological "tonal system" through which the church has historically interpreted the significance of the cross.

[22]Here the teleological trajectory of the sermon comes more clearly into view, as we aim toward the resolution of this question regarding the scoring of our Palm Sunday hymns. An eschatological perspective will ultimately provide the resolution to this question.

and always as our king, and so we sing our songs of triumph even though we know that it all doesn't work out quite the way we wanted it to. It works out better! And we trust that Jesus has truly triumphed through the cross once and for all, and that one day the eternal kingdom of God will come in all its fullness, and all flesh will sing our triumph song together.[23]

I think there just may be a place for us to anticipate the ultimate triumph of God in exultant tones, even as we remember the sense of foreboding that accompanies Jesus' entry into Jerusalem. But there is one thing we must be absolutely clear on if we're going to sing these bright, exultant hymns. This isn't a cheap *hosanna*. This isn't a simple fulfillment of our wishes. This isn't a one-to-one correspondence between the salvation we expect and the salvation we get.[24]

So when we hear ourselves singing *hosanna*, when we hear ourselves saying "if only"—Lord, save us—one of the most important things for us to learn in those moments is that even our most cherished projects, our most dearly held beliefs, our grandest dreams and visions—all of these are subject to redefinition, revision, and crucifixion, in order that God might bring about something so much bigger than we could have ever imagined.[25]

Now to him who by the power at work within us is able to accomplish abundantly far more than all we can ask or imagine, to him be glory in the church and in Christ Jesus to all generations, forever and ever. Amen.[26]

CONCLUSION

The strength of this sermon and its accompanying analysis will be left for readers to assess. The intent of this brief chapter is simply to demonstrate the viability of the musical homiletic developed here. Ultimately, at least two major purposes are envisioned for the conversation between music and preaching developed throughout this project. As noted in the preface, one of the major

---

[23]This eschatological perspective helps to orient listeners within a broader understanding of the reign of God and the salvation Christ brings. This provides the context in which the congregation may sing *hosanna* in exultant tones, trusting that Jesus reigns even now, yet still awaiting the full consummation of God's eternal kingdom.

[24]Even though I allow a place for triumphant *hosannas*, I attempt here to guide the congregation away from receiving this as a cliché resolution, a sentimental understanding of salvation as simple wish fulfillment.

[25]This resolution attempts to reinforce hope inasmuch as it affirms that God's surprising answer to our cries for salvation will ultimately prove to be better than we could have ever imagined.

[26]This Pauline blessing from Ephesians 3:20-21 provides appropriate language by which to conclude the sermon on a note of hope. God's power to redefine our desires and to bring about more than we could ask or imagine is the ultimate eschatological context within which to understand God's answer to our cry, *hosanna*.

aims of this conversation between music and preaching is theoretical: to offer an account of some of the significant ways in which musicology might be found to enrich homiletical theory by providing a unique interdisciplinary perspective. Bringing musicology into conversation with homiletics, one of my major hopes is that homileticians would be afforded a greater understanding of the theological and formative potential of the art of preaching, the specific means by which the practice of preaching might serve as a "conduit of the Spirit's transformative power," a practice by which "the Spirit marshals our embodiment in order to rehabituate us to the kingdom of God."[27] In short, the hope is that homileticians would be given a more comprehensive theoretical tool for understanding the *musical* dimension of preaching.

Yet there is a deeply practical impulse that runs throughout this project as well. At every stage in this musical homiletic, a sustained attempt was made to develop an easily understandable template for use in sermon construction and analysis. Thus each of the three shared characteristics was examined with a range of practical applications always in view. A second major aim of this project is, therefore, the creation of a tool for the construction and assessment of sermons that may be useful for the training of preachers in the classroom setting or in the context of continuing education. For both novice and experienced preachers who may desire a way to draw on the musical metaphor in the development of their practical skills—whether they have previous musical training or not—this book aims to provide an understandable and memorable option for incorporating musical impulses into the practice of preaching.

It must be acknowledged, however, that there is a larger aim that remains constant throughout every Christian practice, including the practice of preaching. The larger aim of every Christian practice, whether in public ministry or in personal discipleship, is the cultivation of spiritual fruit. By calling attention to the presence of these "musical" mechanisms in the practice of preaching—the shared characteristics of synchrony, repetition, and teleology—this book takes its place among other practical theological tools that aim to build unity, patience, and hope in the church. Perhaps the greatest compliment I ever received was from a fellow pastor, who, after listening to one of my sermons, told me, "A congregation that consistently hears

---

[27]Smith, *Imagining the Kingdom*, 15.

preaching like that will be healthy." It is my hope and prayer that God would so use the music of our preaching to produce life and movement and growth in the church, by the power of the Holy Spirit, that the hope of our Lord Jesus Christ may be known throughout the earth.

BIBLIOGRAPHY

Allen, O. Wesley, Jr., ed. *The Renewed Homiletic*. Minneapolis: Fortress, 2010.

Alcántara, Jared E. *Crossover Preaching: Intercultural-Improvisational Homiletics in Conversation with Gardner C. Taylor*. Downers Grove, IL: IVP Academic, 2015.

———. *Learning from a Legend: What Gardner C. Taylor Can Teach Us about Preaching*. Eugene, OR: Cascade, 2016.

Arthurs, Jeffrey D. *Preaching as Reminding: Stirring Memory in an Age of Forgetfulness*. Downers Grove, IL: IVP Academic, 2017.

Augustine, *On Christian Doctrine*. Translated by J. F. Shaw. Grand Rapids, MI: Christian Classics Ethereal Library. Accessed September 13, 2014. http://www.ccel.org/ccel/augustine/doctrine.pdf.

Bartow, Charles L. *God's Human Speech: A Practical Theology of Proclamation*. Grand Rapids, MI: Eerdmans, 1997.

Bauckham, Richard, and Trevor Hart. *Hope Against Hope: Christian Eschatology at the Turn of the Millennium*. Grand Rapids, MI: Eerdmans, 1999.

Begbie, Jeremy, ed. *Beholding the Glory: Incarnation through the Arts*. Grand Rapids, MI: Baker Academic, 2001.

———. "Faithful Feelings: Music and Emotion in Worship." In *Resonant Witness: Conversations between Music and Theology*, edited by Jeremy S. Begbie and Steven R. Guthrie, 323-54. Grand Rapids, MI: Eerdmans, 2011.

———. *Music, Modernity, and God: Essays in Listening*. New York: Oxford University Press, 2014.

———. *A Peculiar Orthodoxy: Reflections on Theology and the Arts*. Grand Rapids, MI: Baker Academic, 2018.

———. *Redeeming Transcendence in the Arts: Bearing Witness to the Triune God*. Grand Rapids, MI: Eerdmans, 2018.

———. *Resounding Truth: Christian Wisdom in the World of Music*. Grand Rapids, MI: Baker Academic, 2007.

———, ed., *Sounding the Depths: Theology through the Arts*. London: SCM Press, 2002.

———. "The Theological Potential of Music: A Response to Adrienne Dengerink Chaplin." *Christian Scholar's Review* 33, no. 1 (Fall 2003): 135-41.

———. *Theology, Music and Time*. Cambridge: Cambridge University Press, 2000.

———. *Voicing Creation's Praise: Towards a Theology of the Arts*. New York: T&T Clark, 1991.

Benson, Bruce Ellis. *Liturgy as a Way of Life: Embodying the Arts in Christian Worship*. Grand Rapids, MI: Baker Academic, 2013.

Borthwick, Alastair, Trevor Hart, and Anthony Monti. "Musical Time and Eschatology." In *Resonant Witness: Conversations between Music and Theology*, edited by Jeremy S. Begbie and Steven R. Guthrie, 271-94. Grand Rapids, MI: Eerdmans, 2011.

Brueggemann, Walter. *Finally Comes the Poet: Daring Speech for Proclamation*. Philadelphia: Fortress, 1989.

Bushnell, Horace. "Pulpit Talent." In *The Company of Preachers: Wisdom on Preaching from Augustine to the Present*, edited by Richard Lischer, 83-89. Grand Rapids, MI: Eerdmans, 2002.

Buttrick, David. *Homiletic: Moves and Structures*. Philadelphia: Fortress, 1987.

Chaplin, Adrienne Dengerink. "The Theological Potential of Music: An Evaluation of Jeremy Begbie's *Theology, Music and Time*—A Review Essay." *Christian Scholar's Review* 33, no. 1 (Fall 2003): 125-33.

Childers, Jana. *Performing the Word: Preaching as Theatre*. Nashville: Abingdon Press, 1998.

Clayton, Martin, Rebecca Sager, and Will Udo. "In Time with the Music: The Concept of Entrainment and Its Significance for Ethnomusicology." *European Meetings in Ethnomusicology* 11 (2005). http://oro.open.ac.uk/2661/.

Cooper, Burton Z., and John S. McClure, *Claiming Theology in the Pulpit*. Louisville, KY: Westminster John Knox, 2003.

Copland, Aaron. *What to Listen for in Music*. Rev. ed. New York: New American Library, 2009.

Craddock, Fred B. *As One Without Authority*. Rev. ed. St. Louis: Chalice Press, 2001.

———. *Preaching*. Rev. ed. Nashville: Abingdon Press, 2010.

Crawford, Evans E., with Thomas H. Troeger. *The Hum: Call and Response in African American Preaching*. Nashville: Abingdon Press, 1995.

Davis, H. Grady. *Design for Preaching*. Philadelphia: Fortress, 1958.

DeVoto, Mark. "Tonality." In *The New Harvard Dictionary of Music*, edited by Don Michael Randel, 862. Cambridge, MA: Belknap Press, 1986.

Dykstra, Robert C. *Discovering a Sermon: Personal Pastoral Preaching*. St. Louis: Chalice Press, 2001.

Edwards, O. C., Jr., *A History of Preaching*. Nashville: Abingdon Press, 2004.

Epstein, David. *Shaping Time: Music, the Brain, and Performance*. New York: Schirmer Books, 1995.

Eslinger, Richard L. "Tracking the Homiletical Plot." In *What's the Shape of Narrative Preaching: Essays in Honor of Eugene L. Lowry*, edited by Mike Graves and David L. Schlafer, 69-86. St. Louis: Chalice Press, 2008.

Fry Brown, Teresa L. *Delivering the Sermon: Voice, Body, and Animation in Proclamation*. Minneapolis: Fortress, 2008.

Graves, Mike. *The Sermon as Symphony: Preaching the Literary Forms of the New Testament*. Valley Forge, PA: Judson Press, 1997.

Green, Joel B. and Michael Pasquarello III, eds. *Narrative Reading, Narrative Preaching: Reuniting New Testament Interpretation and Proclamation*. Grand Rapids, MI: Baker Academic, 2003.

Guthrie, Steven R. *Creator Spirit: The Holy Spirit and the Art of Becoming Human*. Grand Rapids, MI: Baker Academic, 2011.

———. "The Wisdom of Song." In *Resonant Witness: Conversations between Music and Theology*, edited by Jeremy S. Begbie and Steven R. Guthrie, 382-407. Grand Rapids, MI: Eerdmans, 2011.

Hagen, Edward H. and Gregory A. Bryant. "Music and Dance as a Coalition Signaling System." *Human Nature* 14, no. 1 (March 2003): 21-51.

Higgins, Kathleen Marie. *The Music Between Us: Is Music a Universal Language?* Chicago: The University of Chicago Press, 2012.

Hogan, Lucy Lind. "Poetics and the Context of Preaching." In *The New Interpreter's Handbook of Preaching*, edited by Paul Scott Wilson, 173-74. Nashville: Abingdon Press, 2008.

Horton, Michael. *The Christian Faith: A Systematic Theology for Pilgrims on the Way*. Grand Rapids, MI: Zondervan, 2011.

Hulst, Mary. *A Little Handbook for Preachers: Ten Practical Ways to a Better Sermon by Sunday*. Downers Grove, IL: InterVarsity Press, 2016.

Huron, David. *Sweet Anticipation: Music and the Psychology of Expectation*. Cambridge, MA: The MIT Press, 2006.

Jackelén, Antje. *Time and Eternity: The Question of Time in Church, Science, and Theology*. Translated by Barbara Harshaw. West Conshohocken, PA: Templeton Foundation Press, 2005.

Johnson, Todd E., and Dale Savidge, *Performing the Sacred: Theology and Theater in Dialogue*. Grand Rapids, MI: Baker Academic, 2009.

Johnson, Trygve David. *The Preacher as Liturgical Artist: Metaphor, Identity, and the Vicarious Humanity of Christ*. Eugene, OR: Cascade, 2014.

Jones, Kirk Byron. *The Jazz of Preaching: How to Preach with Great Freedom and Joy*. Nashville: Abingdon Press, 2004.

Kernfeld, Barry. "Rhythm." In *The New Harvard Dictionary of Music*, edited by Don Michael Randel, 700-705. Cambridge, MA: Belknap Press, 1986.

Kivy, Peter. "How Music Moves." In *What Is Music? An Introduction to the Philosophy of Music*, edited by Philip Alperson, 149-63. University Park, PA: Pennsylvania State University Press, 1987.

Kramer, Jonathan D. *The Time of Music: New Meanings, New Temporalities, New Listening Strategies*. New York: Schirmer Books, 1988.

LaRue, Cleophus J. *I Believe I'll Testify: The Art of African American Preaching*. Louisville, KY: Westminster John Knox, 2011.

———. *Rethinking Celebration: From Rhetoric to Praise in African American Preaching*. Louisville, KY: Westminster John Knox, 2016.

———. "Two Ships Passing in the Night." In *What's the Matter with Preaching Today?*, edited by Mike Graves. Louisville, KY: Westminster John Knox, 2004.

Levine, Robert. *A Geography of Time: The Temporal Misadventures of a Social Psychologist, or How Every Culture Keeps Time Just a Little Bit Differently*. New York: Basic Books, 1997.

Lischer, Richard. *A Theology of Preaching: The Dynamics of the Gospel*. Rev. ed. Eugene, OR: Wipf and Stock, 1992.

Long, Thomas G. "Out of the Loop." In *What's the Shape of Narrative Preaching: Essays in Honor of Eugene L. Lowry*, edited by Mike Graves and David L. Schlafer, 115-30. St. Louis: Chalice Press, 2008.

———. *Preaching and the Literary Forms of the Bible*. Philadelphia: Fortress, 1989.

———. *Preaching from Memory to Hope*. Louisville, KY: Westminster John Knox, 2009.

———. *The Witness of Preaching*. 2nd ed. Louisville, KY: Westminster John Knox, 2005.

Louw, Daniel. "Preaching as Art (Imaging the Unseen) and Art as Homiletics (Verbalizing the Unseen): Towards the Aesthetics of Iconic Thinking and Poetic Communication in Homiletics." *HTS Teologiese Studies/Theological Studies* 72, no. 2 (December 2016): 125-33.

Lowry, Eugene L. *Doing Time in the Pulpit: The Relationship between Narrative and Preaching*. Nashville: Abingdon Press, 1985.

———. *The Homiletical Beat: Why All Sermons Are Narrative*. Nashville: Abingdon Press, 2012.

———. *The Homiletical Plot: The Sermon as Narrative Art Form*. Expanded ed. Louisville, KY: Westminster John Knox, 2001.

———. *The Sermon: Dancing on the Edge of Mystery*. Nashville: Abingdon Press, 1997.

Margulis, Elizabeth Hellmuth. "Musical Repetition Detection Across Multiple Exposures." *Music Perception: An Interdisciplinary Journal* 29, no. 4 (April 2012), 377-85.

———. *On Repeat: How Music Plays the Mind*. New York: Oxford University Press, 2014.

McKenzie, Alyce M. *Novel Preaching: Tips from Top Writers on Crafting Creative Sermons*. Louisville, KY: Westminster John Knox, 2010.

Meyer, Leonard B. *Emotion and Meaning in Music*. Chicago: The University of Chicago Press, 1956.

Middleton, Richard. "'Play It Again Sam': Some Notes on the Productivity of Repetition in Popular Music." *Popular Music: A Yearbook* 3 (1983): 235-270.

Mitchell, Henry H. *Black Preaching*. Philadelphia: J. B. Lippincott, 1970.

Myrick, Nathan. "Embodying the Spirit: Toward a Theology of Entrainment," *Liturgy* 33, no. 3 (2018): 29-36.

———. "Relational Power, Music, and Identity: The Emotional Efficacy of Congregational Song," *Yale Journal of Music & Religion* 3, no. 1 (2017): 77-92.

Nieman, James R. *Knowing the Context: Frames, Tools, and Signs for Preaching*. Minneapolis: Fortress, 2008.

Patel, Aniruddh D. *Music, Language, and the Brain*. Oxford: Oxford University Press, 2008.

Polanyi, Michael. *Personal Knowledge: Towards a Post-Critical Philosophy*. Chicago: University of Chicago Press, 1962.

———. *The Tacit Dimension*. London: Routledge & Kegan Paul Ltd., 1966.

Porter, Mark. *Ecologies of Resonance in Christian Musicking*. New York: Oxford University Press, 2020.

Postman, Neil. *Amusing Ourselves to Death: Public Discourse in the Age of Show Business*. 20th anniversary ed. New York: Penguin Books, 1985.

Powery, Luke A. *Dem Dry Bones: Preaching, Death, and Hope*. Minneapolis: Fortress, 2012.
———. *Spirit Speech: Lament and Celebration in Preaching*. Nashville: Abingdon Press, 2009.
Ramsey, G. Lee. *Care-full Preaching: From Sermon to Caring Community*. Eugene, OR: Wipf and Stock, 2012.
Randel, Don Michael. "Cadence." In *The New Harvard Dictionary of Music*, edited by Michael Randel, 120-24. Cambridge, MA: Belknap Press, 1986.
Ravignani, Andrea, Daniel L. Bowling, and W. Tecumseh Fitch. "Chorusing, Synchrony, and the Evolutionary Functions of Rhythm." *Frontiers in Psychology* 5 (October 10, 2014). http://dx.doi.org/10.3389/fpsyg. 2014.01118.
Reddish, Paul, Ronald Fischer, and Joseph Bulbulia. "Let's Dance Together: Synchrony, Shared Intentionality and Cooperation." *PLoS One* 8, no. 8 (August 7, 2013): e71182. https://www.ncbi.nlm.nih.gov/pmc/articles/PMC3737148/.
Reid, Robert Stephen. *The Four Voices of Preaching: Connecting Purpose and Identity behind the Pulpit*. Grand Rapids, MI: Brazos, 2006.
Rice, Charles L. *The Embodied Word: Preaching as Art and Liturgy*. Minneapolis: Fortress, 1991.
Rietveld, David. "A Survey of the Phenomenological Research of Listening to Preaching." *Homiletic* 38, no. 2 (2013): 30-47.
Rosenberg, Bruce A. *Can These Bones Live? The Art of the American Folk Preacher*. Rev. ed. Chicago: University of Illinois Press, 1988.
Sacks, Oliver. *Musicophilia: Tales of Music and the Brain*. Rev. ed. New York: Vintage Books, 2008.
Saliers, Don E. *Music and Theology*. Nashville, Abingdon Press, 2007.
Schmit, Clayton J. *Sent and Gathered: A Worship Manual for the Missional Church*. Grand Rapids, MI: Baker Academic, 2009.
———. *Too Deep for Words: A Theology of Liturgical Expression*. Louisville, KY: Westminster John Knox, 2002.
———. "What Comes Next? Performing and Proclaiming the Word." In *Performance in Preaching: Bringing the Sermon to Life*, edited by Jana Childers and Clayton J. Schmit, 169-90. Grand Rapids, MI: Baker Academic, 2008.
Scruton, Roger. *The Aesthetics of Music*. Oxford: Oxford University Press, 1997.
———. *Understanding Music: Philosophy and Interpretation*. New York: Bloomsbury, 2009.
Simmons, Martha. "Whooping: The Musicality of African American Preaching Past and Present." In *Preaching with Sacred Fire: An Anthology of African American Sermons, 1750 to the Present*, edited by Martha Simmons and Frank A. Thomas, 864-884. New York: W. W. Norton & Company, 2010.
Smith, James K. A. *Imagining the Kingdom: How Worship Works*. Grand Rapids, MI: Baker Academic, 2013.
Sparshott, Francis. "Aesthetics of Music—Limits and Grounds." In *What Is Music? An Introduction to the Philosophy of Music*, edited by Philip Alperson, 33-98. University Park, PA: Penn State University Press, 1987.
Spencer, Jon Michael. *Sacred Symphony: The Chanted Sermon of the Black Preacher*. Westport, CT: Greenwood Press, 1987.
Taylor, Charles. *A Secular Age*. Cambridge, MA: Belknap Press, 2007.
Taylor, Gardner C. *The Words of Gardner C. Taylor: Volume 3, 1980-Present*. Compiled by Edward L. Taylor. Valley Forge, PA: Judson Press, 2000.
Taylor, W. David. O. *Glimpses of the New Creation: Worship and the Formative Power of the Arts*. Grand Rapids, MI: Eerdmans, 2020.
Tomlinson, Gary. *A Million Years of Music: The Emergence of Human Modernity*. New York: Zone Books, 2015.
Trappe, Hans-Joachim, and Gabriele Voit. "The Cardiovascular Effects of Musical Genres: A Randomized Controlled Study on the Effect of Compositions by W. A. Mozart, J. Strauss, and ABBA." Translated by Birte Twisselmann. *Deutsches Arzteblatt* 113, no. 20 (May 2016): 347-352. https://www.ncbi.nlm.nih.gov/pmc/articles/PMC4906829/.

Trehub, Sandra E., Judith Becker, and Iain Morley. "Cross-Cultural Perspectives on Music and Musicality." *Philosophical Transactions of the Royal Society B* 370, no. 1664 (February 2, 2015). http://dx.doi.org/10.1098/rstb.2014.0096.

Treier, Daniel J., Mark Husbands, and Roger Lundin, eds. *The Beauty of God: Theology and the Arts.* Downers Grove, IL: InterVarsity Press, 2007.

Troeger, Thomas. "Arts." In *The New Interpreter's Handbook of Preaching*, edited by Paul Scott Wilson, 177-79. Nashville: Abingdon Press, 2008.

———. *Wonder Reborn: Creating Sermons on Hymns, Music, and Poetry.* Oxford: Oxford University Press, 2010.

Turner, William C. "The Musicality of Black Preaching: Performing the Word." In *Performance in Preaching: Bringing the Sermon to Life*, edited by Jana Childers and Clayton J. Schmit, 191-209. Grand Rapids, MI: Baker Academic, 2008.

Viladesau, Richard. *Theological Aesthetics: God in Imagination, Beauty, and Art.* 1999. Reprint. Oxford: Oxford University Press, 2012.

Wells, Samuel. *Improvisation: The Drama of Christian Ethics.* Grand Rapids, MI: Brazos, 2004.

———. *Speaking the Truth: Preaching in a Pluralistic Culture.* Nashville: Abingdon Press, 2008.

Webb, Stephen. *The Divine Voice: Christian Proclamation and the Theology of Sound.* Grand Rapids, MI: Brazos, 2004.

Willimon, William H. *Conversations with Barth on Preaching.* Nashville: Abingdon Press, 2006.

———. *Preaching Master Class: Lessons from Will Willimon's Five-Minute Preaching Workshop.* Edited by Noel A. Snyder. Eugene, OR: Cascade, 2010.

———. *Undone by Easter: Keeping Preaching Fresh.* Nashville: Abingdon Press, 2009.

Willobe, Sondra B. *The Write Stuff: Crafting Sermons that Capture and Convince.* Louisville, KY: Westminster John Knox, 2009.

Wilson, Paul Scott. *The Four Pages of the Sermon: A Guide to Biblical Preaching.* Nashville: Abingdon Press, 1999.

———. *The Practice of Preaching.* Rev. ed. Nashville: Abingdon Press, 2007.

———. *Preaching and Homiletical Theory.* St. Louis: Chalice Press, 2004.

———. "Preaching, Performance, and the Life and Death of 'Now.'" In *Performance in Preaching: Bringing the Sermon to Life*, edited by Jana Childers and Clayton J. Schmit, 37-52. Grand Rapids, MI: Baker Academic, 2008.

Wolterstorff, Nicholas. "The Work of Making a Work of Music." In *What Is Music? An Introduction to the Philosophy of Music*, edited by Philip Alperson, 101-29. University Park, PA: Pennsylvania State University Press, 1987.

Wuthnow, Robert. *All in Sync: How Music and Art Are Revitalizing American Religion.* Berkeley: University of California Press, 2003.

Zahl, David. *Seculosity: How Career, Parenting, Technology, Food, Politics, and Romance Became Our New Religion and What to Do about It.* Minneapolis: Fortress Press, 2019.

Zuckerkandl, Victor. *Sound and Symbol: Music and the External World.* Translated by Willard R. Trask. Princeton, NJ: Princeton University Press, 1956.

GENERAL INDEX

180

New Homiletic, 58-59, 64-65,
69, 104-5, 143
Ollen, Joy, 92
oral engagement with music
and/or preaching 52, 53-57,
60, 62, 67-69, 74, 164
Pasquarello, Michael, III, 149,
156
Patel, Aniruddh D., 66
Polanyi, Michael, 161
Powery, Luke A., 11-16, 25-28,
53, 55-56, 70, 144-45, 149-50,
156
preaching as music, 18-25, 36
See also musical homiletic
preaching as performance, 9,
29-30
predictability
in music, 24, 110, 123-31,
136-37
in preaching 24, 136-37
See also anticipation in
music; expectation
levels of the listener;
repetition
qualia (distinctive sensations)
in a tonal system, 125-26,
135, 137, 146, 154, 156
See also tonal systems
repetition
in forming Christian
character, 82, 111, 116-17,
163, 171
in learning, memory, and
predictability, 83, 85-94,
97, 99-101, 106-7, 110,
112-17
in music, 82-87, 90-100,
106-8, 112-13, 131
in preaching, 82, 97-106,
110-19, 154, 162, 167-68, 171
and tonality, 85-93, 106-8,
167-68
See also expectation levels
of the listener;
predictability
rhythm, 15-16, 40, 43, 46-55,
57-58, 60, 63, 66, 93-95, 99,
108-9, 121-22, 132
downbeat, 49-52
in preaching, 40, 53-55,
57-58, 60, 66-67, 78, 146,
154

syncopation, 51-52
versus beat, 49
See also cadence; meter
Rosenberg, Bruce A., 99-100
Sacks, Oliver, 47
Schmit, Clayton J., 10, 23-26,
31, 36, 97-98, 111, 135-38, 146,
154
Scruton, Roger, 41-42, 45-49,
121, 123, 125, 132-35, 143
sentimentality in art, 133-34
sermon introductions, 54-55,
65, 68, 69-70
Simmons, Martha, 14, 16-17,
25-27
Small, Christopher, 42, 47
sonic-spatial order (vs.
visual-spatial), 74-77
Spencer, Jon Michael, 17,
53-55, 99
"spiritual preaching," 55-57, 70
synchrony, 36, 40-58, 61,
64-74, 77, 79, 161
through preaching, 52-58,
61, 64-71, 73-74, 77-79,
162-64, 166, 171
through singing, 71-74, 77
Taylor, Gardner C., 79-81
Taylor, W. David O., 3-4, 30
teleology / teleological
dynamic, 3, 36, 120-60, 161
and the cultivation of
hope, 13, 150-60, 163,
170-71
of the gospel, 141-42,
145-46, 152, 157-58
in music, 120-26, 128-31,
135-36, 139, 146, 150-51,
153
in preaching, 135-36,
138-47, 149-50, 153-54,
156-58, 160, 162-63,
169-71
temporal organization in
preaching, 52-69, 112-13
temporality in music, 33,
40-43, 46-52, 96, 113, 122
See also meter; rhythm
tension in music, 96-97, 108-9,
112, 121-23, 127-32, 134-35,
146, 151
via compositional
techniques, 127-32

via performative
techniques, 129-30, 132
tension in preaching, 20, 63,
138-40, 144, 146-47, 149-50,
157-58
Theology, Music and Time,
33-34, 41, 85, 94-95, 108-9
theology through music,
32-36, 37
theology through musicology,
35-36
Thomas, Frank A., 154-56
tonal (or tonic) centers
in music, 89-90, 98
in preaching, 89, 98, 100,
106, 167-68
tonal systems, 89-92, 125-26,
131-32, 134, 146
of Christian preaching,
106, 137-38, 169
Western, 121, 131-32, 135
See also tonality
tonality, 16, 83, 85-92, 95-96,
100, 106-10, 121-22, 125,
131-33, 146, 162
See also tonal systems
Troeger, Thomas H., 11-14,
17-18, 20, 25-27, 36-38
Turner, William C., 14-17,
25-27, 54-55, 62-63, 70, 154
Weaver, Lisa, 117-19
Wells, Samuel, 148, 153
Western musical tradition, 12,
42-47, 50, 66, 89, 91-92,
109-10, 121, 123, 125, 128-29,
131, 135
See also cultural
differences in temporal
understanding; cultural
differences in tonal
systems
White mainline worship,
57-59, 62-63, 66-69, 78, 164
"whooping" (overt tonality in
speaking), 7, 16-17
Willimon, William H., 100-103,
111, 117, 145
Willobe, Sondra B., 10
Wilson, Paul Scott, 104-8,
110-11, 146
Zuckerkandl, Victor, 76, 84,
96, 108

SCRIPTURE INDEX

DYNAMICS OF CHRISTIAN WORSHIP

Worship of the triune God stands at the heart of the Christian life, so understanding the many dynamics of Christian worship—including prayer, reading the Bible, preaching, baptism, the Lord's Supper, music, visual art, architecture, and more—is both a perennial and crucial issue for the church. With that in mind, the Dynamics of Christian Worship (DCW) series seeks to enable Christians to grow in their understanding of the many aspects of Christian worship. By harvesting the fruits of biblical, theological, historical, practical, and liturgical scholarship and by drawing from a wide range of worshiping contexts and denominational backgrounds, the DCW series seeks to deepen both the theology and practice of Christian worship for the life of the church.

TITLES INCLUDE

+ John Rempel, *Recapturing an Enchanted World: Ritual and Sacrament in the Free Church Tradition*

+ Glenn Packiam, *Worship and the World to Come: Exploring Christian Hope in Contemporary Worship*

+ Esther Crookshank, *Christ Our Song: Psalms, Hymns, and Spiritual Songs in the History of Worship from the Early Church to Watts* (forthcoming)

ADVISORY BOARD

Constance Cherry, Indiana Wesleyan University
Carlos Colón, Baylor University
James Hart, Robert E. Webber Institute for Worship Studies
Todd Johnson, Fuller Theological Seminary
Trygve Johnson, Hope College
Glenn Packiam, New Life Downtown Church, Colorado Springs, CO
Emmett G. Price III, Gordon-Conwell Theological Seminary
Melanie Ross, Yale Institute of Sacred Music
Lester Ruth, Duke Divinity School
John Witvliet, Calvin Institute of Christian Worship